Strange Natures

STRANGE NATURES

Futurity, Empathy, and the
Queer Ecological Imagination

NICOLE SEYMOUR

University of Illinois Press

Urbana, Chicago, and Springfield

Portions of Chapter 3 were first published as the article
"'It's Just Not Turning Up': Cinematic Vision and Environmental
Justice in Todd Haynes's *Safe*," by Nicole Seymour, in *Cinema Journal*
Volume 50, Issue 4, pp. 26–47. Copyright ©2011 by the University
of Texas Press. All rights reserved.

∞ This book is printed on acid-free paper.

Library of Congress Cataloging-in-Publication Data
Seymour, Nicole.
Strange natures : futurity, empathy, and the queer ecological
imagination / Nicole Seymour.
p.   cm.
Includes bibliographical references and index.
ISBN 978-0-252-03762-7 (cloth : alk. paper)
ISBN 978-0-252-07916-0 (pbk. : alk. paper)
ISBN 978-0-252-09487-3 (e-book)
1. Homosexuality—Philosophy. 2. Human ecology—Philosophy.
3. Human ecology—Study and teaching. 4. Philosophy of nature.
I. Title.
HQ76.25.S4997   2013
306.76'6—dc23   2012040771

Contents

Preface

While in graduate school several years ago, I took the L from Chicago's Midway Airport to a conference downtown. At the time, I was immersed in both queer theory and ecocriticism and had just begun to think about their intersection—or, rather, what I saw as a lack thereof. My intellectual crush of the moment was Lee Edelman; his 2004 book *No Future: Queer Theory and the Death Drive* had captured much attention for its fiery excoriation of "heteroreproductive futurism" in public and political discourse.

So when I looked up inside the L car to see an Environment Illinois ad, I was prepared to critique its deployment of what Edelman terms "the Child"—that innocent and yet implicitly heterosexual[1] emblem of the future. I also noted how the ad's idyllic suburban scene, and the whiteness and maleness of its central figure, frame environmental degradation as a threat not just to a particular child, or even many children, but to a particular way of life. Indeed, the ad matter-of-factly links sentimental heterosexism and environmentalism; its conclusion, "Protect our children's future. Clean up dirty power plants," suggests that one imperative inevitably follows from the other.

Figure 1. Advertisement from environmental advocacy organization Environment Illinois, featured on public transportation in the Chicago area.

But whereas Edelman's targets are homophobic Hollywood films, anti-choice political campaigns, and a Catholic Church embattled over sex-abuse scandals, the project of Environment Illinois is one to which I have long been sympathetic otherwise. And in fact, "the Child" stands to perform much progressive work on the environmentalist front. For instance, in her foreword to Rachel Stein's collection *New Perspectives on Environmental Justice*, indigenous activist and former Green Party vice presidential candidate Winona LaDuke warns, "we know that as each natural element is challenged, transformed, or contaminated, our bodies too will be impacted, our breast milk contaminated, and *our children's* future darkened" ("Foreword" xiii, my emphasis).

A perspective that cleaves closely to Edelman's brand of queer theory might have us dismiss the efforts of environmentalists such as Environment Illinois and LaDuke wholesale—and might also leave us incapable of distinguishing the heterosexism of the former's appeal from the latter's concern for those most vulnerable in terms of environmental problems: people of color, poor people, and their children.[2] But on the other hand, a strictly "environmental" perspective would leave that heterosexism unquestioned. This possibility is particularly problematic, considering how heterosexism in environmentalism often goes unnoticed, and thus unchallenged, because it seems so sensible. To wit: the Environment Illinois ad expects an audience for whom the connection between reproductive futurity and environmental protection is a no-brainer; the replication of the white middle class is natural, and thus its being threatened is bad, and likewise, air and water are natural and thus the pollution thereof is bad. These points suggest that much environmentalist discourse *depends on*, or even *requires*, a white-centric heterosexism, if not homophobia. Thus neither a queer reaction per se, nor an environmentalist reaction per se, seems to be an appropriate response to this ad.

So the questions I had to ask on that train ride were: Is there no queer way of thinking environmentally and ecologically? No environmental or ecological way of thinking queerly?[3] In the years since, several theorists and activists have insisted that there are. This book echoes that view, while considering several additional questions: Can futurism and futurity ever be queer? Can a defense of "nature" or "the natural" ever be queer? Can one redefine those terms such that they effectively, and empathetically, accommodate both the queer and the non-human? And are there ways of being ironic and playful, those qualities often associated with queerness, while also being earnest and dedicated, those qualities often associated with environmentalism? This book attempts to answer these and other pressing questions through new readings of queer literary and filmic texts from the past three decades. The short version of the answer I hope it offers is "Yes."

Acknowledgments

Thank you to all of my friends, family, colleagues, teachers, and students.

I am grateful for the two readers who offered enthusiastic, helpful comments on my initial manuscript; this book is no doubt better for their input. I am also grateful to Larin McLaughlin, the University of Illinois Press's senior acquisitions editor, for her guidance.

Parts of *Strange Natures* began as dissertation chapters, supported by a fellowship from the Robert Penn Warren Center for the Humanities at Vanderbilt University. Carolyn Dever, Dana Nelson, and Paul Young served on my dissertation committee and have been invaluable resources throughout my career. Judith (Jack) Halberstam served as my outside dissertation reader and has been crucial to my work here—even when we disagree. The Department of English at Vanderbilt has always been supportive of my work; special thanks go to Jay Clayton, Mark Schoenfield, and Mark Wollaeger for help of various kinds over the years. I'm also a huge fan of Teresa Goddu—as a teacher, scholar, and coffee date. Vera Kutzinski's graduate course on ecocriticism helped sow many of the seeds for this book; I have to thank her for insisting that I read Shani Mootoo's *Cereus Blooms at Night*.

Susan Ryan and Susan Griffin hired me into the Department of English at the University of Louisville just as I was starting this book project and, for some reason, kept letting me stay. My warmest thanks to them both. My colleagues at Louisville—including Tom Byers (especially!), Amy Clukey, Karen Hadley, Aaron Jaffe, Karen Kopelson, Brian Leung, Kiki Petrosino, and Andrew Rabin—have also been incredibly welcoming. I will miss them but look forward to joining an equally fabulous group of people at the University of Arkansas at Little Rock.

My students at Vanderbilt University and the University of Louisville have been incredible sports as I've foisted my wacky ideas upon them. More importantly, though, they have talked back to me, helping me think through many of the major concepts in this book. Special thanks to my Minority Traditions in American Literature students at Louisville, my queer ecocriticism/ecology students, and the following students in particular: Alex Sugzda, Lauren R. Hall, Shekinah Lavalle, Lana Lea, and Colton Wilson.

I have the best friends in the world. Virginia Allison, Christine Bolghand, Darin DeWitt, Will Funk, Joya Golden, Michelle Horejs, Nathan Ihara, Audra Kudirka, Jeff Morse, Gabriela Nuñez, Sarah Pierce, Erin Tarver, Frances Ulman, Jane Wanninger, and the late, great Jeremy Lespi are particularly precious to me. In addition to being dear friends, Katherine Fusco and Josh Epstein have been motivational writing partners. I have also been blessed with various partners in crime who have passed through Louisville over the years, including Rachel Cobb-Vincent, Anne O. Fisher, Alyssa Knickerbocker, Derek Mong, Heather Slomski, Erin Shaw, Jonathan Vincent, and Cutter Wood. Jonathan, along with Amy Clukey, offered incisive comments on this manuscript. Thanks also to the amazing *Twin Peaks/Northern Exposure*/movie night gang; I'll write the book on Pacific Northwest noir some day, I promise!

Throughout my grad-school years and beyond, I have had the pleasure of eating, drinking, thinking, and being merry with the likes of Beau Baca, Mary Butterfield, Ben Graydon, Sarah Hansen, Justin Haynes, Christian Long, Neal Palmer, Brian Rejack, and Rob Watson. Amanda Hagood, Donald Jellerson, John Morrell, Dan Spoth, and Heather Talley also deserve my thanks for helping me think through queer ecology in various ways over the past several years.

My parents, Michael and Cecilia, and my brother, Philip, have loved and supported me from afar and from up close whenever possible. I'm pretty sure that our family's obsession with Alfred Hitchcock and *The Twilight Zone* is somehow to blame for much of my work.

Finally, perhaps it will not seem exceedingly strange, in the acknowledgments for a book focused on environmental concerns, for me to express my appreciation for the environment in which it was written. I adore the many quirks and charms of the place I've called home for the last three years; they've inspired and sustained me in countless ways. Louisville, I love you!

Introduction

Locating Queer Ecologies

[E]nvironmentalism and queer politics seldom seem to
intersect. This dislocation rests on a narrow association of
ecology with visible landscapes and sexuality with visible
bodies bounded by skin. In the pages of journals, as in popular
culture, attractions may range far afield, but the field itself
merely offers a place to suffer or to frolic, a simple backdrop
for the playing out of sexual politics.
—Kath Weston, "A Political Ecology of 'Unnatural Offences'"

The task of a queer ecology is to probe the intersections of
sex and nature with an eye to developing a sexual politics that
more clearly includes considerations of the natural world and
its biosocial constitution, and an environmental politics that
demonstrates an understanding of the ways in which sexual
relations organize and influence both the material world of
nature and our perceptions, experiences, and constitutions of
that world.
—Catriona Mortimer-Sandilands and Bruce Erickson,
    Queer Ecologies: Sex, Nature, Politics, Desire

Strange Natures identifies a tradition of queer environmentalism
in contemporary fictions: I find that novels and films generally categorized
as queer—including Leslie Feinberg's *Stone Butch Blues* (1993), Todd Haynes's
Safe (1995), Ang Lee's *Brokeback Mountain* (2005), and Shelley Jackson's *Half
Life* (2006)—explicitly link the queer to the natural world through an empathetic, ethical imagination. These works understand oppressed humans
(including working-class individuals and people of color, in addition to
queers) and oppressed non-humans (degraded landscapes, threatened natural resources, and other flora and fauna) to be deeply interconnected, and
they promote politicized advocacy on behalf of both. My focus on contemporary work from the Americas is crucial to my intervention in the emerging
paradigm known as "queer ecology": I maintain that the ecological stances

of the works I treat here are striking precisely because of the contexts from which they emerge—including postmodernism, poststructuralism, and the "post-identity" era—and *precisely because they are so self-consciously queer*. That is to say, these works manage to conceive of concrete, sincere environmental politics even while remaining, to varying degrees, skeptical, ironic, and self-reflexive. And they do so even while, as I detail below, queer fictions and theory are known for their cynicism, apoliticism, and negativity, such that "queer environmentalism" sounds like an oxymoron.

My readings thus make a unique contribution to the queer-ecology paradigm, while taking up what Mortimer-Sandilands and Erickson define in the second epigraph of this chapter as its general task. More broadly, these readings perform what David Mazel calls *poststructuralist ecocriticism*: "a way of reading environmental literature *and* canonical landscapes . . . that attends concurrently to the discursive construction of both . . . environment and . . . subjectivity" and that analyzes environment "as a powerful site for naturalizing constructs of race, class, nationality, and gender" (*American Literary Environmentalism* xxi). In rereading contemporary queer literature and film *as* environmental literature and film, I add "sexuality" and "gender identity" to Mazel's list of dominant identity constructs. And I show that the environment can function as a site not just for *establishing* such constructs, but for *challenging* them.

This book draws on the insights and methodologies of queer theory and ecocriticism—as well as on critical race theory, environmental and social-justice studies, feminist theory, transgender studies, and areas of philosophy such as environmental ethics. Mine is not an arbitrary attempt to join together the already diverse and already interdisciplinary fields of queer theory and ecocriticism: these fields are known for focusing on the concept of nature. But they have historically done so in very different ways, ways that suggest that the "naturalness" of a category such as heterosexuality is largely unrelated to the "naturalness" of a category such as wilderness. "Natural" has actually become something of a dirty word in queer theory, as I outline below, though one that it seems unable to do without. One of *Strange Natures*'s major projects is challenging this conceptual disconnect. I show that contemporary queer fictions ask the question, "What counts as 'natural'—and why?" in regard to *both* gender/sexuality and environment— as well as race, immigration status, health status, ability, and class—and that they do so in a way that illuminates the imbrication of those categories. In what follows, I offer a genealogy of this book's iteration of queer ecology. I specify how I intervene in, and draw on, queer theory and ecocriticism— thereby suggesting that queer ecology exists not only to provide a new lens, but to make use of the gaps in and overlaps among existing lenses. I also specify what *Strange Natures* offers more broadly as a scholarly work: not just a reconceptualization of the human relationship to the non-human natural world, but a reassessment of how we draw critical-theoretical boundaries.

Queer Theory and Ecocriticism: An Unnatural Union?

Queer Theory

Queer theory and its (arguable) precursor, gay and lesbian studies, have long wrestled with the concept of the natural. Jeffrey Weeks's *Against Nature: Essays on History, Sexuality, and Identity* (1991) is a prominent early example, and one worth considering here in some depth. Weeks nicely summarizes the stalemate at which nature-versus-nurture debates arrive, noting that "the textbooks used to tell us that homosexuality was unnatural. Lesbians and gay men, on the contrary, assert that homosexuality is natural. Who is to tell us which of these two 'truths' is true?" (88). He seeks to step out of the stalemate by historicizing sexuality, as have other theorists, such as Michel Foucault and Eve K. Sedgwick. First, Weeks declares that "sexuality in general, and homosexuality in particular, has been shaped in a complex, and ever changing history over the past hundred years. At the centre of that history has been the making of sexual identities—identities we so readily take for granted now as rooted in nature, but which in fact have a variety of determinable sources and points of origin" (vii). He then goes on to maintain that "lesbian and gay history has led the way in challenging the conventional view that sex is a private, unchanging, '*natural*' phenomenon" (89, my emphasis); that "what we should use history for is to . . . try to see whether what we assume is *natural* is not in fact social and historical" (91, my emphasis); and that "identity is not inborn, pregiven, or '*natural*'" (94, my emphasis).

Some curious things have happened to "nature" in these discussions. For one, the concept of nature itself, rather than the dehistoricizing and discriminatory processes of *naturalization*, has come under fire. "Nature" thus starts to look like something that can function only oppressively—or, at best, naively; it is rendered monolithic even as it is decried for being farcical. For another, Weeks makes strange bedfellows of an anti-discriminatory, anti-essentialist, historicist position, and a discriminatory, homophobic one; both positions agree that queerness is "against nature." Of course, they agree for different reasons. And, of course, Weeks has nothing like anti-gay discrimination as his goal. But we might object to the undertheorization and underhistoricization of "nature," in comparison to the theorization and historicization of "sex." We might object, further, to how Weeks's foundational work speaks from a poststructuralist stance to create an antipathy between "the queer" and "the natural" that potentially exacerbates the antipathy already engendered by the dominant culture. (And all this despite the fact that, as Weeks acknowledges, "lesbians and gay men" have deployed the concept of nature to combat oppression.) We might then say that "nature" occupies a particularly strange position within queer theory: both abhorred and needed, as a kind of conceptual whipping boy.

It is in fact striking how regularly queer scholarship targets designations of "nature" and the "natural" while failing to theorize or contextualize the terms themselves; to acknowledge that the terms have multiple meanings, not all of which apply to the human or the social; or to acknowledge what the rejection thereof might mean for nature qua the non-human world. Indeed, at times "nature" or "natural" function in queer theory as synonyms for heteronormativity or political conservativism, while at other times they are benign synonyms for something like "character" or "status." Consider, for example, that one of Weeks's other stated aims is "to show that sexual identities are historical in *nature*" (viii, my emphasis)—while, above, "historical" was his *antonym* for "natural." Weeks's work is not unique in this regard; consider José Esteban Muñoz's reference to "the relational and contingent *nature* of sexuality" ("Thinking Beyond" 825, my emphasis). To be fair, both theorists seem to mean something like "status" here. Moreover, "nature" is one of the most elastic words in the English language; one could make the case that if such theorists sometimes mean "nature" as in "essence" at some points, and "nature" as in "status" at others, then they might very well talk about nature in respect to the human without implying, or being expected to imply, anything about nature in respect to the non-human. But what I show throughout this book is that such divisions are disingenuous, as the two are always co-implicated. If "nature" is the foundational point of departure for queer theory, then, it is a departure that has left much to be resolved.

The texts in my archive, and this book itself, heed this call. Rather than simply ignoring the fact that the same concept that applies to human sexualities and gender identities also applies to the non-human world, they approach that overlapping application head-on. But they refuse to collapse "nature" qua the threatened natural world into "nature" qua the threats of heteronormativity and homophobia. Instead, these texts and this book consider that queerness might be progressively articulated through "the natural" more broadly, or the non-human world more specifically. For instance, in Chapter 4 I show how *Brokeback Mountain* frames wilderness and the queer human as equally threatened by capitalist domestication, and develops in response a portrait of anti-domestic, non-urban queer living. Through such depictions, the texts in my archive imply that it is a mistake, rather than a radical provocation, for queers to embrace the charge of "unnaturalness" and align themselves with culture, against nature. And they suggest that it is a tragedy to allow queer criticism of "the natural" to render us silent, or even scornful, about the natural qua the non-human world.

This is not to suggest that the texts in my archive embrace "nature" or "the natural" unreservedly. They interrogate these concepts, but they do so very carefully. And with good reason: there is much more at risk for queers than for heterosexuals and other dominant groups in calling into question the naturalness of sexual, gender, or other types of identity. While these texts agree that ideas of nature are constructed, they take aim less at "nature" than at the processes of construction.[1] They suggest that, while it may not be possible to escape altogether the construction of some things as natural and some as unnatural, it might at least be possible to combat the kinds of naturalizations and denaturalizations that enable exploitation and discrimination, or that deny the complexities of humans and non-humans. My archive thus engages, as does this book on the whole, with the question posed by Mei Mei Evans: "When it is said that women are 'by nature' maternal . . . or that it is 'unnatural' for people of the same gender to be sexually attracted to one another"—or, I would add, when queer theorists say that sexual and gender identities are not "natural"—"what role is being assigned to [non-human] nature? . . . What is at stake for these groups of human beings, and what is at stake for nature [the non-human] itself?" (184).

In addition to queer theory's general disdain for the "natural," its so-called negative turn—including the "anti-social thesis"—has worked against the development of queer ecological stances. A 2005 *PMLA* roundtable article on the anti-social thesis paints a picture of a hostile climate for queer ecology—and, ironically, of the need for just such a perspective. The MLA panel that prompted the *PMLA* article traced the anti-social thesis to Leo Bersani, who has outlined a concept of queer sexuality as "self-shattering" in essays such as "Is the Rectum a Grave?" and argued that "homo-ness" represents "a potentially revolutionary inaptitude—perhaps inherent in gay desire—for sociality as it is known" (as quoted by Caserio 819). Theorists such as Edelman and Michael Warner have extended Bersani's ideas in order to critique mainstream gay bids at respectability, such as same-sex marriage, and in order to highlight queer forms of existence that do not seek to reproduce the dominant social order. Similar to Weeks's ironic embrace of the "against nature" designation, these theorists have celebrated the charge of anti-sociality and reclaimed concepts such as "failure" and "shame."[2] However, like the aforementioned embrace, these recent moves leave the queer at a curious impasse: as Tim Dean argues in the PMLA article, "the antisocial thesis originates not in queer theory but in right-wing fantasies about how 'the homosexual agenda' undermines the social fabric" (826). Again, though the motive of the queer theorist and the right-winger may differ, their messages and potential effects are troublingly similar.

One could imagine, however, that these concepts of self-shattering and anti-sociality might open out onto something else entirely, such as queer interest in the natural world. After all, a measure of self-renunciation and anti-sociality is central to many if not most forms of environmentalism, including ecocriticism; the renunciation of anthropocentrism and the adoption of bio-centric or ecocentric viewpoints are veritable prerequisites for participation in either. In fact, as I discuss in Chapter 3, some radical environmentalists, such as those associated with deep ecology and ecoanarchism, abhor hu-manism and humans themselves. I take serious issue with ecological mis-anthropy in that chapter, and I believe, along with ecophilosopher Patrick Curry, that humanism can be rehabilitated for ecological purposes—as he argues, "humanism . . . has strong roots in Montaigne, and later Voltaire, Bentham and Mill, for whom it implied almost the opposite of its modern meaning: the need to be humane, including but extending beyond humanity, in order to be fully human" (54). But the point nonetheless remains: if queer-ness is anti-social, might radical environmentalists' targeting of society as we know it—say, through tree-sitting, tree-spiking, or destroying fast-food restaurants—not be the anti-social move de résistance? And if even mainstream environmentalist groups ask us to put the ecosystem ahead of individual hu-man desires, might environmentalism as an impulse then be queer at its very core? At the very least, if queer theorists are interested in "[a]pproaching the humanities without any need to preserve the subject of humanism" (Edel-man, "Antagonism" 822), might they not find something in common with figures such as author/environmental activist Edward Abbey, who lamented the fact that "in the classicist view only the human is regarded as significant or even recognized as real" (as quoted in McKibben 177)? But such elabora-tions of the anti-social thesis have not happened. Many who promulgate it have, arguably, devolved into nihilism, or, at least, "cast[ing] material political concerns as crude and pedestrian" (Halberstam, "The Politics of Negativity" 824).[3] Among other things, such thinkers thereby leave the health and future of the planet looking like a frivolous concern.[4]

The anti-social thesis has also led some queer theorists to critique futurity, which just so happens to be a fundamental rhetoric of environmentalism at large. Edelman's No Future is now (in)famous for its takedown of "reproductive futurism," which entails the staging of politics and reality itself through the figure of "the Child." In the PMLA roundtable on the anti-social thesis, Edelman observed that one question dominated the roundtable discussion: "do our narratives of political efficacy, historicist analysis, and pedagogical practice *naturalize* what No Future designates as reproductive futurism, thus compelling us all, regardless of political affiliation or critical method, to prostrate ourselves at the altar of what I call the Futurch?" (821, my emphasis). Aside from the fact that Edelman hereby shows an attunement to the processes that determine what counts as natural, his question leaves no room for any consideration of futurity qua the planet and its resources.[5] Again, a deep suspicion of all that is deemed natural abides.

This is not to say that Edelman's critique of reproductive futurism cannot be put to ecological use. For one thing, it certainly has the potential to spark objections to environmental agendas grounded in heterosexist, pro-reproductive rhetoric. In a recent course I taught on queer theory and ecocriticism, I juxtaposed images targeted in No Future—Tiny Tim in Charles Dickens's A Christmas Carol, for one—with images from the many environmental campaigns that use the image of the child. The latter included the Environment Illinois ad cited in my preface and the logo of the World Health Organization Europe, which features a feminized figure atop a globe, holding the hand of a childlike figure, with the heading "The Future for Our Children." Such sentimentalized rhetoric, as my students and I discussed, suggests that concern for the future qua the planet *can only emerge*, or *emerges most effectively*, from white, heterosexual, familial reproductivity. Moreover, it potentially privatizes issues of environmental health by locating them within that domestic framework, rather than tracing them to larger structures such as racism and classism, which make for unequal distributions of risk.[6]

But despite this potential of the queer critique of futurism and futurity to function for anti-racist, anti-classist, anti-sexist environmentalist ends, it still proves problematic on many levels. For one thing, while Edelman critiques capitalism in his PMLA comments, he fails to acknowledge that, more often than not, it is corporate and governmental *disregard* for the future that enables the (paradoxical) reproduction of capital, and, more specifically, environmental degradation and destruction in the name of capital accumulation. Indeed, anyone who has seen a "Drill Offshore Now" bumper sticker, or heard the chants of "Drill, Baby, Drill" during the John McCain–Sarah Palin campaign, would be suspicious of the idea that concern for future generations, or for the future more broadly, is a sacred tenet of the conservative Right.

Similarly, recent work on "queer time" characterizes concern for the future as a normative impulse—again, in effect maligning environmentalist values and quashing queer ecological thought. For instance, Halberstam observes that "Western cultures . . . pathologize modes of living that show little or no concern for longevity" (*In a Queer Time and Place* 4). Halberstam's 2005 book goes on to consider modes of queer cultural production that challenge this pathologization by championing ephemerality and refusing legacy as imagined in heterosexist, patriarchal terms. While I do not want to suggest that "queer time" is anti-environmentalist per se, the fact remains that a mindset that connotes "concern for longevity" as heteronormative leaves environmental concerns floundering. Indeed, while Halberstam's point about longevity is spot-on in terms of social norms and the logic of capital accumulation, it is off-base in conservationist, environmentalist, and even certain economic terms. The planned obsolescence of so many consumer goods, and environmental catastrophes such as the 2010 British Petroleum oil spill—the result of shortsighted cost cutting and inadequate testing[7]—attest to that fact. Perhaps more prominently, George H. Bush's declaration at the United Nations Conference on Environment and Development in 1992 that "we cannot permit the extreme in the environmental movement to shut down the United States"[8]—echoed by George W. Bush several years later—illustrates the dominance of "modes of living that show little or no concern for longevity." It seems, then, that many queer theorists have reached a point at which they cannot imagine a queer futurity and, by extension, where they cannot imagine environmentalism, much less a queer one.

These shortcomings are particularly troubling from both an anti-racist and an environmental-justice standpoint. Both of those movements have long been concerned with the future—as well as with present injustices and suffering—but not in the white-supremacist, heteronormative way that many queer theorists would imagine. (Indeed, the queer critique of futurity threatens to make us look at such advocacy as a normative or even conservative phenomenon.) Consider, for instance, how indigenous activist Winona LaDuke sees futurity as a necessary mindset: "Dump dioxin into the river, and *you will inevitably* eat or drink it. Assent to acceptable levels of radioactive emissions, and *sooner or later*, those sensitive cells in the human body will likely respond" (*All Our Relations* 197, my emphasis). Environmental-justice advocates have long told us that such "inevitable" outcomes have a disproportionately greater impact on the poor and people of color. Perhaps less dismally, LaDuke also reminds us that "[one] teaching of the Six Nations Iroquois Confederacy recognizes the importance of future generations. 'In each deliberation, we must consider the impact on the seventh generation from now,' they say; that is, undertake conservative [conservationist] thinking and use careful deliberation. Such consideration would have preempted thousands of decisions made by the U.S. government" (198). Clearly, the Iroquois's and LaDuke's perspective complicates the understanding of futurity—even heterosexual reproductive futurity—as an oppressive, hegemonic orientation. This is not, in other words, the territory of Lauren Berlant's "cruel optimism," in which we find that future-thinking and "fantasy isn't a plan. It calibrates nothing about how to live. It is the *action* of living . . . [a] way of passing time, not trying to make something of [oneself] in a system of exploitation and exchange" (9, emphasis original).[9] For LaDuke, future-thinking and optimism are the means of changing that system. Now, of course, many readers will recognize "seventh generation" not from Iroquois teachings or LaDuke's book, but from the massive marketing campaign launched by the (unrelated) eponymous corporation in 2010. A queer ecological perspective attuned to issues of social justice—which I model here—could, among other things, discern between a progressive invocation of futurity that benefits the seventh generation and a superficial one that benefits Seventh Generation, Inc. Chapter 2, for instance, details how Shani Mootoo's novel *Cereus Blooms at Night* contrasts the loving act of raising plants for the sake of their eventual blooming with the act of seizing them for the sake of immediate profit.

The queer failure to conceptualize a viable environmentalism is troubling in a different sense when it comes to environmental justice. As Andil Gosine points out, "[i]n Euroamerican-dominant cultural contexts, *two* kinds of sex have been (are) said to be toxic to nature: reproductive sex between non-white people, and sex between men" (149, my emphasis). He finds, further, that "overpopulation propaganda [in the name of environmental protection] and its material offshoots . . . and the criminalization and policing of sexual acts between men" are not "distinct phenomena, [but] intimately interwoven through the projects of colonialism, development, and nation building" (150). Homophobia, in other words, has been allowed to flourish where racism, classism, and colonialism have held great sway—and vice versa. But perhaps more importantly, we can see from Gosine's comments that environmental *protection* is often the guise under which both environmental *destruction* and forms of social oppression, such as homophobia, operate. Thus this book insists that there must be a way to bring together mainstream environmentalism and its concerns with ecological relationships and sustainability; environmental justice and its concerns with racism, classism, and colonialism; and queer theory and its concerns with homophobia and the regimes of normativity. And I insist that there must be a way to question "nature" and "environmentalism" while still caring for the non-human natural environment.

But this book doesn't just take issue with queer-theoretical ideas; it attempts to adapt some and put them to use in the framework of an anti-racist, -classist, and -sexist queer ecology. For example, I am taken with how Muñoz calls anti-utopianism and anti-relationality "failures of imagination" ("Thinking Beyond" 825), and with how he suggests that we might use the past and the future to combat the kind of here-and-now logic that allows capitalism, among other things, to flourish. I would insist that there are ways of thinking about the here and now that are, in fact, crucial: the belief that environmental devastation is a *possibility*, rather than a current and impending *reality*, or that we have to clean up the planet for *future* generations, rather than for *present* ones, allows for the kind of complacency that authorizes such degradation in the first place. But Muñoz's idea of queer utopianism, outlined more extensively in his recent book-length study *Cruising Utopia* (2010), could inspire environmentalist agendas that seek to achieve positive ends without resorting to heterosexist, homophobic, or pro-reproductive ideologies. Similarly, Tim Dean theorizes queer utopia by noting that the "plung[e] into an experience of the nonrelational represents but the first step in Bersani's account of relationality. The second, correlative step is to trace new forms of sociability, new ways of being together, that are not grounded in imaginary identity or the struggle for intersubjective recognition" (827). Dean is talking about new ways of *humans* being together, whereas ecologists, and of course this book, talk about humans and the non-human world. But the novels and films I look at in *Strange Natures* employ these same understandings of ontology and "being together": they show how humans might interact with non-humans in empathetic and ethical ways despite their irresolvable differences.

Muñoz's phrase, "failures of imagination," is also particularly pertinent to this book. I argue that the texts in my archive represent remarkable *achievements* of imagination, achievements that have much to offer to both queer theory and ecocriticism, as well as to gay, lesbian, bisexual, transgender, queer, and intersex (GLBTQI) politics, and environmentalism more broadly. They allow us to think beyond the stalemates and impasses described above, suggesting that there are ways to care about the natural, ways to expand the social, and ways to think about the future, that are not heteronormative. Indeed, this book suggests that, with a queer ecological perspective attuned to social justice, we can learn to care about the future of the planet in a way that is perhaps more radical than any we have seen previously: acting in the interests of nameless, faceless individuals to which one has no biological, familial, or economic ties whatsoever. This kind of action operates without any reward, without any guarantee of success, and without any proof that potential future inhabitants of the planet might be similar to the individual acting in the present—in terms of social identity, morality, or even species, if some doomsday predictions are to be believed. It is invested in the ends (survival of the non-human alongside the human) but emphasizes the means (caring for the non-human alongside the human). Chapter 2, for instance, highlights how the characters in Mootoo's novel focus on the present and ongoing well-being of a night-blooming cereus plant and a late-blooming transgender character—rather than on the specific end results of their transformations.

Queer theorist Michael Snediker's concept of "queer optimism," proffered in his recent book of the same name, is also inspirational to me here. While Snediker turns to lyric poetry to rethink heteronormative futurity, I have, of course, turned to contemporary queer novels and films that engage with the natural world. But his concept speaks directly to the understandings of time and care that my archive puts forth; as he declares, "[q]ueer optimism . . . is not promissory. It doesn't ask that some future time make good on its own hopes. Rather, queer optimism asks that optimism, embedded in its own immanent present, might be *interesting*" (2). I take Snediker's term "interesting" to mean both something that draws one's attention ("interesting" as in "fascinating") and something that inspires care ("interesting" as in "provoking interest or investment"). Queer optimism, then, is definitely not valuable because one can gain something by it. But it's also not valuable "in and of itself," because there is no such thing as value without a valuer. Rather, its value is determined by the communal and empathetic process of valuing. That is precisely the kind of ethical model that the texts in my archive offer for our encounters with the non-human.

We might test these claims about queer empathy and optimism by considering a recent survey by *Echelon* magazine that found that "two-thirds (66 percent) of lesbian, gay, bisexual, and/or transgender adults say that it is important to support environmental causes, compared with 56 percent of non-LGBT adults. Three-quarters (75 percent) of LGBT adults (compared with 53 percent of heterosexuals) believe global warming is happening right now" (as quoted by Connell). At least one media report on the survey mentioned the idea that this "[g]ay concern about protecting the environment for future generations is especially admirable given the fewer numbers of gay parents" (Bolcer), while another noted "the moral implication of continued dependence on carbon energy to fuel our lives and economy," arguing that "[t]here is also another moral struggle going on by which this generation will be judged[:] . . . the continuing dehumanization, discrimination, hate and violence directed at LGBT people" (Connell).

All this might sound well and good from a queer ecological standpoint. But the claim that gay concern for the environment is "especially admirable" because of the relative dearth of gay parents reveals a problematic lack of empathetic imagination. As I have noted, "imagination" is a key term in this book, and one that has great resonance for queer ecology: since humans cannot always see the consequences of their actions on the environment immediately, nor the intricate interrelationships among all components in an ecosystem, they must be able to *imagine* them in order to act empathetically and ethically. Indeed, empathy is by definition a largely imaginative act, a point I stress throughout *Strange Natures*. Thus, while being concerned about the environment despite not having children may be "especially admirable" to some, the texts I consider insist that it should simply be the status quo.

The aforementioned reports also fail to explain how awareness of the "continuing dehumanization" of GLBTQI people could allow for, rather than prevent, concern for the non-human. Critiques of "dehumanization" often, though not always, rest upon liberal humanist values around the importance of the individual—values that are not particularly ecocentric. The texts I consider in this book propose that environmentalism might involve a decentering of anthropocentrism, such that the dehumanization of queers and other populations would not be considered wrong in and of itself—because the non-human is not worthless—but dehumanization *as a justification for violence would* be. After all, environmental exploitation is often justified by the non-human status of "nature." The texts I consider imagine that queers might empathize with the likewise non-human, instead of (just) fighting for human status, or fighting for it on unethical terms.

In sum, *Strange Natures* hopes to redress queer theory's more glaring blind spots, such as anti-futurity, while extending its more dynamic ideas, including self-shattering, optimism, and utopianism. I agree that the value set of normative, reproductive heterosexuality establishes strict, moralized limits to futurity, but I refuse the idea that it has a monopoly on futurity, or on environmental ethics rooted in futurity. I propose, in fact, that any kind of environmentalism that does not operate within those limits—that is, that does not operate out of immediate or extended self-interest—is "queer." As I detail in my last chapter, on Shelley Jackson's novel *Half Life*, such points can be conveyed with good humor, rather than defensiveness or despair. In that spirit, I offer in closing the "Deep Thought" from *Saturday Night Live*'s Jack Handey series that I show to my queer theory/ecocriticism students each semester: "I believe in making the world safe for our children, but not our children's children, because I don't think children should be having sex."

Ecocriticism

Comparatively speaking, there has been less conceptual resistance to queer ecology or queer ecocriticism from the field of ecocriticism, as compared to queer theory. (Work in queer ecology tends to emerge from ecocritical rather than queer-theoretical scholarly backgrounds, though that is certainly not predictive of the kind of work that might emerge in the future.) That said, the relationship between the natural and the queer is still a new area of focus for those in environmental activism and literary studies, one that has not yet infiltrated all quarters of those fields. As of this writing, a search for the term "queer" in ISLE, the journal of the Association for the Study of Literature and Environment, and the most prominent journal of its kind, returns twenty-five hits—at least five of which include the term as a synonym for "strange," not as a reference to issues of gender and sexuality. (We might compare this statistic to the one hit that GLQ, the most prominent GLBTQI studies journal, returns for "ecocriticism,"[10] the sparse handful of hits for "ecology" that refer to the non-human natural world, and the one hit for the term "environmentalism"—which finds Kath Weston lamenting that "environmentalism and queer politics seldom seem to intersect" [231].) The majority of ecocritical monographs and edited collections give queer issues, and sexuality more broadly, no mention. Some, such as Lawrence Buell's *The Future of Environmental Criticism* (2005), acknowledge the importance of sexual orientation in critical considerations of the natural world but do not treat it in depth. For example, he opines that "Skittishness at modernization's aggressive, accelerating, inequitable transformation of 'natural' into constructed space . . . giv[es] ecocriticism . . . its edge of critique. This is ecocriticism's equivalent as it were to queer studies, which some environmental writers and critics have in fact begun to affiliate (see Sandilands 1999): to unsettle normative thinking about environmental status quos" (24). Buell's comment glosses over a glaring paradox: queer theory actually *underwrites*, rather than *resists*, the move from the natural to the constructed. That is, it seeks to show that heterosexuality, the association of male biology with masculine gender, et cetera are social constructs rather than natural phenomena.

We might also note that Buell *parallels* the two paradigms—"ecocriticism's *equivalent* . . . to queer studies"—rather than gesturing toward their intersections. Similarly, while David Mazel draws on the work of Judith Butler to inform his poststructuralist ecocriticism, he ends up drawing an *analogy* between postructuralist feminist/queer theory and a poststructuralist ecocriticism: he proposes to "treat the wilderness landscape *the way* Butler treats the 'naturally' sexed human body" (*American Literary Environmentalism* xvii, my emphasis)—"'not as a site or surface, but as *a process of materialization that stabilizes over time to product the effect of boundary, fixity, and surface we call matter*'" (*American Literary Environmentalism* xvii, emphasis original). Buell and Mazel do not admit the possibility of a paradigm that would draw on all of the aforementioned schools of thought at once, and that would show us that dominant beliefs about the "'naturally' sexed," and sexual, human body are inextricable from beliefs about the non-human natural world. However, in putting poststructuralist ideas into conversation with more traditional ecocritical approaches to nature, they have undeniably paved the way for queer ecological scholarship such as this book.

One strong historical barrier to the emergence of queer ecology from ecocritical quarters has been the existence of some strains of environmentalism and ecocriticism that are hostile to "special interest" concerns. For example, as I discuss in Chapter 3, many radical environmentalists have taken anti-anthropocentrism to such an extreme that they fail to consider that there might be anything like problems *among* humans, or humans who actually *suffer*. Moreover, many prominent idols of ecocriticism happen to be privileged, straight white men whose disregard for problems of social inequality might be confidently termed racist, sexist, classist, and homophobic.[11] We can surmise that such idolizing has turned at least a few queer, non-white, and/or working-class people away from ecocriticism and environmentalism.

Relatedly, ecocriticism has long been characterized by essentialisms of various kinds—which stand at odds with queer theory's staunch anti-essentialism and anti-identitarianism. This has been true even when the goal has been the liberation, rather than oppression, of "special interest" groups. For one thing, as Timothy Morton observes, "[e]cofeminism . . . arose out of feminist separatism, wedded to a biological essentialism that, strategic or not, is grounded on binary difference and thus unhelpful for the kinds of difference multiplication that is queer theory's brilliance" (274). The models for care that have emerged from ecofeminist quarters have therefore often been based in essentialist beliefs—say, that women, being sensitive creatures, are uniquely equipped to care for animals.[12] In the same way, masculinist brands of ecocriticism have upheld fundamentalist beliefs about maleness.[13] And it likely goes without saying at this point that nature is essentialized in much ecocriticism, posited as pristine, primal, or at least self-evident. We can see this when, for instance, ecocritic Karl Kroeber claims that "no one old enough to remember life before antibiotics will march under the new historicist banner 'There is no nature.' Nor should anyone who has encoun-

tered a forest fire . . . or been out in a middle-western thunderstorm" (42).
Morton catalogues the popularity of such "common-sense," experience-
based responses to poststructuralist and social-constructionist scholars of
all stripes, including feminists and Marxists. We may be disturbed by the
anti-intellectualism such responses display, and by their unwillingness to
listen to the actual claim at hand. (After all, no one who ever said gender was
constructed said gender didn't exist.) But these responses also indicate a real
failing on the part of poststructuralist frameworks such as queer theory to
make their ideas comprehensible to people who may have more challenging
and more visceral lived experiences of gender, sexuality, race, or nature.

As I demonstrate throughout *Strange Natures*, my texts both speak to those
kinds of people and are influenced by the postmodern, poststructuralist
insights of fields such as queer theory, post–Second Wave feminism, critical race studies, and New Historicism; they are skeptical of identity and
question the natural bases of sexuality, gender, and race. This fact points
toward another potential antagonism between queer theory/politics and
ecocriticism/ environmentalism—and, in turn, toward yet another reason
why the texts in my archive have not been widely recognized as ecologically
minded. As Simon Estok observes, "what has popularized and expanded
the hermeneutic range of ecocriticism"—an activist, direct-action orientation, among other things—"has in some ways also made ecocriticism
seem immune to the challenges presented by so much of poststructuralism" (203). Estok points to Peter Quigley, who declares that "the academic
environmental community in the USA has done a poor job of responding
to the challenge of poststructuralism," noting, "after poststructuralism, it
is impossible to take a term like 'nature' at face value; it is impossible not
to see the fissures of contradiction and the fault-lines of history that criss-
cross the term" (205). Ecocriticism's historical lack of a poststructuralist
position, or even something like a strategic essentialism—wherein, just
as Gayatri Spivak has suggested that ethnic minorities might identify col-
lectively to achieve certain goals, we might act as if there really is a simple,
self-evident thing called "nature," to the extent that the non-human world
might be defended[14]—has made queer ecocriticism and queer ecology all
but impossible until recently.

Many ecocritics, in fact, actively object to anything that looks like theory.
This resistance is perhaps best exemplified by S. K. Robisch, who declares
that theory—which he calls the "sleazy uncle of poststructuralism and
cultural criticism"—is "regularly ecophobic" and that it "regularly indicts
itself as a participant in the destruction of biospheric health by promoting
a thought process that renders the biosphere an immaterial idea subject to

the laboratory of abstraction" (702). Robisch thereby sabotages his own sentiment: his statement is aligned exactly with ecologically minded theorists (or theory-minded ecologists) who have taught us that our ideas about nature have authorized environmental destruction. At the same time, his statement gives most, if not all, of the credit for environmental destruction to abstract "thought process[es]"—not consumers, corporations, or even human beings. And he thereby focuses even less on the "real world" than have self-described poststructuralist ecocritics such as Mazel.[15]

Poststructuralist ecocriticism is just one example of the broader shifts that have been taking place in the field of ecocriticism; others include the interest in dissolving the nature–culture boundary, or registering its already-extant dissolution, and the interest in attending to social problems such as racism and poverty, in part through increased attention to minority texts and viewpoints. Just as queer theory needs to see "nature" in a context other than the social and the human, ecocritics have come to see "nature" and "the environment" in contexts other than the organic and the non-human. This "second wave" of ecocriticism,[16] I argue, has been instrumental in making queer ecology possible. In attending to environmental injustice as it plays out through homophobia and transphobia, in addition to racism, classism, sexism, and xenophobia, and in tracing in how the queer has been framed in opposition to the natural, *Strange Natures* builds on the insights of this second wave and, as I discuss further below, on previous queer ecology scholarship more specifically.

Resistant Receptions; or, "Why Should I Care?"

Since this book presumes that the persisting gaps between queer theory and ecocriticism need to be bridged, and that we should both embrace and build upon queer ecological thought, I will offer a few answers to that dreaded question so often asked of critical theorists: "Why should I care?" Someone like Robisch might say that the solution to theory's potential hindrance to the environmentalist agenda would be to simply ignore theory. But that would mean, as I have intimated in my preface, dismissing the anti-homophobia and anti-transphobia of queer theory, among its other insights, as well as the anti-misogyny and anti-racism of paradigms such as feminist theory and critical race studies. It would also mean brushing aside the momentous question asked by Mortimer-Sandilands and Erickson: "What does it mean that ideas, spaces, and practices designated as 'nature' are often so vigorously defended against queers in a society in which that very nature is increasingly degraded and exploited?" (5) Finally, it would mean ignoring the fact that so many literary and filmic texts influenced by poststructuralism and postmodernism actually take "nature" qua the non-human quite seriously. In short, without a perspective that is at once ecological and queer, we cannot intervene in some of the most pressing intellectual and political conflicts of the contemporary era; we cannot adequately address oppression, especially interrelated oppressions; and we cannot effectively interpret a great deal of the cultural and artistic output of the past several decades.

We must note that ecocritics and environmentalists on the one hand, and queer theorists and activists on the other, have formulated very different versions of the "Why should I care?" question. The ecocriticism/environmentalism camp has formulated this question in terms of the "sinking ship hypothesis"—asking, essentially, why we should prioritize the queer in queer ecology, when the environment is at such dire risk. As Peter Barry summarizes:

"Seeking to contribute to rectifying injustices in the areas of gender, race and class is a praiseworthy aim for critics and theorists to have, but it isn't sensible to ignore the fact that making a difference in these presupposes that we can manage to avoid environmental catastrophe. Otherwise, it might seem like working . . . to secure improved working-conditions for the crew as the Titanic speeds towards the iceberg" (248).

Or, as David Orton quips more succinctly: "There can be no social justice on a dead planet."[17] Some environmentalists take an even more extreme view, suggesting that attending to factors such as race, class, gender, and sexuality actually *keeps us* from fighting environmental degradation. But this view, I argue, represents a failure of imagination. Not only am I unclear as to why we can't attend to both social and environmental concerns, I'm not convinced that the two are separate. Social ecologist Murray Bookchin is likewise unconvinced; he argues that, "based on considerable anthropological evidence, [we can see] that the modern view of nature as a hostile . . . 'other' grows historically out of a projection of warped, hierarchical *social* relations onto the rest of the natural world" (57, my emphasis). Even if such evidence were lacking, the fact remains that a considerable number of individuals do not have the luxury of choosing environmental concerns over social concerns. Further, the suggestion that one should confront environmental problems in a "gender-blind" or "color-blind" way is highly problematic, even offensive: it asks that we all be more like the white, straight, privileged men who have, historically, been at the forefront of environmental destruction in the first place.

Conversely, queer theorists and activists have, though much less directly, asked why we should prioritize the ecology in queer ecology. Consider Halberstam's contribution to a *GLQ* roundtable on "Queer Temporalities":

> I am in a drag king club at 2:00 a.m. and the performances are really bad, and some kid comes onstage and just rips an amazing performance of Elvis or Eminem or Michael Jackson and the people in the club recognize why they are here, in this place at this time, engaged in activities that probably seem pointless to people stranded in hetero temporalities. . . . Queer time for me is the dark nightclub, the perverse turn away from the narrative coherence of adolescence—early adulthood—marriage—reproduction—child rearing— retirement—death, the embrace of late childhood in place of early adulthood or immaturity in place of responsibility. ("Theorizing Queer Temporalities" 181–82)

Like the queer embrace of the "unnatural" and the anti-social, the queer embrace of a "live in the now" attitude draws on familiar stereotypes of queers as preoccupied with the frivolous, and with meaningless and fleet-ing pleasures. More to the point, this embrace resonates poorly in an envi-ronmental framework; it allows for a dismissal that runs something like, "Why should I care about the environment? If the world falls apart in the future, I'm not going to be there to see it." Such dismissals also happen to inform "Drill, baby, drill"–style politics—and the contemporary political climate, in which environmental regulation has been (falsely) positioned as a contributing factor to financial crisis.[18]

To be fair, long-term environmental problems would quite understand-ably be a low priority for many of the queer "kid[s]" whose only refuge is the "dark nightclub." And of course, my claims are extrapolative; Halber-stam's version of queer time does not seem intent upon articulating any relationship, positive or negative, to the environment or nature as such, and Halberstam has been a prominent critic of queer-theoretical elisions of racial, class, and gender inequality. But perhaps all of the above is to the point. The texts I treat in *Strange Natures* tell us that failures of queer eco-logical empathy—in the dismissal I've cited above, the failure to imagine someone or something to whom environmental destruction *would*, and *does*, matter—can have disastrous results not just for the environment, but for those individuals who fail. It produces a devastating isolation, a discon-nection from human and non-human others alike. And it prevents those individuals from recognizing how their everyday experiences of oppression might be bound up with ecological destruction. My texts, in response, ask a galvanizing set of questions around empathy: What if we could imagine that environmental catastrophe *does* matter, even, or perhaps especially, if we are not going to witness its effects? How might that imagination func-tion as a form of queer survival? How could we develop, and strengthen, that imagination? I argue that a concept of queer time that is attuned to environmentalism's focus on futurity—on the long- and short-term effects of policies and products; on health outcomes for humans and non-humans alike; on sustainable practices—is one place to start.

Building Queer Ecology

Popular and Political Challenges

It may go without saying at this point that the disconnect between "the queer" and "the natural" is not confined to the academic paradigms of queer theory and ecocriticism. Indeed, this disconnect is pervasive in contemporary Western culture, and oftentimes in very concrete, not just conceptual, ways; its pervasiveness provides a larger explanation for why scholars have not considered the queer alongside the ecological until quite recently.[19] In briefly outlining this disconnect here, I further indicate the "real-world" purchase of this book, and the alternative ways of thinking and feeling that it proposes. To begin with, the concept of "nature" has been used in religious, political, and other public discourses to invalidate queerness and, in turn, validate heterosexuality. To take a prominent example, George W. Bush addressed the nation in 2004 in support of a constitutional amendment to ban same-sex marriage, declaring, "Marriage cannot be severed from its cultural, religious and *natural roots* without weakening the good influence of society" (my emphasis).[20] Bush hereby collapses human nature and the natural world—not to indicate their interconnection, but instead to discriminate against an instance of the former by rhetorically exploiting the latter. (So far as we know, plants have no vested interested in whether or not Adam and Steve marry.) Likewise, one of the most common arguments against same-sex marriage has rested upon the inability of two men or two women to "naturally" reproduce, like other humans, and like other mammals. These examples indicate not just that the battle over queer acceptance has been waged largely along "nature-versus-nurture" lines, but that that battle actually constructs and calcifies the two categories—with "nature" the "right" answer to the "wrong" one of "nurture," and the two conceptually separate. Scientists have been laboring against this fallacious separation for the past several decades.

Queers also have a vexed relationship with "nature" in a different sense: popular media and news media have largely associated them with urbanity or "unnatural" spaces, despite realities to the contrary. As Katie Hogan points out, queers "are presumed to be located in decadent cities, as having no place in rural landscape" ("Detecting" 251). Catriona Sandilands has argued, further, that this "lack of a strong representation of queer rurality

impoverishes both ecological and GLBTQI culture and reinforces an articulation of queer-urban-artifice against straight-rural-nature" ("Sexual
Politics" 122). In recent years, a few projects have worked to overturn this
assumption, from Will Fellows's memoir collection *Farm Boys: Lives of Gay
Men from the Rural Midwest* (2001) to the documentary *Small Town Gay Bar*
(2006). But the ameliorative character of much of these projects suggests
that the connection of queerness and urbanity is predominant, even in media produced by GLBTQI people.

When popular media and news media *do* associate queers with the non-
urban, those associations are often admonitory, or even damning. Take, for
example, the rape and murder of transgender man Brandon Teena in rural
Nebraska, captured in Aphrodite Jones's sensationalist true-crime account
All She [sic] Wanted and the acclaimed 1999 film *Boys Don't Cry*. Such depictions
have served as cautionary tales of queer unsafety in rural areas, although
research suggests that urban and suburban areas may have much higher
incidence of hate crimes.[21] Perhaps more disturbingly—or laughably—religious conservatives such as Pat Robertson have linked queers to destructive
acts of nature. Robertson once warned his television audience, "When you
see the rise of blatant open homosexuality and lesbianism, what you also
know is God has given a society up . . . and we're at the mercy of the elements."[22] After Orlando, Florida, city officials flew gay pride flags during
Disney World's "Gay Days" in 1998, Robertson declared that "earthquakes,
tornadoes and possibly a meteor" would follow.[23] Of course, it brought
none of the above. But interestingly enough, even a satirical response to
Robertson, which drew on meterological data to show that more natural
disasters strike areas populated by straight Protestants, featured the title
"Do Unnatural Acts Cause Natural Disasters?"[24]—thus maintaining the
association of queerness with "unnaturalness."

Lest Robertson's seem like a fringe opinion, Noël Sturgeon has recently
noted that popular children's texts such as *Captain Planet*, *The Lion King*,
Pocahontas, and *White Fang 2* regularly feature "an association . . . between
homosexuality, evil, and environmental destruction, coupled with . . . anxiety about the successful reproduction of the white, middle-class, nuclear
family form[, which] is presented as 'normal' and 'natural' without any
critique of its complicity in the overconsumption of corporate products in
an environmentally destructive system in which the toxins, waste, pollution
and radiation produced are visited on the poor, the people of color, and the
tribal peoples of the world" ("The Power Is Yours" 263). Not to mention,
I would add, that those who preach concern for the natural along with
homophobia are rarely concerned for the natural in practice; despite his

appeals to "natural roots," George W. Bush has been widely recognized as the most destructive president in U.S. history when it comes to the environment.[25] Among other things, he bears the distinction of having received an "F" on his environmental "Report Card" from the bipartisan League of Conservation Voters.

Against this political and pop-cultural background, the works I consider in *Strange Natures* explicitly link queerness to the environment and the natural world. But they concentrate less on the shocking juxtaposition of the queer and the natural, and more on the importance of positively staging the relationship thereof. With the exception of the thoroughly self-conscious and -reflexive postmodern novel *Half Life*, the rest of the texts in my archive are likewise modest about their meaningful endeavors; they presume that environmentalist and environmental-justice work are logical extensions of queer approaches.

State of the Field:
Whence, and Whither, Queer Ecology?

In the past few years, queer ecology has emerged as a burgeoning area of interdisciplinary study. (Depending on the emphasis of study, practitioners and affiliates occasionally use more specific terms, such as "queer eco-criticism," "queer ecofeminism," or "queer biology," if they systematically categorize such work at all.) Several scholars have explicitly or implicitly taken up the queer ecological paradigm in full-length works—including Bruce Bagemihl and Joan Roughgarden, whose respective books *Biological Exuberance* (1999) and *Evolution's Rainbow* (2004) theorize the evolutionary role of sexual diversity among non-humans, which they claim as widely underreported; Scott Herring, whose *Another Country: Queer Anti-Urbanism* (2010) uncovers a tradition of rural queer life and style in the United States; Noreen Giffney and Myra J. Hird's *Queering the Non/Human*, a collection of essays that use queer-theoretical interest in fluidity and indeterminacy to demonstrate the unstable distinction between human and non-human; Catriona Mortimer-Sandilands and Bruce Erickson, whose *Queer Ecologies: Sex, Nature, Politics, Desire* (2010) offers a complex picture of queer ecology by collecting work from a variety of fields; Rachel Stein, whose edited collection *New Perspectives on Environmental Justice: Gender, Sexuality, and Activism* (2004) asks, "How might our conception of environmental justice be expanded so as to foster alliances and help promote queer ecologies?" (7); and Noël Sturgeon, whose *Environmentalism in Popular Culture: Gender, Race, Sexuality, and the Politics of the Natural* (2009) claims that various media naturalize white heterosexual family life and its attendant ecological behaviors. Additionally, several articles and book chapters affined with queer ecology have appeared in the past few years, in the wake of Sandilands and Greta Gaard's respective groundbreaking articles "Lavender's Green?: Some Thoughts on Queer(y)ing Environmental Politics" (1994) and "Toward a Queer Ecofeminism" (1997). These include Cynthia Chris's "Animal Sex" chapter in *Watching Wildlife* (2006), which laments the fact that "[h]omosexuality is, within the bounds of wildlife TV, not a natural act to be understood on its own terms, but a phase of foreplay prior to the real reproductive deal" (165), and Jill E. Anderson's "'Warm Blood and Live Semen and Rich Marrow and Wholesome Flesh!': A Queer Ecological Reading of Christopher Isherwood's *A Single Man*," which appeared in the *Journal of Ecocriticism* in 2011.

   Strange Natures builds on the spirit and the momentum of this work while making unique contributions to queer ecology, to contemporary literary, filmic, political, and cultural studies more broadly, and to non-academic areas such as social justice and environmental activism. I might begin, then, by clarifying what this book does *not* seek to do. First, it does not endeavor to analyze rural queer life or the activities of queer environmental activists, as Herring and Sandilands have. Nor does it investigate the queerness of the non-human through a queer science framework, as found in Bagemihl, Roughgarden, or Giffney and Hird's collection. And nor is *Strange Natures* a work of queer geography—a look at queer spaces, or at queer ways of occupying spaces—which David Bell and Gill Valentine and several other scholars have produced.[26] Like Giffney and Hird, I probe queer theory itself even as I apply it to the relationship of the human to the non-human—but unlike in their collection, my primary task is not to examine the philosophical and ontological bases of those two categories. (I am concerned, instead, with how literature and film teach us about both the oppressive experiences and ethical implications of the slippage between the two—say, how transgender persons are violently punished for being "less than human," and how such individuals might respond in a biocentric, rather than anthropocentric, manner.) Like Stein, I take up social and environmental justice—but my primary intent is not to expand those paradigms to include (homo)sexuality, as many of the essays in her collection do. (I follow up on the work of that collection by presuming from the very start that queerness is an environmental-justice issue, and vice versa.) And while it offers queer ecological readings of film and literature, as scholars such as Anderson and Alice A. Kuzniar already have, this project is not solely a work of queer ecological textual analysis, or queer ecocriticism. Finally, *Strange Natures* is not, at least primarily, an examination of queer ecology as a field; no book-length publication in this vein exists yet, though the introduction to Mortimer-Sandilands and Erickson's *Queer Ecologies* offers one overview.

Rather, *Strange Natures* is a study of how contemporary queer novels and films from the Americas have imagined empathetic, ethical interrelationships between the queer and the non-human—and, thereby, addressed some of the most abiding cultural, political, and intellectual divides of the postwar period. In conducting this study, of course, I necessarily think about the field of queer ecology itself. But my intention is not to define or even describe it. Rather, I theorize its arrival and point to what it might accomplish. In terms of the former, I show how post-1960s conceptual tendencies have allowed, or not allowed, for the kind of queer ecological empathetic thought that the texts in my archive model. I identify these tendencies as postmodern/poststructuralist skepticism (with which queer theory has been closely associated) on the one hand, and pragmatism and activism (with which ecocriticism has been closely associated) on the other. (Above, I have shown how queer theory and ecocriticism specifically have allowed, or not allowed, for the development of queer ecological thought.) While some queer ecology scholarship has discussed the *why-now* of the paradigm, then, *Strange Natures* also offers a look at the *why-not-before*. And while queer ecological work tends to focus on its social, scientific, and/or political implications—precisely because of theory's abstract tendencies, and thus its frequent disinterest in "real world" problems like environmental degradation—*Strange Natures* insists that we understand the theoretical as well. This book is thus a story of how queer ecological thought emerges out of two very different sets of impulses, to be synthesized in art.

In the first place, then, *Strange Natures* is distinguished by its archive. Certainly there are earlier fictional works, and works from other cultural traditions, that synthesize queer concerns and ecological concerns, and/ or to which the application of a queer ecological lens would be productive. Robert Azzarello, for example, has performed an exemplary queer-ecocritical reading of Irish writer Bram Stoker's *Dracula*, published in 1897,[27] while Mortimer-Sandilands and Erickson recover the queer ecological impulses of late nineteenth- and early twentieth-century writers such as Sarah Orne Jewett and André Gide, and of older traditions such as the pastoral. But the twenty years I focus on here have unique implications in terms of queer ecology. For one thing, these texts manage to take seriously the well-being of the environment and the natural world at a time at which the very concept of the natural has been vigorously interrogated, and skeptically framed, in both intellectual and popular circles—and at which technological advancements have prompted some to declare the arrival of the "post-natural" era.[28]

And they manage to care about the natural world despite being *themselves* skeptical of "nature." Indeed, all of my texts demonstrate an awareness of, and affinity for, intellectual traditions that question the construction and naturalization of fundamental categories such as gender and race, and the dehumanization/animalization of poor people and people of color. My work thus concurs with Mazel's belief that "the constructivist approach need not impede environmental politics; it does not wipe out the possibility of effective political agency, but rather reconfigures such agency" (*American Literary Environmentalism* xvii).

My historical context is important in another sense: as I will briefly sketch out, contemporary environmentalism in the United States (including the so-called second and third waves, stretching from the 1960s to the 2000s[29]) has been marked by contradictions and combative elements. The paradox-laden texts in my archive are in many ways creatures of these environmentalisms and thus are uniquely suited to comment on them. To begin with, environmental historian Philip Shabecoff observes on the one hand links between environmentalism and the radical countercultural movements of the 1960s, including feminism, antiwar, and civil rights, and on the other environmentalism's appeal to many moderate, white, middle-class Americans. Understanding themselves as empowered consumers, the latter group saw environmentalism as an opportunity to demand healthy products and clean spaces to live and recreate. In contrast to those members of countercultural movements, then, environmentalism appeared to such individuals as a relatively nonthreatening, even traditionalist pursuit.[30] (These different takes on environmentalism just happen to overlap with the different iterations of "gay liberation," from moderate assimilationism to radical queerness.) Shabecoff also observes that "[e]nvironmentalism is a kind of platypus among social movements—it is not easy to classify. . . . Environmentalism is progressive in that it believes that human society can be changed for the better to curb pollution, husband resources, and protect life. It is conservative because it strives to conserve the natural world" (238–39). Environmental historian Samuel P. Hays looks more broadly to environmentalism's reception, to find that "[r]egions of lower environmental [political] support tend to be those in which extractive industries, including agriculture, have long played a significant role in the region's economy," while "[r]egions of higher environmental [political] support tend to have newer economies in which service, high-technology, and consumer-oriented economic activities dominate" (187). Considering his additional finding that inhabitants of the former areas tend to hold traditional social views, while those of the latter hold nontraditional social views, a larger picture of paradox appears: communities known for understanding certain behaviors (feminism, homosexuality) as "unnatural" are less likely to demonstrate concern for the non-human natural world—even as they work more closely with it. And, conversely, communities that are known for "unnatural" behaviors voice greater concern for the natural world, yet are further removed from it. Thus the contrarian work performed by my archive—texts that develop conceptions of nature that include "unnatural" queers—and the larger work of queer ecology as a field, emerges from, and responds to, a long history of political paradox.

In historicizing and theorizing the emergence of both queer ecology and that of the works in my archive, I offer several new approaches and concepts. These have purchase for queer ecology specifically and critical theory generally, and, even more broadly, for environmental ethics and other such points at which the sciences and the humanities meet. First, I attempt to model a more thoroughly queer and intersectional reading practice than have previous works in queer ecology. (This type of intersectional consciousness has been largely lacking in the separate fields of queer theory and, to a lesser extent, ecocriticism.[31]) To take just one example, Jill E. Anderson's recent article on *A Single Man* connects the queer lifestyle preferences of Isherwood's protagonist to his disapproval of California coastal development but leaves his white male privilege and arguable misogyny untouched. I would argue, in fact, that the novel is as much about the changing racial dynamics of postwar California as it is about its changing landscape. This book, then, insists that a queer ecological focus on sexuality and environment should open out onto other foci, and I therefore take up not just the central queer-theoretical tenets of anti-heteronormativity and anti-essentialism, but also principles of social and environmental justice, anti-racism, -classism, -capitalism, -sexism, -xenophobia, and -colonialism. In each chapter, I show how such concerns intersect. For example, in Chapter 5 I discuss how Shelley Jackson's *Half Life* indicates that the desert has been framed as a barren, useless, and otherwise "queer" space in part because of racist attitudes toward its indigenous populations.

My reading practice is also distinguished by my critique of homonormativity. This critique is part of my effort to model an expansive, and thoroughly queer, queer ecology—and to ensure that GLBTQI identities or behaviors do not become overly idealized through queer ecological inquiry. Thus, whereas scholars such as Herring and Sandilands have investigated pagan gay male communities and lesbian-separatist communes, and whereas non-scholarly publications such as *The Advocate* highlight mainstream "gay environmentalists," I keep my focus on queer iterations of ecology that are anti-essentialist, anti-assimilationist, and heterogeneous. Chapter 4, for instance, rereads *Brokeback Mountain* not as a fantasy of gay separatism, nor as a bourgeois gay tragedy of failed assimilationism, as have many critics, but rather as a document of class-conscious queer resistance to neoliberalism. Through such critique, I challenge the idea that GLBTQI texts and perspectives are *necessarily* progressive, environmentally or otherwise.

Environmental justice, and not just environmentalism, is a particularly important paradigm for this reading practice and this book as a whole, especially considering the former's concern with human rights, and how mainstream environmentalism in the United States has often been characterized by, and linked to, discrimination and social inequality.[32] Environmental justice, as defined by leaders in the field such as Bunyan Bryant, Robert Bullard, and Ben Chavis, is the view that inequalities of race and class put people of color and poor people at greater ecological risk. For instance, in his groundbreaking *Dumping in Dixie: Race, Class, and Environmental Quality* (1990), Bullard demonstrates that dangerous waste sites in southern U.S. communities have been overwhelmingly located in low-income black communities. Bullard and others have thereby expanded the narrow, traditional definition of "environment" that has kept mainstream environmental activism a white movement, at least in name.[33] Thus the "environmentalism" of which I speak throughout this book should be understood as one that goes beyond a general concern for the non-human's well-being, to scrutinize how issues such as racism, classism, homophobia, and transphobia are tied up with that well-being—or, as it were, ill-being. I thus claim that sexuality is a central vector through which humans understand the non-human world, while stressing that that vector cannot be isolated from other concerns.

I offer such reading practices as a means of identifying queer texts that might not otherwise seem environmental but that espouse environmental justice and/or social-justice values; these reading practices could be applied, conversely, to environmental texts that might not otherwise seem queer but that denounce forms of inequality that intersect with transphobia or homophobia. I thereby suggest that "nature writing" and "ecocinema" might be even more expansive categories than ecocritics and other scholars have previously thought: if, as I show, naturalization is a process that operates on both humans and the non-human world, then queer texts that ask what counts as natural in terms of gender and sexuality can help us interrogate what counts as natural in other senses and contexts. I thus follow Katie Hogan's belief that "queer skepticism is good for queers, nature, and environmentalism"—and, I would add, people of color and economically disadvantaged people—"because it questions how all of these terms can be put to use in harmful ways" ("Undoing Nature" 250). The skepticism found in queer fictions toward that which dominant forces deem "natural" could help us see, to take just one example, the disingenuousness of categorizing Hurricane Katrina as a "natural disaster," when in fact most of its greatest harms resulted from social inequalities.

In modeling an expansive queer ecological practice of reading, *Strange Natures* also proposes futurity as a queer concept. I track how my texts think in terms of the future well-being of the human and the non-human world—and how those futures are interconnected. Specifically, I show that queer values—caring not (just) about the individual, the family, or one's descendants, but about the Other species and persons to whom one has no immediate relations—may be the most effective ecological values. This proposal counters the anti-futurist and "negative" strains in queer theory discussed above, ongoing strains that I see as opposing the crucial environmentalist value of sustainability. Thus "futurity" functions in this book in much the same way that "nature" and "environmentalism" do: as a paradigm that has value but that must be reconceptualized from a queer, biocentric standpoint. I show that troubling the views of nature and the future that queer theorists have held, and troubling the views of nature and the environment that eco-critics and mainstream environmentalists have held, may, ironically, be the best path to an effective and inclusive queer ecological practice.

Strange Natures also contributes to queer ecology, and to literary and film studies more broadly, by considering how contemporary fictions represent queer ecological concerns through form and style, in addition to content. I elaborate a theory of queer ecological form and style applicable to both literature and film. For instance, Chapter 3 studies how Todd Haynes's queer filmic techniques produce a formal commentary on environmental injustice, while Chapter 5 points to the queerness of Shelley Jackson's ambiguous narrative voice, and the ironic playfulness of her speculative fiction novel *Half Life*, as environmentalist modes. I argue that these queer formal/stylistic techniques are uniquely suited to dealing with environmental issues that cannot otherwise be represented through classical narrative form—such as slow-building toxins or slow-growing cancers, or threats to generations far in the future. Moreover, in the latter chapter, focused on Jackson's *Half Life*, I claim that the detachment allowed for by irony allows humans to imaginatively occupy the place of the non-human. I thereby counter the idea that a "post-identity" age of ironic detachment is necessarily an apolitical age.

Ironic environmentalism is just one iteration of the complex of imagination, interconnectedness, empathy, and ethics upon which *Strange Natures* focuses—a complex that I see as a crucial foundation for queer ecological thought. Each of my chapters discerns an ethical interconnected ecology in the work or works in question; I show how, in each context captured by the literary or filmic work, this type of ecology advocates for oppressed humans of various stripes, as well as oppressed non-humans. I thereby go beyond queer theoretical work that sees compassion and optimism as dangerously normative elements in American political life, as well as beyond previous work in ecofeminism that sees such kinds of care as the province primarily of women, or as sufficient unto itself.[34] As I suggest, the works in my archive offer a political model that we might extend to the "real world": one in which imagination and empathy allow humans to build political coalitions across divides such as race and sexuality, and to identify across species in ways that benefit the biosphere rather than the individual, the nation, or the corporation.

Queer Literature
as Environmental Literature

The tradition of queer environmentalism I find in my archive entails a consideration of the human relationship to the non-human entities that usually fall under the categories of "nature" or "the environment." More specifically, it entails the dramatization of problems ranging from air pollution, to the takeover of indigenous lands, to nuclear fallout. In exploring these relationships and problems, the texts I consider rethink "the natural" as it pertains to both gender/sexuality and the environment. They find that, just as "natural" genders/sexualities are social constructs—a finding that marks these texts as queer—so are many of our visions of the natural world. But these novels and films do not stop with that insight: they reveal how dominant constructions of the natural world have allowed for its real-life abjection while, paradoxically, also privileging it as implicitly white and heterosexual. I show how they respond to this oppressive paradox by modeling ethical, queer human relationships to the non-human. Through their uniquely empathetic imaginations, which employ queer experiences and affect to transport the human closer to the non-human, these texts foment urgent environmentalist agendas.

In this book, I employ "queer" as most queer theorists do: to describe that which questions the naturalness, and undermines the stability, of established categories of sex, gender, and sexuality. The texts in my archive are queer in that sense, staging incoherencies among those categories and indicting heterosexist ideals of health, reproductivity, individuality, domesticity, and capital accumulation. They also strike anti-identitarian stances, focusing on *performances and experiences* of gender and sexuality rather than on coherent identities based in firm categories of gender and sexuality. Thus *Strange Natures* does not claim that queer *individuals* necessarily have a particular kind of relationship to the non-human; it focuses primarily on the queer *relationships* that humans might develop with the non-human, and how environmental ethics might emerge from queer practices and perspectives.

Compared to "queer," "eco" is a slightly more slippery term. Many scholars have debated the usefulness of the prefix vis-à-vis "environment" or "enviro," with some believing that the latter are more capacious, and thus more effective.[35] But I believe that "eco" as in both "ecological" and "ecocriticism" importantly specifies interrelationships. While the primary OED definition of "ecology" is "[t]he branch of biology that deals with the relationships between living organisms and their environment," its "extended use" denotes "the interrelationship between any system and its environment"; "eco," in turn, derives from the ancient Greek for "house," or "dwelling." These definitions allow me to understand the relationships between, say, immigrant labor and insular suburban communities, or homophobia and nuclear-irradiated landscapes—not to mention between the human and the non-human, more broadly—as "ecological" concerns.

My archive consists of works that appeared between 1987 and 2006. With the exception of two novels by binational Caribbean-raised authors, these works were produced by American artists. These texts' diegeses cover the period from before gay liberation in the United States (1950s), to the rise of radical queer politics (1980s), to the "post-gay" period (2000s and forward), a span that also includes the so-called second and third waves of environmentalism. All of my novels and films respond in some way to these historical events, as well as to the often-problematic legacy of first-wave or nineteenth-century environmentalism, including the creation of the National Parks and the National Forest Service. Thus, more explicitly than queer ecological work focused on "pre-environmentalist" eras, this book comments on the imbrication of fiction and real-life environmental politics. My texts also provide critical queer perspectives on other uniquely American concerns, such as the Manhattan Project, Second Wave feminism, the rise of global capitalism, the AIDS crisis, and the widening income gap between whites and non-whites. All such issues are interdependent, they suggest—proving their queer thinking to be truly, extensively, ecological.

My second chapter, "Post-Transsexual Pastoral: Environmental Ethics in the Contemporary Transgender Novel," offers a definitive example of

ecological thinking in contemporary queer fictions. I read American author
Leslie Feinberg's *Stone Butch Blues* (1992) alongside two narratives set in the
Caribbean: Jamaican American Michelle Cliff's *No Telephone to Heaven* (1987)
and Trinidadian Canadian Shani Mootoo's *Cereus Blooms at Night* (1998). These
novels depict what I call "organic transgenderism": a spontaneous, non-
commodified, and self-directed process likened to the life-cycle changes of
plants and animals. I claim that they thereby challenge the common view of
gender transitioning as an "unnatural" medical intervention.

In so doing, these texts outline a unique environmental ethics. I show
how they view trans people and natural landscapes in the same empathetic
light, as threatened biological entities. Their protagonists, in coming to
consciousness as trans people, and in grappling with their concomitant status as less-than-human, begin to forge strong bonds with the non-human.
These characters also begin to see the connections among various forms
of oppression—poverty, pollution, sexual abuse, police brutality—and to
view coalition politics as the most effective response.

I link these novels' visions to a major development in GLBTQI politics:
the shift in the 1990s from the older sexological model of "transsexuality" to
the current community-derived umbrella term of "transgenderism." I argue
that, through their depictions of organic transgenderism, these novels stage,
and thus help facilitate, this shift. This chapter thereby offers a new contribution to the history of sexuality, as well as to the history of environmental
thought: it confirms that new models of gender and sexuality emerge not
just out of shifts in areas such as economics and medicine, but out of shifts
in ecological consciousness.

Finally, this chapter demonstrates how a queer ecocritical lens can help us
trace the transnational circulation of queer ecological thinking. I show how
the concept of organic transgenderism has unique purchase for the Third
World settings of Cliff and Mootoo's novels, in which voluntary surgery
is an unthinkable expense, and where Western medical and technological
interventions have framed the culture as "underdeveloped" or "backward."
At the same time, I demonstrate that a queer ecocritical lens can illuminate
otherwise unrecognized commonalities among diverse texts: despite their
differing cultural contexts, Feinberg, Cliff, and Mootoo all use their concern
with the well-being of gender/sexual minorities to raise questions about the
well-being of the natural world, and vice versa.

Chapter 3, "'It's Just Not Turning Up': AIDS, Cinematic Vision, and Environmental Justice in Todd Haynes's *Safe*," examines a very different context in which queer ecological thinking appears. This chapter moves from
the rural and urban landscapes of transgender novels to those of American

suburbia, where we meet a white housewife suffering from an ambiguous illness. While many critics read Haynes's 1995 "New Queer Cinema" film as an AIDS allegory, I argue that it also tells a story about environmental injustice: its queer filmic techniques draw our attention away from our privileged protagonist to the film's literally and figuratively marginal figures and the disproportionately large envirohealth risks they face. The film thereby interrogates how we recognize suffering, and how certain types of suffering are framed as "natural" and, therefore, not worthy of public attention.

In arguing for *Safe* as a formal treatise on environmental justice, this chapter accounts for the 1995 film's setting in 1987, at the height not just of the AIDS crisis, but of Reaganomics, the self-help movement, the so-called War on Drugs, and deep-ecology-influenced environmentalism. I draw new attention to the relationship among these contemporaneous paradigms: all are known for championing personal responsibility while dismissing structural violence and institutionalized inequality. For instance, some adherents to deep ecology, which the film explicitly references, insist that ecological well-being can be achieved only when individual humans transform their relationship to the earth.[36] I claim that the film works against these ideologies: it highlights the larger forces that oppress the vulnerable—from the medical complex that dismisses women's and gay men's claims to illness, to the systems of immigration and capitalism that put Latina/o and Chicana/o day laborers at risk with little compensation—and exposes how those forces, in turn, blame the individual victim for such oppression.

This chapter indicates how environmental concerns obtain even, or perhaps especially, in spaces construed as *refuges from* the environment, such as the suburban home. It also reminds us that environmental injustice occurs not just in the homes and workplaces of the lower classes, but in the spheres of privilege where those individuals operate. I thereby help to expand basic ecocritical definitions of "environment" and environmental injustice. In showing how queer artistic sensibilities can take us far beyond those definitions, and far beyond issues of gender and sexuality, this chapter illustrates the wide applicability of queer ecological thought.

In Chapter 4, "'Ranch Stiffs' and 'Beach Cowboys' in the Shrinking Public Sphere: Sexual Domestication in *Brokeback Mountain* and *Surf Party*," I look at a text that seems to stand outside the bounds of my argument. Ang Lee's 2005 big-budget Hollywood film is widely perceived as "gay" in content, but not particularly "queer" in outlook; most critics have characterized it as either a simplistic pastoral that romanticizes the American West, or a universal love story in service of gay normalization. I counter these readings by highlighting how the film accounts for its historical setting and by focusing on how it frames its protagonists in relation to the natural world. I show how it alludes to federal Reclamation efforts in the American West, which entailed the harnessing of natural resources under the imperative of "homemaking." *Brokeback* places its protagonists in opposition to these developments, detailing Jack and Ennis's poverty and subsequent exploitation by land developers, and creating in Ennis a character who rejects private domesticity as a solution to public homophobia. More explicitly, through a series of visual and thematic parallels, the film presents the queer as vulnerable to the same capitalist imperatives that threaten the natural landscape.

I argue that the film thus offers the possibility of a queer, anti-capitalist relationship to land and explicates the paradox observed by ecofeminist Greta Gaard: the claim that queer sexualities are "against nature" "[implies that] nature is valued—. . . [while, i]n Western culture, just the contrary is true: nature is devalued just as queers are devalued" ("Toward a Queer Ecofeminism" 120). *Brokeback Mountain* suggests that the charge of queer "unnaturalness" is actually a reaction to *queer resistance to the domestication of nature*, both human and non-human. This chapter, then, explains not just how contemporary queer texts oppose the "queer"/"nature" binary, but how that binary comes into being in the first place. And it identifies a twofold project for queer ecological fiction and scholarship: to both revalue nature where it is unjustly devalued, and challenge "nature" where it becomes the rationalization for injustice.

This chapter also brings new attention to the 1964 film *Surf Party*, which *Brokeback Mountain* briefly excerpts. Through a comparative reading, I show this seemingly frivolous beach romp to be a crucial intertext: like *Brokeback*, it depicts the policing of illicit desire in a natural context. But unlike *Brokeback*, it features delinquent characters who eventually conform, enthusiastically policing their own desires and cleansing natural spaces for the purposes of private ownership. I thus claim the later film as a critical rewriting of the earlier one.

I conclude this chapter by exploring how, through its commentary on access to natural public space, *Brokeback Mountain* critiques the contemporary state of Western and, especially, U.S. gay politics—wherein the fight for private rights in the form of marriage has replaced the fight for an expanded public sphere. Thus, whereas my previous chapters focus on my archive's resistance to oppressive regimes such as homophobia, transphobia, and racism, this chapter focuses on homonormativity as a target of queer ecological critique.

Chapter 5 deals with the far-reaching implications of queer ecological thought in contemporary fictions. This chapter, "Attack of the Queer Atomic Mutants: The Ironic Environmentalism of Shelley Jackson's *Half Life*," examines the alternate reality of that 2006 novel, wherein the United States has implemented a program of self-bombing to atone for Hiroshima and Nagasaki, thus wreaking havoc on the Nevada desert. This bombing gives rise to a politicized minority of conjoined twins—modeled satirically on, and overlapping with, queer communities—who then serve as emblems of peaceful, post-nuclear coexistence. Jackson thus commemorates the actual history of nuclear testing in the U.S. desert, while framing its ongoing effects on indigenous residents and landscape as a matter of queer concern. Indeed, I claim that the novel highlights how the desert has historically been maligned as queer—and, accordingly, targeted for destruction. In response, Half Life renegotiates, rather than disavows, queer connections to this space.

In examining Half Life's revision of Atomic Age history, I focus on the queer ecological implications of its narrative form. Our guide for much of the novel is a conjoined lesbian narrator whose madcap quest to separate herself from her twin fails on both a diegetic and an extradiegetic level: as the quest falls apart, it becomes impossible for the reader to differentiate between the narrative contributions of the protagonist and those of her sister. I argue that the novel thereby questions the anti-ecological ideal of the human individual as a sovereign, self-contained unit—an ideal that, in Western culture, has long justified non-human exploitation—and literally voices the kind of empathetic interconnectivity that my other texts have depicted.

But where Half Life diverges sharply from the rest of my archive is in its irreverent affect, which includes humor, satire, grotesquerie, and irony. This chapter studies what I call the novel's ironic environmentalism; in so doing, I build on previous work in environmentalist rhetoric and establish irony as a new topic of inquiry for queer ecology. I show how irony allows Half Life to ridicule Atomic Age rhetorics that frame nuclear fallout as a threat to the white heterosexual body and family,[37] and popular rhetorics and representations that frame environmental health and safety as solely heterosexual concerns. But I also claim that Jackson's irony has important implications for activism, for how we do politics: she satirizes everyone from academic theory-heads to GLBTQI activists to tree-hugging hippie mystics, while also taking their importance as a given. Her vision of an ultra-P.C. queer minority born of nuclear fallout thus elicits a kind of laughing-at-while-laughing-with when it comes to queer and ecological politics. This mode of response rejects the tendency of activist movements to poke fun at the enemy while leaving their own foibles unexamined, and it complicates environmentalism's reputation for humorless stridency.

More extravagantly and self-reflexively than the rest of my archive, then, Jackson's novel melds the skepticism of queer theory and other postmodern and poststructuralist modes with the pragmatism of ecocriticism and environmental activism. This melding lets *Half Life* critique environmentalist tactics without undermining environmentalist convictions, as well as question "nature" even as it defends it. I thereby claim the novel as an instructive political model. It imagines a scenario in which a playful but politicized queerness literally grows out of, and effectively responds to, ecological devastation. Such alternate realities, this book suggests, might just be our own future.

Post-Transsexual Pastoral

Environmental Ethics in the Contemporary Transgender Novel

Transsexual gender identities and homosexual/bisexual orientations are . . . typically viewed as being inherently questionable, unnatural . . . and less socially and legally valid than their cissexual and heterosexual counterparts.

—Julia Serano, "Rethinking Sexism: How Trans Women Challenge Feminism"

The environmentalists' silence about the body is all too familiar. My worry is that this silence reflects that traditional and dangerous way of thinking that the body is of no consequence, that our own corporeal nature is irrelevant to whatever environmentalists are calling "Nature."

—Deborah Slicer, "The Body as Bioregion"

In a prefatory note for the 2003 edition of the 1993 queer literary landmark *Stone Butch Blues*, author Leslie Feinberg recounts that

> at the eleventh hour when the novel was almost due at the publisher's, I tore up the ending and set out to create a new character, Ruth. I [culled from a friend] . . . memories about the tiny rural community of Vine Valley where she was raised. We took a trip there to meet and talk with people whose lives are rooted in the vineyards. As a result, I was able to write Ruth . . . from the immersion pool of memory, the dark and rich organic soil, the bouquet of concord grape, the basin lake that mirrors a changing sky, and the hard-scrabble lives of Vine Valley. (1)

These memories inform the penultimate chapter of the novel, in which Feinberg's autobiographical protagonist Jess Goldberg, a female-born "he-she," accompanies hir[1] male-born, female-identified sweetheart Ruth home to Vine Valley after the two meet in New York. Feinberg's commentary on this episode is notable from a queer ecological standpoint on two counts. First, it shows how the natural world informs the human imagination; Feinberg likely does not mean to pun when ze[2] says ze "talk[ed] with people whose lives are *rooted* in the vineyards," but the statement has both literal and figurative resonance. Perhaps more importantly, Feinberg's decision to add the Vine Valley episode indicates a desire to locate queerness in a natural context. While Jess and Ruth meet in the city, Feinberg traces each character's formative moments to rural spaces with strong indigenous histories. For Ruth, it is these valleys of western New York, connected to the Seneca Nation, while for Jess, it is an unspecified Southwest desert area originally populated by the Dineh.

For the most part, though, the novel's most frequent settings are grim indoor urban spaces such as factories, gay dive bars, and jail cells. The novel's main action centers on the Jewish, working-class Jess as ze transitions from female, to male, to ambiguously gendered person in 1960s–80s Buffalo and New York City. Over this period, ze also becomes increasingly involved in industrial labor activism. The aforementioned rural spaces thus appear at first as anomalous detours, or intentional contrasts to the dominant urban milieu. But I argue that these sections are a crucial part of the novel's overall project: a synthesis of the cultural and the natural, and the subsequent dissolution of related binaries (male–female, rational–fantastical, self–Other) from a queer perspective. Specifically, *Stone Butch Blues* develops a vision of what I call "organic transgenderism": gender transitioning as a phenomenon that is at least partly natural—that is, innate and spontaneous—rather than primarily cultural, or constructed.[3] Organic transgenderism, as I will describe, involves the treatment of gender transitioning as a biological phenomenon on the same order as puberty; an obviation of the medicotechnological complex and its commodification of the body, in favor of "homegrown" and psychic solutions to bodily problems; the characterization of self-knowledge as equal, if not superior, to medical knowledge; and a focus on individual will as transformative. Works that articulate this vision of transgenderism insist that the perceived "unnaturalness" of that process is the result of simplistic binary thinking—thinking that victimizes trans people as well as the natural world.

Thus this shift toward a partly natural rather than purely cultural vision of transgenderism is not a cynical or random bid at justifying that process. Rather, it is part of a broadening ecological consciousness. The novel illustrates how the principles that shape Jess's post-transsexual identity—self-determination, anti-hierarchism, anti-consumerism, et cetera—apply to a wide range of individuals and spaces, urban and rural. Jess comes to realize that ze is part of a larger web of human and non-human interactivity to which ze has ethical responsibilities. And, in turn, ze sees the interconnections among forms of oppression ranging from transphobia to racism to pollution, and how a politics of solidarity might ignite effective responses.

Ecofeminists and activists such as Carol J. Adams and Karen J. Warren have long thought about interconnections among certain humans and non-humans; as Greta Gaard explains, "at the root of ecofeminism is the understanding that the many systems of oppression are mutually reinforcing. Building on the socialist feminist insight that racism, classism, and sexism are interconnected, ecofeminists [have] recognized additional similarities between those forms of human oppression and the oppressive structures of speciesism and naturism" ("Toward a Queer Ecofeminism" 114). These structures rely at once on dualistic thinking—self–Other, culture–nature, human–animal, male–female, white–non-white and, as Gaard argues, straight–queer—and hierarchism, in which each of the second terms is lower than each of the first terms. As these thinkers have noted, while coalition is most effective against such interlocking oppressions, oppression often obfuscates those very connections, pitting marginal groups against other marginal groups.[4] Moreover, the enforced alienation of oneself from one's body, which many transgender people, women, and people of color experience, is a major obstacle to recognizing interconnectivity. That is, if one is disconnected from oneself on a primary level, one cannot see oneself as, in turn, empathetically and ethically connected to other things and persons.

In contrast, in coming to terms with their own bodies, *Blues*'s characters come to achieve great empathy for the non-human as well as for diverse groups of humans. We see that Jess's respect for the natural world is ineluctably intertwined with hir recognition of hirself as a valued part of that world—while ze also insists upon justice in the urban, "artificial" world of which ze is, likewise, a part. Thus while Siobhan Somerville is right to note that "the emergence of . . . transgendered . . . subjectivity is mediated through racial discourses in the text, specifically . . . through repeated invocations of analogies to Native American and African American culture and identity" (171), I argue that it is more broadly through a classically ecological imagination—one that thinks in terms of relationships, rather than in terms of distinctive entities, and specifically in terms of the relationship of the human to the non-human natural world—that the trans figure emerges.

I focus here on *Blues*, but put it in a transnational context by reading it alongside two contemporaneous works, Jamaican American novelist Michelle Cliff's *No Telephone to Heaven* (1987) and Trinidadian Canadian novelist Shani Mootoo's *Cereus Blooms at Night* (1998), set primarily in Jamaica and the fictional Caribbean island of Lantanacamara, respectively. I thereby draw attention to organic transgenderism as a counterdiscourse that circulates throughout the Americas: each of these novels also features a major character who undergoes a gender transition, and they bring to the fore the natural dimensions of that process as I have described above. In all three novels, the transgender character is a mediator, a figure who moves among several different worlds. "Baby butch" Jess enters the queer community as the older generation of butches, femmes, and drag queens have begun to struggle with accusations of gender conservatism; ze is also a labor activist with ties to radically different groups of laborers—straight white men, Native Americans, white and black butch lesbians. *Cereus*'s Tyler is an ambiguously raced native of Lantanacamara who goes abroad for nursing training but returns to care for an ailing Indian woman who is part of the island's uneducated lower class. *Heaven*'s Harry/Harriet is a dark-skinned Jamaican medicine woman-cum-revolutionary who counsels the novel's privileged, light-skinned Jamaican protagonist on how to reconcile her conflicted identity. Despite being largely shunned by their fellow islanders, and despite their acquaintance with Western/European culture, Tyler and Harry/Harriet strongly identify with their homelands, following local folkways and communing with plants, animals, and the natural landscape. These characters are, simultaneously, insiders and outsiders.

These texts thereby obviate the nature–culture schema, wherein Western/European rationality tames "backward" indigenous traditions and the natural world with which they are associated, and wherein the human is the subject and the natural world is the object. Instead, they participate in what Bruno Latour calls "nonmodern" thinking. As Eric Todd Smith explains,

> In his explanatory model, which he terms "nonmodern" (as opposed to modern or postmodern) . . . [he] proposes that we imagine "mediators" . . . A mediator is not subordinate to other, more ontologically valid entities, but rather is an entity, like all others, existing in and through relationships. Once mediation is taken to be not only the [character] of relationships between entities, but also the *constitutive activity* of entities, "we notice that there is no longer any reason to limit the ontological varieties that matter to two" (79), such as culture and nature or subject and object. Because mediation is the nature of existence, purity is not valued, much less possible. Nothing can be entirely of nature or entirely of culture. (36)

These characters, by Latour's definition, are consummate mediators. And both they and their creators resist arguing for the rights of trans people on the basis of a human subjectivity from which they've been excluded. Instead, they advocate a respectful and responsible stance whenever one encounters alterity, and the belief that all life, human and non-human, is connected. This stance seems all-important considering that transgender people are often considered less than human and thus are vulnerable to extreme violence:[5] rather than insisting that they *are* in fact human, and thereby underwriting an anthropocentric humanist worldview, these novels establish the transgender person as a valuable part of an all-encompassing web of life. They are thus obligated to treat other entities, and to be treated, ethically.

It must be noted that these texts are very careful in articulating this vision of interconnectivity. For one thing, homophobic and transphobic discourses have been known to conflate "nature" in terms of the human with "nature" in terms of the non-human in order to persecute the queer human, specifically— sometimes because s/he does not display characteristics of animal biology (heterosexual reproduction, for example), at other times because s/he relies upon synthetic and manmade resources (sex-change operations, sex toys, fertility treatments, to take more examples). (Of course, several ecologists and theorists have shown that not all animals demonstrate heterosexual behavior, and that cisgender[6] and heterosexual persons also augment their bodies and lifestyles with manmade resources.) Moreover, since time immemorial, humans have attributed human desires and impulses to nature, often to justify exploiting it.[7] But these three novels, instead, acknowledge that human nature and non-human nature are unique in their own rights, while simultaneously refusing the kind of binary thinking that limits our ability to recognize points of connection, or that authorizes domination of one side over the other. As David Wiggins puts it, "We ought not to pretend (and we do not need to pretend) that we have any alternative, as human beings, but to bring to bear upon ecological questions the human scale of values. . . . [But] [t]he human scale of values is by no means exclusively a scale of human values" (as quoted in Curry 54). These novels reduce the perceived distance between the queer and the natural for the express purpose of arguing for ethical responsibility. Organic transgenderism thus refrains from exploiting the concept of nature, or leaving it unquestioned, as it (re)claims it for the queer.

Like my other chapters, this one seeks to show how a poststructuralist, constructionist-leaning position—that is, one that is suspicious of the "natural" bases of categories such as race, gender, and so forth—can actually honor "the natural." While I follow the spirit of critics who claim that novels such as *Stone Butch Blues* "destabilize 'natural' categories of sex and gender" (Somerville 170), I believe that such characterizations can obfuscate the critical interest in natural paradigms, processes, and landscapes that such texts express. This chapter explicates this interest, revealing an environmentalist and anti-capitalist imagination that has yet to be recognized as a component of transgenderism or queerness more broadly. I show

how a concern for the natural, so rare among queer theorists and many queer activists, can work toward queer ends. Finally, in outlining an organic transgenderism that emerges from a truly ecological imagination, I bring new attention to these post-transsexual works as part of a unique literary subgenre. They draw from multiple traditions, including nature writing, proletarian literature, indigenous storytelling, and the Bildungsroman, to recast the lines of embodiment in queer ecological terms.

Transgenderism in Context

Over the past two decades, major shifts in the public profile of gender transitioning have taken place. Stephen Whittle outlines these shifts in The Transgender Studies Reader, explaining that the anthology includes "work from before the 1990s that is representative of the vast majority of work of those times, when the primary concern was the psychology and medicalization of transsexualism. In the 1990s, a new scholarship, informed by community activism, started from the premise that to be trans was not to have a mental or medical disorder" (xii). Ariadne Kane explains further that

> "Transsexualism" was coined by D. O. Cauldwell, an American sexologist, and popularized by Harry Benjamin in the 1950s and 1960s. . . . [I]n 1980 . . . transsexualism and gender disorders were recognized in the American Psychiatric Association's Diagnostic and Statistical Manual III. In 1988, transsexualism was defined by the DSM-III-R as having the following diagnostic criteria: 1. persistent discomfort and sense of inappropriateness about one's assigned sex; 2. persistent preoccupation for at least two years with getting rid of one's primary and secondary sex characteristics and acquiring the sex characteristics of the other sex; and 3. having reached puberty . . . DSM-IV has [since] replaced the term "transsexual" with the generic term "gender disorder." (my emphasis)[8]

The wave of activism to which Whittle refers was crucial in bringing the community-initiated term "transgender" to the Western lexicon starting in 1992. An umbrella term, "transgender" widens the scope to include everyone from those who undergo gender-reassignment surgery and take hormones to ambiguously gendered individuals who shun any kind of intervention and identify as "genderqueer." Informing this changing picture is the increased visibility of female-to-male (FTM) trans people, many of whom have deep roots in lesbian communities and who often eschew genital reconstruction.[9] These individuals have helped throw the male-centric and heteronormative foundations of medicalized transsexualism into question. As Sandy Stone and others have explained, the goals of medical practitioners working with trans individuals have historically been to make a "proper" female or male out of a patient, one who conforms to the sexual and aesthetic norms of her or his chosen gender. In sum, then, the late twentieth century constitutes a contentious period in which the dominant history of transsexualism continues to loom over trans individuals' efforts at self-determination. After all, there is no significant distance between the 1988 date of transsexualism's DSM definition cited by Kane and Whittle's "post-medical" 1990s date. It is in this period of debate that works like *Stone Butch Blues*, *No Telephone to Heaven*, and *Cereus Blooms at Night* emerge, and intervene.

Feminist theory can provide us with a useful index of these overlapping cultural moments, the one of medicalized transsexualism, and the other of "post-transsexualism," or transgenderism, and of what is at stake in the shift from one to the other. To begin with, despite Whittle's suggestion that this shift has been clean and complete, much feminist work well into the 2000s has continued to imagine the trans body only, and negatively, as transsexual—as a medicalized, technological figure, usually male, that has been forged into the "opposite" sex. Such connoting leaves these feminist texts at a curious impasse. For example, Elizabeth Grosz's *Volatile Bodies* (1994) usefully re-visions the body as a historically specific object but bluntly refuses to validate the historical specificity of the *trans* body. She maintains that "processes and activities that seem impossible for a body to undertake at some times and in some cultures are readily possible in others. What are regarded as purely fixed and unchangeable elements of facticity, biologically given factors, are amenable to wide historical vicissitudes and transformation" (190). A mere seventeen pages later, however, she declares that "[m]en . . . can never, even with surgical intervention, feel or experience what it is like to be, to live, as women. At best the transsexual can live out his fantasy of femininity—a fantasy that in itself is usually disappointed with the rather crude transformations effected by surgical and chemical intervention" (207). The female body—initially, on her account, a differentially inscribed object rather than an essentializable fact—has suddenly become the valorized, essentialized, and natural "real" vis-à-vis the transsexual's fantastical and unnatural synthetic body.

Grosz thereby participates in the long tradition of feminist antagonism to gender transitioning, specifically on the grounds that it necessarily entails a fetishizing, cynical exploitation of Western medical technologies. This tradition is perhaps epitomized by Janice Raymond's infamous *The Transsexual Empire: The Making of the She-Male* (1979), which claims that "all transsexuals rape women's bodies by reducing the real female form to an artifact, appropriating this body for themselves" (104). In 2005, radical feminist Sheila Jeffries echoed these claims, but in relation to female-to-male gender transitions—arguing that they constitute "an extension of the beauty industry [that] offer[s] cosmetic solutions to deeper rooted problems [i.e., misogyny]" (Bindel). In such views, gender transitioning is not only a capitulation to a mass-consumerist, technomedical system that trades on anti-female social and aesthetic standards; it is an agent of that system.

However, such views are not universal. Many feminist theoretical texts, including Judith Butler's *Gender Trouble* (1990), Judith Halberstam's *In a Queer Time and Place* (2005), and Stone's "The Empire Strikes Back: A Posttranssexual Manifesto" (1987–2004)—a direct response to Raymond—offer more nuanced accounts of gender transitioning and indicate how theories of transgenderism are both indebted to feminist theory and primed to contribute to it. Moreover, Halberstam questions the assumption that postmodern cultural formations—such as transgender film and visual art—necessarily endorse late capitalism and consumerism. Meanwhile, Susan Stryker describes transgender studies as an inherently postmodern field—and not just because the term "transgenderism" appeared in the late twentieth century, encompassing and going beyond the "transsexual" label. As she explains, transgender studies "takes aim at the modernist epistemology that treats gender merely as a social, linguistic, or subjective representation of an objectively knowable material sex. Epistemological concerns lie at the heart of transgender critique" (8).[10] By her view, "transgender critique," and perhaps transgenderism itself, represents a liberatory move beyond institutionalized knowledges based in cold, hard facts and material proof.

But these critical texts still maintain the association, found in Grosz and Raymond, between transgenderism and postmodern technology, and they still focus heavily on transgenderism's visual and material manifestations. Stone, for example, draws on Donna Haraway's work to champion a vision of the trans body as politicized cyborg, while Halberstam claims that the "body in transition indelibly marks late-twentieth- and early-twenty-first-century visual fantasy"—a fantasy that, while imagined through the science fiction of *Terminator 2*, *The Matrix*, and the like, is "powerfully realized . . . in transgender film" (76).[11] More generally, these critical texts tend to cement the link between transgenderism and postmodernity—a link that, while useful and accurate on many levels, still requires careful examination. (After all, Jean Baudrillard has taken this link so far that he can title one of his essays "We Are All Transsexuals Now.") Rita Felski summarizes the problematic postmodernity/transgenderism connection thusly: "The destabilization of the male/female divide is seen to bring with it a waning of temporality, teleology, and grand narrative; the end of sex echoes and affirms the end of history, defined as the pathological legacy and symptom of the trajectory of Western modernity. Ineluctably intertwined in symbiotic relationship, phallocentrism, modernity, and history await their only too timely end, as a hierarchical logic of binary identity and narrative totalization gives way to an altogether more ambiguous and indeterminate condition" (566).

Felski criticizes conversations about "the end of history" as being, ironically, temporal and teleological in character, and for privileging "good" postmodernism over "bad" modernism—when postmodern thought otherwise militates against simple models of genealogy, moralized progressivism, and teleology. Moreover, she warns that such talk about the end of "grand narrative" elides the existence of individuals who have never fit into that narrative in the first place.

Like Felski, I want to probe the association among (trans)gender liberation, postmodernity, and late capitalism. Specifically, I want us to consider the possibility that transgenderism's rise to prominence in postmodernity might occasion criticism of postmodern conditions, including the devastation of the natural world. And I want us to consider that viewing transgenderism as a quintessentially postmodern phenomenon, as something based primarily on fantasy and perception rather than reality and materiality, can problematically characterize the trans body as a futuristic product of medical and technological experimentation, and thereby paper over local, indigenous, and self-driven articulations of transgenderism. The textual imaginings that I treat here boldly offer such articulations and critique postmodern conditions such as globalization, ecological devastation, the long afterlife of colonialism, and the increased obfuscation of labor relations in late capitalism. They also demonstrate the persistence of materialist medical discourses—a modern phenomenon not yet vanquished, apparently, in postmodernity. And they draw our attention to the existence, and importance, of *non*-technological potentialities when it comes to bodily modification.

Trans Nature versus the Medical Complex

Through a series of graphic episodes, *Stone Butch Blues* illustrates the fraught relationship between trans people and the medical complex—both contextualizing and justifying the emergence of an organic transgenderism. Most notably, the novel highlights how medicine functions as a gatekeeper: Jess and hir friends frequently find themselves at the mercy of disdainful, even abusive caregivers in their attempts to modify their bodies. While this dynamic obtains in many patient–caregiver relationships, it proves particularly oppressive to the trans person on at least two specific levels.

First, it alienates hir from hir body, even as the goal of intervention for most individuals is self-reconciliation. Second, it creates a paternalistic dynamic in which the medical professional controls the mobility of the "unedu-cated" trans person—who is, in many if not most cases, already socially and economically immobile. (As Jess laments, after a series of brutal gay-bar raids set in the era before the Stonewall and Compton's Cafeteria riots,[12] "We didn't seem to have any of our own places to gather in community, to immerse ourselves in our own ways and our own languages" [248].) Indeed, Feinberg, Cliff, and Mootoo indicate that the medical procedures associated with transgenderism are exorbitantly expensive, and rarely cov-ered by insurance—which many individuals might not even have in the first place. When Jess and hir butch friend Grant begin to take hormones from a "quack" doctor whom they pay under the table, Grant reflects, "It would be a lot easier if we went to the sex-change clinic. They give you hormones for free. The only thing is you have to take all these tests and they interview your family and everything" (158). This "only thing" is actually a major barrier, considering that it positions the trans person as a medical specimen—and considering that the families of people like Jess have violently rejected their children for gender nonconformity.

Medicalized transsexualism, in rendering the body a commodity to be obtained from "authorized" sources, also exacerbates the sense that the trans person does not own hir own body, whether pre-operative, post-op-erative, or somewhere in between. That person in turn becomes objectified and dehumanized and may suffer extreme abuse. Authority figures of all kinds inculcate this sense of objectification throughout *Stone Butch Blues*: at one point in the novel, Jess sees a pair of white cops assault two black drag queens and squeeze the breasts of one, while staring directly at hir and laughing. This act singles out aspects of the trans body as artificial and thus literally up for grabs by others. Likewise, those medical professionals in *Blues* who offer services to trans people are depicted as doing so out of a lust for power. Upon entering the office of the "quack" doctor, Jess asks, "Where are all your diplomas?" Ze recounts that the man then "looked me up and down. God, he hates us, I thought to myself" (162). Later, after ze undergoes a mastectomy in the office of another "quack," ze is immediately kicked out by a nurse, who declares, "You people make some arrangement with [the doctor] on the side, that's your *business*. But this bed and our time is for sick people" (177, emphasis mine). The nurse justifies her inhumane treatment by characterizing Jess's experience as frivolous—essentially, just a shady "business" transaction.

The work of trans activist Sandy Stone can help us further understand the historical reality to which these visions of self-directed transgenderism respond. First, as ze explains, medical practitioners have traditionally insisted upon psychic and body alignment for trans people, often as a precondition for desired hormonal or bodily modifications. A male-to-female person, for example, is compelled to get rid of hir penis and acquire a surgically constructed vagina. Even when trans people agree to these norms, medical authorities try to ensure that genital reconstruction is understood as utterly integral to their transitioning. Access to surgery, in fact, has often been contingent upon the proper response to the question, "Suppose that you could be a man [or woman] in every way except for your genitals; would you be content?" (Stone 13). Ze explains, "there are several possible answers, but only one ['no'] is clinically correct . . . Under the binary phallocratic founding myth by which Western bodies and subjects are authorized, only one body per gendered subject is 'right.' [Thus] the transsexuals for whom gender identity is something different from and perhaps irrelevant to physical genitalia are occulted by those for whom the power of the medical/psychological establishments . . . is the final authority for what counts as a culturally intelligible body" (13). This kind of single-mindedness renders transitioning something shameful to be downplayed after the fact. And, somewhat ironically, it suggests that retaining one's male body while living with a female identity (or vice versa) would somehow be *more* unnatural than changing both one's body and one's identity.

In response to these oppressive dynamics, trans people in *Stone Butch Blues*, *No Telephone to Heaven*, and *Cereus Blooms at Night* downplay the importance of medical intervention, stress their self-determination and self-possession, and proudly embrace—rather than seek to hide—their trans status. We watch Jess change hir own bandages after being forcibly discharged immediately after hir mastectomy, and hir drag queen friend Peaches declare of hir newfound breasts, "That's hormones made them swell up like that, but *they're mine now*" (66, my emphasis). Similarly, in Cliff's *Telephone*, Jamaican revolutionary Harry/Harriet tells hir best friend, protagonist Clare Savage, "Cyann [can't] afford [genital reconstruction]. Maybe when de revolution come . . . but *the choice is mine*, man, is made. Harriet live and Harry be no more . . . you know, darling, castration ain't de main t'ing . . . not a-tall" (168, my emphasis). *Cereus* gives us a pair of transgender lovers, female-to-male Otoh and male-to-female Tyler, whose transformations also occur spontaneously, outside of medical and parental prescription. As Mootoo describes it, Otoh's parents "hardly noticed [at first] that their daughter was transforming herself into their son . . . [Then] Elsie fully expected that he (she) would outgrow the foolishness . . . But the child walked and ran and dressed and talked and tumbled . . . so much like an authentic boy that Elsie soon apparently forgot she had ever given birth to a girl" (109–10).

This miraculous transition is treated as quite credible: Mootoo reports that "hours of . . . exercise streamlined Ambrosia [Otoh's given name] into an angular, hard-bodied creature and tampered with the flow of whatever hormonal juice defined him. So flawless was the transformation that even the nurse and doctor who attended the birth, on seeing him later, marveled at their carelessness in having declared him a girl" (110).

Such descriptions do not deny the machinations involved in transgenderism, but they shift the emphasis from the external to the internal, from prosthetic addition to organic self-transformation. They position the trans body as generally replete, and largely autonomous, in the face of medical and other claims to the contrary. In fact, these authors go so far as to satirize medical authorities as clueless and incompetent rather than expert and unassailable. Mootoo's equivocal diction has the nurse and doctor merely "attending" Otoh's birth, like passive spectators at an event. It imagines that the doctor and nurse do not stand between the trans person and hir desired body, the way that the doctor and nurse in *Stone Butch Blues* do. And Harry/Harriet's declaration of self-sovereignty, while not disavowing surgery completely, critiques the fixation on a surgically normalized, coherent body as the end-all endpoint. In thus reclaiming transgender agency, these texts characterize transgenderism as a process that anyone might undertake at any time. Considering the high cost and potential pitfalls of medicalized transsexualism, and the fraught social and economic status of many trans people, this characterization has material as well as ideological implications.

Through these depictions, Feinberg, Cliff, and Mootoo locate the "problem" of transgenderism in outside institutions rather than in the individual body. Specifically, they implicate the medical establishment in the characterization of trans people as artificiality incarnate; aside from the undeniable fact that surgeons and psychiatrists often help construct trans bodies, the real issue is that their gatekeeping insists upon transgenderism as externally granted, as opposed to internally driven—cultural, and not natural. Thus criticism of trans people's focus on "the genitals as obsessive or fetishistic" (Judith Shapiro, as quoted in Stone 13) is misguided: this fetishization might be more accurately traced to a technomedical complex that literally capitalizes on bodily transformations.

Feinberg's novel also draws our attention to the ubiquity of external gendering mechanisms and gender policing, which further necessitates a counterdiscourse of organic, self-willed gender transitioning. The examples abound: when Jess visits a women's clinic, ze is virtually thrown out for hir masculine appearance despite having a vaginal infection (235); when ze goes to visit hir friend in the mental hospital, ze has to lie about hir gender to gain entry (285). And even when Jess has begun passing as male, ze is still immobilized: ze cannot pass over the nearby border to Canada from Buffalo, New York, because ze lacks a male ID—and, of course, using hir female ID would make hir vulnerable to punishment or violence. Feinberg's inclusion of these episodes, along with those related directly to transitioning, illuminate the pervasive institutional strictures on gender variance. Similarly, trans autobiographer Jamison Green puts transgenderism in the broader context of a gender-rigid society, arguing that "Changing one's sex is just one way of changing one's body, and a sex change is not necessarily part of a *search for perfection* or a reification of stereotypes. The reality of gender is that anyone who has not opted for androgyny has . . . accepted the binary gender system . . . so why imply that transsexual people have any greater share of responsibility for reinforcing that binary?" (90, my emphasis). Both Green and Feinberg oppose the characterization of gender transitioning as unnatural by highlighting gender binaries. These binaries, they suggest, more properly deserve the charge of unnatural, because they encourage cisgender and transgender people alike to undertake ongoing, sometimes extreme, programs of modification.

Denaturalizing Human Development, Renaturalizing the Trans Body

While *Blues*, *Cereus*, and *Heaven* respond directly to medicalization, they also take a separate tack, describing transgenderism as a lifelong experience that begins at birth and unfolds organically, along the same lines as puberty. One's transgenderism is thus shown to be *prior*, or at least *parallel*, to medical intervention, not a product thereof. To begin with, these novels show the characters presaging their transgender adulthoods: Jess recalls a "time I was about fourteen and I saw this he-she . . . [with a] femme [at the shopping mall] . . . I wanted to run after them and beg them to take me with them. And all the while I was thinking, *oh shit, that's gonna be me.*" Jess's girlfriend Angie remarks, "It's tough when you see it coming, ain't it?" (69). Perhaps more positively, after starting on male hormones, Jess declares, "this was almost the body I'd expected before puberty confounded me" (171). The normative schema outlined for body development does not, apparently, apply to everyone. Likewise, Ruth's simple comment about hir childhood, "I wasn't growing up to be a man" (262)—rather than, "I didn't *want to* grow up to be a man," or "I knew I would change into a woman"—shows the contingency, and not the inevitability or universality, of normative human growth. Girlhood is not inextricably linked to womanhood, Feinberg suggests, nor is boyhood a predictor of manhood.[13] And, most importantly, the "I" is valorized over institutionalized wisdom about the body.

Blues builds on this questioning of normative development by further naturalizing the transgender body and its accoutrements. Shortly after visiting a gay bar for the first time—and being sexually assaulted by the policemen who raid the bar—Jess has hir first sexual encounter with a woman:

> Angie rolled me over and began unbuttoning my shirt, leaving my T-shirt on. . . . She slid my pants off but left on my BVD's. I struggled to slip on the harness and the dildo. Angie pushed me back on the pillow and took the rubber cock in both her hands. The way she touched it mesmerized me. "Feel how I'm touching you?" she whispered with a smile. . . . Her mouth was very near my cock. "If you're going to fuck me with this," she said, stroking it, "then I want you to feel it. This is an act of sweet imagination." (71)

The move here from inanimate to animate object—"the dildo" to "my cock"—is quick and almost imperceptible. Angie naturalizes that which is perceived as artificial, and Jess immediately takes up that move, treating the dildo as a natural extension of hir own body. The trans body is hereby figured as capable of operating sufficiently without medical or professional help. It is no coincidence, then, that this scene takes place shortly after a sexual assault that alienates Jess from hir body—positioning hir as female, against hir own self-conception, and asserting dominion over hir person. The text subsequently re-members the body as belonging to the self, and as physically replete through the power of imagination.

This notion of willing one's body into the desired shape suffuses both *Cereus Blooms at Night* and *No Telephone to Heaven*. While *Cereus* participates in a magical realist tradition vis-à-vis transgenderism much more so than *Stone Butch Blues*, the same general elements exist: a defiance of the body's perceived limitations, and an insistence on the imagined as just as meaningful as the material—and, in fact, on the two as interrelated. Through their respective magical-realist modes, these texts demonstrate a pointed skepticism of the modern Western equation between materiality and truth, but they do not come down solely on the side of the imaginary. For example, after Tyler's patient Mala brings hir a nurse's dress, ze describes an astonishing, spontaneous transformation: "I reached for the dress. My body felt as if it were metamorphosing. It was *as though* I had suddenly become plump and less rigid. My behind *felt* fleshy and rounded. I *had* thighs, a small mound of belly, rounded full breasts and a cavernous tunnel singing between my legs" (76, my emphasis). Mootoo's diction allows this metamorphosis to be a fantasy, but it focuses on the "real" feelings that the fantasy evokes in Tyler.

Tyler, like Jess, has an empathetic witness to hir transformation, one who has experienced gendered violence despite having a normative gender identity. While Angie, Jess's girlfriend, is a prostitute who has suffered abuse at the hands of police and clients, Mala is a survivor of physical and sexual abuse by her father and presently suffers from mental illness. These characters perform crucial work on many levels. First, their presence allows the novels to identify shared Otherness as a grounds for mutual care. (As I detail further below, the characters in Feinberg and Mootoo's novels recognize this kind of shared Otherness across species divides, not just across those of race, gender, sexuality, and class.) Mootoo, for instance, suggests that Mala intervenes in the mistreatment that Tyler suffers as a feminine person in a homophobic, patriarchal framework, because she has had her own experience of abuse and subsequent social exile as a female person within that framework. Importantly, this is a history that Tyler will come to understand only when ze begins to patiently attend to hir patient. Indeed, while *Cereus* is narrated by Tyler, the ostensible aim of hir narration is to probe Mala's mysterious past. However, ze frequently slips into hir own life story and chides hirself rather disingenuously, and charmingly, when ze does so; rather than growing impatient, the reader comes to realize that the two individuals' stories are ultimately inseparable. This inclusion of empathetic cisgender characters also allows the authors to suggest that gender transitioning might be initiated through a simple, egalitarian exchange between loving persons, rather than negotiations between a patient and medical authorities. Finally, the inclusion of individuals who have experienced gendered and sexual violence, yet identify as cisgender, points away from transgenderism as a result of trauma, and toward it as an almost intrinsic bodily state. That is, if Mala and Angie are not transgender, then the trans statuses of Jess, Tyler, and Harry/Harriet may serve as *excuses* for abuse, but they cannot be its result.

Cereus provides an even more complex articulation of the latter idea, suggesting that we look at transgenderism as a quasi-inherited trait— something natural that is nonetheless shaped by individual will. In a humorous, touching encounter, Ambrose Mohanty rubs his child Otoh's face and says, "Son, perhaps if you were to use a razor on your face, you might encourage the growth of some hair" (145). This encounter follows Otoh's decision to act in hir father's place to bring Mala food—which Ambrose had been doing to atone for his abandonment of her decades before, when he realized her father was abusing her. (The lovers Otoh and Tyler meet later in the story, when Mala comes under Tyler's care and Ambrose and Otoh come to visit her.) Gratefully, Ambrose observes, "you are indeed a reincarnation but not of a person per se, merely of a forgotten memory. You are a perfect replica of me in my prime" (144). In fact, Ambrose named his child Ambrosia at birth; hir subsequent transformation into a young man who carries out hir father's good work makes transgenderism both a logical necessity and a revered wonder. Like the sheer will invoked in the image of shaving in order to grow hair, the positive forces of penitence, responsibility, and love override Otoh's biologically female body. This scenario resonates with Feinberg's novel: Ambrose suggests that Otoh, like Jess, is not some new creature of technology, but the biologization of deferred dreams. But Otoh is not merely paying for the sins of hir father. Ze takes pride in hirself as a male who acts ethically and empathetically toward a female—who also happens to be a person ze has not yet met. These are notable individual accomplishments in a larger context marked by sexual, racial, economic, and environmental exploitation.

Besides treating gender transitioning as natural, and as something enacted through empathy and respect for alterity, all three authors explicitly connect their visions of transgenderism to ecological concerns. Again, we see that organic transgenderism is not just a reaction to abuse, but a result of the insight that nothing and no one is wholly of nature, or wholly of culture; if the human and non-human world are connected, these texts tell us, then one should strive for the least negative impact and for a positive ethics of care. I stress these insights because I want to clarify that Feinberg, Mootoo, and Cliff do not merely naturalize the trans body *conceptually*, or as a humanist/social-justice effort. To do so would be to rhetorically exploit non-human nature, to value "nature" only insofar as it helps the (queer) human. So while these three novelists "fin[d] in the natural world an antidote to heteronormative oppression" (301)—as Rachel Stein writes of a speaker in Minnie Bruce Pratt's poem sequence *Crime against Nature*—their goal of queer well-being is no more primary than, and in no way separable from, their goal of ecological well-being. More specifically, they insist that "heteronormative oppression" extends itself to the non-human natural world, as well as to GLBTQI people, poor people, and people of color.

We see these beliefs in operation when Jess equates a world free from gender policing and what ze perceives as the consequent, necessary evils of medicalized transsexualism with a world free from environmental degradation. When ze discusses passing as a man (rather than embracing the transgender identity ze alternately refers to as "butch" and "he-she"), ze asks hir friend, "Does it just last for a little while? I mean can you go

back to being a butch later, *when it's safe to come out?*" (145, my emphasis).
Shortly thereafter, ze takes hir friend's children to the zoo and "point[s]
to the golden eagles nearby. 'You know there's not many eagles left. The
food they eat got all poisoned with chemicals, and sometimes people shot
at them. You know what the eagles did? . . . They flew high up into the
mountains, way above the clouds, and they're going to stay up there and
fly around in the wind *until it's safe to come visit*'" (167, my emphasis). In
Cereus, Tyler's slow-growing acceptance of hir female identity parallels
the blooming of the titular desert plant. The cereus appears ugly to the
casual eye but blooms once a year at nighttime; its beauty, in a phrase,
operates undercover. Tyler's adult femininity is, likewise, belated and un-
usual by normative standards. And just as characters such as Tyler's mute
patient Mala and the alms-house gardener Mr. Hector carefully tend to the
slow-growing cereus plant, so do they lovingly accept Tyler's increasingly
overt attempts at femininity. Thus, when Tyler announces that "*my own
life* has finally—and not too late I might add—begun to bloom" (105, my
emphasis), we realize that this is not a cheap deployment of an ecological term. "Bloom" is not totally figurative, as "human nature" is not fully
distinguished from the nature of plants, animals, and landscape.

Indeed, *Cereus*'s ethics of care encompasses the natural, the cultural, and
everything in between: when Mala gives Tyler the dress that first inspires
hir to begin identifying as a woman, ze states appreciatively that "she was
not one to manacle *nature*, and I sensed that she was permitting mine its
freedom" (77, my emphasis); we later learn that, in the chaotic ruins of
Mala's overgrown house, "flora and fauna left her to her own devices and
in return she left them to theirs" (128). The same ethics of care that can and
should be applied to the natural landscape can and should be applied to
humans: patience, attentiveness, and appreciation for the ephemeral and
unfamiliar, rather than for the visible, "useful," or "normal." Loving care
for the different, in short, allows the latter to be different. Greta Gaard and
Patrick D. Murphy's definition of "ecology" proves relevant here: "ecology
is a study of interrelationship, with its bedrock being the recognition of
the distinction between things-in-themselves and things-for-us" (6). *Blues*,
Cereus, and *Heaven* validate "things-in-themselves" as self-sovereign but still
insist that a nonviolent, loving stance can allow "us" to have meaningful
interactions with "them." Moreover, the cultural aspects of nature, as well
as the natural aspects of culture, are subtly stressed in *Cereus*, further questioning the disjuncture between the two: while cereus plants are native to
the New World, those featured in the novel have been transplanted to the
alms house and therefore require human care before they can grow. Mootoo

thus asks us to look at someone like Tyler as naturally transgender, but just in need of some additional care so ze can "bloom."

Environmental Injustice and the Trans Person

Stone Butch Blues explicitly takes up the issue of environmental justice, illuminating how minority individuals face disproportionately greater health risks in their work and living environments. These experiences are compounded, the novel suggests, by the alienation and lack of self-determination experienced by workers under global capitalism—not to mention by trans people in a medicalized framework. In one of the novel's more gut-wrenching scenes, a foreman purposely sets Jess up with a faulty machine and ze loses hir finger. Jess's straight male coworker, Duffy, accompanies hir to the hospital, only to view with horror "how they treated you, how they talked about you." He later tells hir, "I felt so helpless, you know? I kept yelling at them that you were a human being, that you mattered. . . . I couldn't do anything to help you and I couldn't make them take care of you the way I wanted" (93). While Duffy's lament seems to relate to Jess's status as a transgender person (as opposed to his straight, non-ethnic, white cisgender male identity), it resonates at least as much with Jess's growing awareness of the dispensability of working-class bodies. On an earlier work assignment, ze reports: "my head was frozen and my ears burned like fire. That's when I noticed with horror that both of the men we were working with were missing pieces of their ears. Frostbite. In some plants the men were missing a finger down to the second joint, or a thumb. Out here on the docks, which butt up against the frozen lake, the men gave up little exposed pieces of their bodies. It frightened me. I wondered what I would be forced to sacrifice in order to survive" (76). In part, Jess seems to be alluding to hir experience of gender—foreshadowing hir period of "giving up" hir transgender identity in order to pass as a biological man. But ze is also recognizing that alienation, lack of self-determination, and physical violence, so common to the trans experience ze outlines, are also common to those living under environmental injustice.

It is tempting to parallel the missing body parts in the novel, and to read Jess's "incomplete," non-phallic body as pathos-inducing in the same manner as these examples of bodily loss. But the novel wards against such a reading. Jess's lack of a penis is not treated as a cause for concern, just as Mootoo and Cliff's characters brush aside certain attributes, and the lack of certain attributes, of the bodies with which they were born. But the loss of bodily integrity experienced by Jess and the men described above is not only externally enforced, it is more explicitly the product of unjust relations. Such relations are clearly what the novel considers "unnatural," because they alienate the individual from the body ze desires.

Even as the novel focuses on Jess's shared experiences of environmental injustice, it makes clear that ze is relatively privileged. When ze gets sick on the job, "Jimmy came over to clean up my vomit. Jimmy was Mohawk. All the other guys on the maintenance and set-up gangs were white. 'Can I help you clean it up?' I asked him. 'It is my mess, after all'" (198). Despite the misogyny and anti-Semitism aimed at Jess, hir work skills and white skin allow hir some dominance in the workplace. The novel thus reveals the existence of a hierarchy in which some are seen as more human than others, and some have the opportunity to benefit from the oppression of others. Ecofeminists and other such thinkers seek to dismantle this kind of hierarchism, for it disadvantages people of color on the basis of their being "uncivilized," closer to animals and the natural world. Further, as I show in the next chapter, labor injustices are often justified through dominant discourses of naturalization. But Jess refutes the naturalization of Jimmy's subordinate position and does not take the opportunity to benefit from it. Hir heightened sense of empathy leads hir to make a cooperative connection to him—not "Can I do it *for* you?" but "Can I *help* you?"

Elsewhere, the novel connects transgender experiences of alienation and degradation with raced experiences of alienation and degradation. One of its ongoing threads is Jess's friendship with Ed, an African American "he-she." Ed gives Jess a copy of Du Bois's *The Souls of Black Folk*, which Jess puts off reading. When Ed commits suicide, Jess returns to the book—perhaps realizing that connectivity and empathy do not immediately produce a full understanding of another's experience. Here, we might take note of Karla Armbruster's claim that "relying *only* on connection . . . risks simply incorporating the other into the self, a move that Jim Cheney warns leaves no room for 'respecting the other *as other*'" (101). Indeed, as I have suggested, these three novels take pains not to *equate* one experience of oppression with another, even if the two may be usefully compared; they demonstrate a nuanced eye for difference, even as they highlight similarities for progressive political purposes. Thus, while Somerville proposes that the novel makes an "analogy between Ed's double consciousness as a 'Negro'/'American' and the split subjectivity that ze experiences as a he-she, or transgendered subject" (173), we should note that each experience exists in its own right within the diegesis. But perhaps the more important point is that the connection *Blues* draws between race and gender allows us to see that neither transgenderism nor blackness necessarily constitutes a split subjectivity in and of itself.

Rather, a culture that both exalts whites above non-whites and insists people be either male or female, and that polices those categorical borders forcefully, inculcates split subjectivity. Traditional discourses of transsexualism can in fact underwrite this split subjectivity by focusing on the trans person as always already self-alienated ("trapped in the wrong body"). *Blues* works to shift our attention, pointing out that such people are frequently prevented from occupying the bodies they *wish* to occupy, and punished for treating their bodies as they choose. The novel thereby renders self-alienation an imposed state, one not natural or endemic to transgender people, working-class people, people of color, women, or anyone else. And it shows how a non-binaristic embrace of alterity—that would find someone, for example, accepting aspects of hir male body along with hir female identity—inculcates a more capacious sensibility with which to relate to the Other. Beyond issues of environmental injustice, the novel's depiction of bodily alienation has further ecocritical implications—perhaps rather unexpected ones. Environmental philosopher Deborah Slicer remarks, "We will probably never know which was the historical first and paradigm for the other: the violation of a woman's body or of the land. In a culture that defines both the human female body and the land as 'resource,' as someone else's 'property,' such violations are conceptually guarded secrets" (107); thus, she elaborates, "the deep metaphysical belief that the land does not, *cannot*, own itself is a belief from which the Wilderness Act and the Endangered Species Act have never fully freed us. And the belief that women do not own themselves is one from which the Nineteenth Amendment or even *Roe v Wade* haven't freed us" (111). Though Slicer's observation too easily establishes the monolithic category of "women" as the oppressed, and "men" as the oppressors, it illuminates the importance of including the human body in ecological discussions. In insisting upon the body as bioregion, Slicer counters the nature–culture divide that puts (some) humans above (most of) nature, and she argues for an ideal of self-ownership that would counteract all manner of degradation.

This ideal of self-ownership is pressing for Jess as both a trans person and a working-class laborer. We have already seen how medical, legal, and economic forces enact depersonalization and self-alienation. Simply put, Jess's body is not fully hir own for the majority of *Stone Butch Blues*. In response, Slicer and Feinberg propose that, like nature, bodies always own themselves first. The "natural" is thereby (re)defined as self-possession—not necessarily something in its original state. The "natural" might change or evolve, and it might incorporate "unnatural" elements. Indeed, those who critique transgenderism as "unnatural" likely forget that "nature" is dynamic and ever-changing. By this logic, the transgender body—the body type perhaps most often perceived as postmodern, constructed, technologized, fetishized, and thus unnatural—can and, for various political purposes, *should* be recognized for its natural properties. So while Slicer presumably did not have transgender people or queers in mind, the visions of transgenderism with which Feinberg, Mootoo, and Cliff provide us nonetheless take up her insistence that the body should be considered within the same scope as the natural landscape—not in order to produce a facile comparison, but instead to help us see both bodies and landscape as self-same, self-sufficient, and yet threatened and managed at so many junctures.

It is no coincidence, then, that Jess attempts to escape mentally to the desert, not just a natural space but hir place of birth, after hir sexual assault by the police. As ze describes it, "the mountains rose to meet me. I walked toward them, seeking sanctuary, but something held me back" (63). As the officers continue their assault, ze reconnects to that desert space: "wind blew through my hair. I closed my eyes and turned my face up to the desert sky. And then, finally, it released—the welcome relief of warm rain down my cheeks" (63). These tears exemplify hir insistence upon experiencing hir body as hirs, despite the officers' attempts to control it. And the tears are particularly meaningful to hir as a "stone butch": ze is learning to respect emotion as something human, rather than something feminine—or, *if* something feminine, as no cause for disavowal. But this relief can come only when Jess sees hirself as part of nature, as intertwined with it; ze finds frustration when ze first "seek[s] sanctuary" in the desert as a romanticized, separate place. Once again, Jess's coming-to-self-embodiment both requires and enacts an empathetic ecological stance: a willing connection with alterity.

Indeed, the novel suggests that the ability to forge such connections is as much a sign of self-acceptance as it is of acceptance of the Other. The first time Jess sleeps with someone of hir own volition, the woman tries to get hir to open up hir "stone" exterior by telling a seemingly non sequitur tale: "I remember when I was a little kid, I saw a bunch of the older kids in a circle in the playground. I went over to see what they were doing." [Jess] got up on one elbow to listen. "'There was this big beetle. The kids were poking it with a stick. The bug just kind of curled up to protect itself.' She snorted, 'God knows I been poked with enough sticks'" (73). This reminiscence resonates almost exactly with one in *Cereus*: as Ambrose Mohanty tells his transgender child Otoh many years after the fact, "[Mala and I] fancied ourselves protectors of snails and all things unable to defend themselves from the bullies of the world" (119); as children, they saved a "colony of periwinkle snails . . . vulnerable to the [schoolyard] torture squad's delights. One clean blow with a heavy boot or the blunt end of a guava rod could shatter the snails into a gooey green, yellow and pink jigsaw" (92). The coincidences between the two novels are striking: cisgender individuals (Mala and Ambrose of *Cereus* and Angie of *Blues*) who care for transgender individuals (Tyler and Otoh of *Cereus* and Jess of *Blues*), and who help facilitate supposedly "unnatural" transformations, express great empathy for the non-human natural creatures who literally cross their paths. The transgender character is thus naturalized to some extent, shown to be connected to the natural world through ethical treatment. In turn, ze is inspired to come into contact with the natural world through a strongly ethical and empathetic framework.

Anti-Capitalism and Productive Desire

Stone Butch Blues's vision of organic transgenderism entails a critique of capitalism—a critique that, like the environmental-justice framework, brings corporeal concerns and labor concerns together with ecological concerns. To begin with, a strict insistence on transsexualism (acquiring the characteristics of the "opposite sex" through surgery and hormone therapy) over transgenderism (changing one's given gender to a gender of one's choice, which may or not approach a clear or consistent "opposite sex," and which may or may not entail surgery and hormone therapy) positions the genitals, and the phallus in particular, as central. And it also makes the body into a consumer object. In that scenario, the trans person can be whole only if ze participates in the medical circuit, wherein ze would be positioned as passive patient-consumer. In naturalizing the dildo and other bodily accoutrements, Jess and hir partner render negligible Jess's "real" genitals and thus preclude any alienating commodification of hir body.

The novel also highlights the alienating aspects of corporeal consumerism by paralleling it with the alienating aspects of labor in a capitalist economy. While working at a computer parts factory, Jess observes, "it's *weird* to spend half my waking day making something and *I don't even know what the hell it is*" (198, my emphasis). Later, once Jess decides to stop trying to pass as a man and instead be visible as a trans person, ze says, "I didn't regret the decision to take hormones. I wouldn't have survived much longer without passing. And the [mastectomy] surgery was a *gift* to myself, a coming home to my body. But I wanted more than to just barely exist, a *stranger* always trying not to get involved" (224, my emphasis). Jess recasts hir purchase of a mastectomy as something removed from the capitalist system of exchange value and, in fact, as something not really exchanged at all—a "gift to [hir]self." Ze also notes that to obsessively maintain manhood would render hir a "stranger," alienated from hir body and at the mercy of more powerful people, just as ze is in hir job.

The estrangement associated with capitalism is also of concern in Tyler and Harry/Harriet's milieux, but for different reasons. Both characters live in postcolonial locations that have been ravaged for the profit of others and that are characterized by racial and economic segregation—with the extremely wealthy few, largely of European descent, existing in a self-enclosed world apart from the extremely poor masses, largely of African and Indian descent. Cereus's depiction of organic transgenderism is, in response, animated by anti-capitalist values. For one thing, Tyler's emphasis on the fact that hir "bloom[ing]" has not come "too late" (105) suggests a way of approaching humans, animals, and other biological species not based on dominant imperatives of productivity and time—in effect, what, and when, they can produce for "us," or how they can become something useful and legible within "our" systems. This point becomes most obvious when policemen invade Mala's ruinate house and disrupt the reciprocal relationship between her and nature. They see the cereus plant and exclaim, "The blossoms on this thing so big! I wonder if it will catch if I break off a piece and take it home?" (176)—clearly not recognizing the plant's unique properties, or the fact that they just happened to catch it in rare bloom. A band of profiteers descends immediately thereafter: a band of men with birdcages, four each, approach the back fence. Following them are three men with saws. As the bird catchers pass, they observe, "In a pinch ten birds could live for about two, three days in one cage." "You know how much one peekoplat fetching these days?" "Divide up, a third each, a mudra that size would make each one of us a rich man. I myself putting in a bid for the lower third of the base" (187). These scenes offer us the Marxist insight that "under capitalism[,] nature is more complexly mediated, by exchange value as well as use value" (Buell 143).

In response to such exploitation, the novel offers a very different value system, one informed by aspects of trans life as well as the existence of flora. To begin with, the glimpse of beauty the cereus offers is so brief as to be unquantifiable—meaning, we might say, that it confounds capitalistic logic. It forces one to realize that attentiveness, patience, and, as Tyler puts it, "promise" (72), must be largely their own rewards. Tyler and Mala treat each other similarly to how they treat the cereus: they act ethically and even lovingly toward each other not because they want, or expect, to get anything back, but because it is fulfilling in and of itself to do so. They think about the future, but specifically in terms of care, not in terms of profit or compensation. For example, without knowing for sure if the mute and dazed Mala will ever respond or improve, Tyler takes on hir care with good humor and gentle fortitude. Tyler, in turn, requires that others consider the "promise[s]" that normative puberty might actually defer (hir feminine body), rather than the product of that puberty (hir masculine body). And as hir adult body takes much longer to be realized than the average one does, ze requires patience. Were it not obvious by now, Mootoo is punning extensively on the terms "patient" and "patience." Mala is literally Tyler's patient, and ze is in many ways hers; they are two patients who teach each other patience.

This new value system, then, is a way of looking toward the future that is not based on exchange value or use value. That is to say, *Cereus* develops a queer definition of futurity that can combat the logic of capital accumulation. It draws in part on the notion of intrinsic value but focuses more on value as something lovingly and communally constituted, rather than as the property of a given thing. Indeed, the novel stresses the positive social aspects of valuing. We might turn here to Patrick Curry, who has developed a view that he calls "ecopluralism," which draws upon both ecocentrism and poststructuralist non-essentialism to put forth an environmental ethics. As he maintains,

> in ecopluralist terms, there is no intrinsic value "out there" in the objectivist sense; value can have no meaning, or even reality, without a valuer (although not necessarily a human one). But the necessary involvement of valuers in value does not therefore mean it is purely or merely subjective in the sense of being arbitrary, and so requiring some kind of "objective" (usually scientific) support. Nor does it mean that value is "not really there"; it really is there, but not in the absolutist and therefore untenable sense, demanded by objectivists, of only "there," or else not "there" at all. (56)

Cereus, like *Stone Butch Blues*, stresses the idea that value is created largely by valuers. But it insists that that creation of values must take place through an ethical framework—not as a means of punishing some and exalting others. In both novels, then, we see that the valuing of nature, and the very apprehension of nature *as* nature, is the result of a process of construction—but that that construction can have real, and positive, effects on both the human and the non-human.

Recognition of interconnectedness is key to this process of ethical valuing. Writer-activist Al Young makes this point in his semi-fictional essay on environmental justice, "Silent Parrot Blues." "Silent" contains the following conversation between two middle-aged African American men, a conversation that resonates with my transgender archive on multiple levels:

"[I]f you believe the earth is alive, and the waters, and the trees and the sky, and you're related to it all—then you treat all of it with respect. . . . But if you don't believe those things are alive, and if you don't believe they have anything to do with you—" "Except," Briscoe broke in and said, "*except* provide you with the means to turn a quick buck . . ." "In which case," I said, picking up where I imagined he'd trailed off, "it's OK to dump pesticides and nuclear waste and PCBs and anything at all into the earth." "Right," said Briscoe. "Dump it round where black people and Mexicans and Indians live." "And poor whites," I added. (121)

Importantly, Young stages this conversation as a collaboration—with the speakers playing off of each other's ideas and finishing each other's sentences. Similarly, the story Tyler relates in *Cereus* is inspired largely by the mystery of hir patient Mala Ramchandin, and by Mala's gentle encouragement of Tyler to find hir voice as a transgender person.

Interestingly enough, Young's essay centers around a parrot captured for profit, as does the scene discussed above from *Cereus*. This particular creature, we might say, symbolizes that process of finding one's voice against injustice. But equally as relevant is how both "Silent Parrot Blues" and *Cereus Blooms at Night*, along with *Stone Butch Blues*, use non-human creatures to lament the exploited human's exploitation of others as a means of improving his or her lot. In "Silent," the speaker/narrator's coming-to-environmental-consciousness revolves around the discovery that his building superintendant, a transient person of little means, has been mistreating a "fancy parrot from Bolivia" (115) that he keeps in a closet; the super has bragged that the bird will "fetch me five thousand dollars if he'll fetch a nickel" (114). Likewise, the plunderers described in *Cereus* are poor men who ignore their connection to exploited non-humans—tragically so, Mootoo would say. The speaker/narrator of "Silent" equivocates about his responsibility to have the super reported and probably jailed, until he realizes that his bigger responsibility is to report his environmental epiphany to us, his readers. The last line of the piece reads, "Remembering the pens people used to fashion from feathers . . . I knew I would one day follow Briscoe's suggestion and get some of it down in black and white" (123). Like Tyler, this sensitive speaker/narrator has indeed succeeded, metafictionally speaking, in producing the narrative that we as readers can now behold, and without continuing the cycle of oppression and incarceration he has witnessed.

Compared to *Blues* and *Cereus*, *Heaven* dramatizes its environmentalist, anti-capitalist ethics through more militant figures: its overarching plot finds Harry/Harriet leading a diverse band of civilians-turned-guerillas who fight economic inequality and segregation as they "redo" the colonial development of the island. (Importantly, we have by now learned that Harry/ Harriet is a survivor of sexual abuse, like *Stone Butch*'s Jess and Angie and *Cereus*'s Mala—and that his abuser was a figure not just of patriarchal power, but of colonial power: a white British solider.) The novel's first chapter is titled "Ruinate"—a "distinctive Jamaican term . . . used to describe lands which were once cleared for agricultural purposes and have now lapsed back into . . . 'bush'" (as quoted by Cliff 9). The guerillas take over empty ruinate lands and clear them,

> sometimes singing songs they remembered from the grandmothers and grandfathers who had swung their own blades once in the canefields. . . . Swinging their blades against the tough bush, some of them thought about their grandparents, thought: yes, this is for them too. . . . As the land cleared, it turned black—blackness filled with the richness of the river and the bones of people in unmarked graves. . . . When [the land] was prepared they planted some acres of ganja and, later, they planted food. They found, in the process of clearing the land, things that had been planted long before . . . which had managed to survive the density of the wild forest. Cassava. Afu. Fufu. Plantain. (10–11)

Cliff makes clear that this band is changing the landscape not for profit through exploitation, but as a way to repair that exploitation. And, interestingly enough, they leave a layer of ruinate to keep their operations under cover—a human–non-human reciprocity that is engineered, but reciprocal nonetheless.

Though less explicitly militant, Harry/Harriet's refusal of outside medical intervention constitutes an anti-capitalist, anti-colonial statement of its own. In declaring that "the choice is mine, man . . . castration ain't de main t'ing" (168), ze embraces the organic and innate over the foreign and externally imposed, just as ze does as an anti-colonial guerilla. The trans body, like Jamaica, is presented as independent and self-sufficient: close to nature in an *ideal* sense, rather than underdeveloped, primitive, and in need of outside help. In fact, the novel nearly collapses organic transgenderism and anti-colonial militance into each other.[14] While away in England, Clare receives a postcard from Harry/Harriet that states, "I find myself closer to my choice, girlfriend. How about you? Jamaica needs her children—I repeat myself, I know" (140). The phrase "my choice" privileges self-determination but does not specify exactly what that choice entails. Gender freedom and freedom from colonial domination thus become inseparable goals. We might recognize the same intertwining in *Cereus*, though on a more subtle level: the novel's depiction of transgenderism has folk wisdom trumping not just medical expertise, but received scientific wisdom—thus questioning the inferiority of local, indigenous cultures as compared to "developed" Western culture.

We might turn to Marxist theory to illustrate more explicitly how organic transgenderism can militate against dominant materialist[15] and capitalist epistemologies. In their *Anti-Oedipus: Capitalism and Schizophrenia* (1977), Gilles Deleuze and Félix Guattari explore the story of Daniel Paul Schreber, a schizophrenic whose *Memoirs of My Nervous Illness* (1903) describes the spontaneous growing of breasts on his body—part of Schreber's belief that he was turning into a woman. Referring to this description, Deleuze and Guattari state, "Nothing here is representative; rather, it is all life and lived experience: the actual, lived emotion of having breasts does not resemble breasts, it does not represent them" (19). They thereby collapse the privilege of the signifier: it is not just that the signifier (breasts) and signified (the feeling or knowledge of having breasts) are equivalent, but that the signifier might be irrelevant. Schreber's breasts are, we could say, the anti-penis vis-à-vis the phallus. Literal anti-matter, they cannot be assimilated into a signifying economy, much less one that ratifies gender binarism.

This example validates desire as productive. That is, Schreber has breasts because he *believes* he has breasts, just as with Tyler in *Cereus*—and just as Jess has a penis because Angie's "sweet imagination" says ze does. This claim is troubling not only to the paradigm of medicalized transsexualism, which sees the coherent-looking, normative body as the tangible goal to be pursued to the end, but to capitalism's mechanisms of commodification. As Deleuze and Guattari argue,

> When the theoretician reduces desiring-production to a production of fantasy, he is content to exploit . . . the idealist principle that defines desire as a lack, rather than a process of production . . . Clement Rosset puts it very well: every time the emphasis is put on a lack that desire supposedly suffers from as a way of defining its object, "the world acquires as its double some other sort of world, in accordance with the following line of argument: there is an object that desire feels the lack of; hence the world does not contain each and every object that exists; there is at least one object missing . . . hence there exists some other place that contains the key to desire." (26)

What results is an ever-insatiable quest for the object, a quest that fetishizes material/visual entities such as "real" (or "better") breasts, only to find them lacking. Deleuze and Guattari's analysis reminds us of how Feinberg has suggested that childhood expectations and desires produce adult bodies. In turn, to say that the expected or desired is not actually absent from the world (for example, that Jess's modified adult body was never "missing") is to refuse to reduce it to a commodity fetish and to make an autonomous, self-determined transgenderism conceptually possible. (After all, if something was never "missing," it cannot be so odd that one "finds" it.) Sheer desire can minimize or even supplant the need for intervention.

All this is not to say that transgender people are necessarily anti-capitalists, or that transsexuals are the consummate consumers. And nor is it to position transgenderism as somehow more progressive than transsexuality. Rather, I am suggesting that what we now term "transgenderism" has emerged at least in part from an imaginary in which the materiality of body parts is incidental, if not negligible, and in which desired body parts do not necessarily become commodities. Through this imaginary, the body can be moved out of the purview of a medical establishment from which one might purchase it, and (back) into the purview of the self, where, even if not yet fully extant, it can still be seen as sufficient. For those in low-wage jobs who cannot afford surgery, and for those such as Harry and Tyler in supposedly "backward" Third World countries, this imaginary is crucial. But perhaps more important is the fact that Feinberg, Mootoo, and Cliff show how this imaginary contributes to a biocentric worldview, one that rejects the characterization of bodies and landscapes as commodities or commodities-to-be.

Indigeneity and Transgender Pastoral

Of course, the fact that queer life bears a direct relationship to the rise of capitalism cannot be denied. John D'Emilio's groundbreaking 1983 article "Capitalism and Gay Identity" explains how capitalism produces the conditions necessary for individuals, and queer individuals in particular, to live outside of familial and reproductive structures—but also produces homophobia and other forms of regulation to maintain the family and biological reproduction, thus reproducing itself by ensuring the next generation of workers.[16] As D'Emilio clarifies, "[e]very society needs structures for reproduction and childrearing, but the possibilities are not limited to the nuclear family. Yet the privatized family fits well with capitalist relations of production. Capitalism has socialized production while maintaining that the products of socialized labor belong to the owners of private property" (109). D'Emilio's schema generally holds true for Jess, who initially identifies as a lesbian. Hir ability to leave home at sixteen and support hirself through blue-collar labor is undeniably a function of capitalism. And Stone pays particular attention to the crucial second part of D'Emilio's analysis, which outlines the ways in which capitalism produces punishments for the lifestyles it enables.

But Feinberg wants to tell a very different story about GLBTQI life than D'Emilio does. He observes that "there is . . . [a] historical myth that enjoys nearly universal acceptance in the gay movement, the myth of the eternal homosexual. The argument runs something like this: gay men and lesbians were and always will be. We are everywhere, not just now, but through-out history, in all societies and all periods" (101). Meanwhile, *Blues* traces transgenderism to pre-capitalist, nature-based societies and thus offers a transhistorical rather than strictly historicist view; Jess insists that "women like me [have] existed since the dawn of time, before there was oppression, and . . . those societies respected them" (6). D'Emilio's concern is that the belief in the "eternal homosexual," or the eternal GLBTQI individual, leaves unexamined those contradictory conditions that allow for the visibility of such individuals. But Feinberg clearly believes that we can use the concept of the "eternal homosexual" or "external transperson" to imagine forms of relations and identity formation outside of capitalism, and in natural spaces in particular.

Thus, whether or not Feinberg actually believes in social construction and the historicity of sexual/gender identities (it appears, generally speaking, that ze does), her transhistorical appeal must be taken seriously. For one thing, I have suggested that the perception of transgenderism as the product of postmodern late capitalism and medico-technological innovation—the ultimate consumer good in a world where we can supposedly choose gender identities at will—simplifies the trans experience and understates the per-sistence of gender inequality and misogyny. And it also positions the trans body as particularly "unnatural," for better or worse.[17] In the "real world" of Jess's factory jobs and jail cells, this perception of the trans body is another occasion for disciplinary acts of violence and humiliation—just as those who perceive the female presence in the factories as a disruption of the natural gendered order retaliate with sexual harassment and violence. The corre-lation of transness/queerness to the rise of capitalism is also problematic in that it obfuscates capitalism's role in the destruction of nature qua the environment—or, at least, subordinates environmental concerns to those of gay "liberation" and visibility by way of consumerism. *Stone Butch Blues*'s transhistoricism, then, asks us to imagine alternate scenarios of transition-ing and liberation, and to be skeptical of concepts of "the natural" that serve to underwrite exploitation. In (re)claiming the queer/trans person as at least partly natural, and tied to pre-capitalist societies, the novel sparks empathy for the environment's exploitation under capitalism.

Stone Butch Blues's vision of transgenderism as pre-capitalist specifically focuses on Native American existence. In one scene, when Jess's partner

Ruth is reading *Gay American History*, ze enthuses, "Look at this whole section about Native Societies. . . . This whole part is about women like you who lived as men" (266). This description broadens our view beyond the family-centered economies D'Emilio refers to as preceding capitalist ones. Capitalism as the double-edged escape from heterosexual/cisgender family life, *and* as a way of life, generally speaking, was not inevitable—but, following the suppression of indigenous societies, it has been American history. Importantly, Jess identifies hir makeshift Native American family as a viable alternative to the abusive nuclear one into which ze was born. Ze traces the latter relationship to hir birth, and in fact even earlier—further underscoring the idea of transgenderism as a lifelong process rather than a late-in-life medical decision. As ze describes it, "Rain and wind had lashed the desert while my mother was in labor. That's why she gave birth to me at home. The storm was . . . violent . . . [T]he Dineh¹⁸ grandmother from across the hall knocked on the door to see what was wrong, and then, realizing my birth was imminent, brought three more women to help" (14). When hir parents reject hir for hir inherent masculinity, ze finds solace with these Native Americans—until hir "father grew alarmed when he heard . . . [hir answer one of the Dineh women] with words he'd never heard before. He said later he couldn't stand by and watch his own flesh and blood be kidnapped by Indians" (14). Hir father's comment alludes to the "captivity narrative" tradition, distorting the more widespread action by which Native Americans were slaughtered and resources seized, destroyed, and/or taken over by whites.

As Jess prepares to modify hir body as an adult, ze draws once again on this connection to pre-capitalist and nature-based societies. Before undergoing hormone treatment and a double mastectomy, ze has a dream in which ze discovers a hut in a forest and crawls in to discover Rocco, a legendary female-to-male individual, "sitting next to me. She reached forward and stroked my cheek. I touched my own face. I felt the rough stubble of beard. I ran my hand across the flat plain of my chest. I felt happy in my body, comfortable among friends. . . . I looked up. The hut had no roof" (142). Ze later explains the setting as a "place that felt very old," and that ze "didn't feel like a man or a woman, and I liked how I was different" (143). At the end of the novel, Jess has a variation on this dream. Sitting again in the hut among a group of people, "[o]ne of the oldest in the circle caught my eyes. I didn't know if she was a man or a woman at birth. She held up . . . the ring that the Dineh women gifted me with as an infant. . . . She pointed to the circle the ring cast on the ground. I nodded, acknowledging that the shadow was as real as the ring" (300). This acknowledgment echoes, whether intentionally or not, the earlier scene with the dildo: the material object is subordinated to what it represents, and the signifier is made redundant in the face of the signified—rather than, as many theorists of postmodernity would have us believe, the opposite.[19]

Ruth, likewise, understands hir gender transitioning as a natural process on par with puberty, and as one inseparable from the natural world and nature-based societies. Ze describes how, rather than doing hard labor in the vineyards with hir uncle and other men, "[my mother] and my aunt and my grandma took me to work with them. They already knew my nature" (261). This comment recalls *Cereus Blooms at Night*, when Tyler remarks that Mala "was not one to manacle nature, and I sensed that she was permitting mine its freedom" (77). Even though ze does not work in the vineyards, Ruth nonetheless develops a close connection to nature. Ze recounts to Jess how her uncle Dale would "come by to take me hunting," but

> [m]ostly we just walked in the woods. He taught me to *respect* Bare Hill—that's the birthplace of the Seneca nation. *The government cut a road right through the burial grounds there.* Anyway, Dale used to get more and more upset about the way I was growing up. There certainly wasn't anything manly about me, and I think he felt it was his fault . . . One spring day we were walking on Bare Hill . . . At the top of the hill I saw a man whose hair was long and chocolate brown . . . They stood there talking. Then Dale nodded toward me and said, "I'm trying to teach the boy to be a man." . . . [T]he man put his hand on my uncle's shoulder and he said, "Let the child be." After a minute Dale hung his head and nodded. He looked at me different after that, like he was seeing me for the first time. (262, my emphasis)

Just as the Dineh women form a more loving family for Jess than hir own, the Seneca man prompts Ruth's family to fully accept hir. But Feinberg's employment of Native American cultural motifs runs deeper than legitimation or historical validation. It allows hir to trouble the association of gender transitioning with (post)modern medical technology and capitalism, and to link the destruction of indigenous lands to the rise of the rigid social formations that pathologize gender deviance. In response, Ruth's uncle teaches hir to respect the land that has been commandeered and exploited, and he learns a concomitant lesson about respecting gender variance.

The novel's moves here are remarkable, as it seems nothing short of contradictory to argue for a respectful, limited-interference stance toward nature, and to align those values with transgenderism—which usually *does* involve "interference."[20] But organic transgenderism allows us to see gender transitioning as a process involving relatively little interference from the outside world, and to focus on its self-directed, spontaneous, and internal mechanisms. Moreover, *Stone Butch Blues*, along with *Cereus* and *No Telephone*, shifts the somatic paradigm altogether: in linking transgenderism to the natural world, these novels establish the former as a state that, simply, exists in its own right, regardless of physical or visual proof, and regardless of validation from outside authorities. Thus they challenge the belief—widespread when it comes to trans people—that any machinations to the body are bad or, at least, very "unnatural." Instead, they suggest that the kinds of interference that are undertaken in a spirit of violence—without regard for an entity's autonomy, for its unique properties, or for the effects of that interference—are cause for concern.

Ruth does admit that ze is not entirely sure that the episode with hir uncle actually happened as she recalls it. Moreover, Jess's story of the Dineh women sounds apocryphal at best, within the context of Feinberg's otherwise realist novel. While we could therefore write off these episodes as intrusions into an otherwise realist story, I believe we should focus on their queer ecological implications. To begin with, these episodes participate in an alternative value system linked to, but not limited to, indigenous forms of spirituality that see that natural world and the human world as interconnected and that assume there are phenomena that exist outside the realm of so-called rational thought. To state, for example, that Jess does not actually have a penis, or that Ruth was born a man, is therefore utterly beside the point; such statements assume that the manifest is preeminent, that all events can be explained rationally, and that all other ways of thinking are "superstitious" and irrelevant. All three novels work against those assumptions. Ruth's tale, and Jess's story, then, are *Blues*'s equivalent to the magical realism found in *Cereus* and *Heaven*—which treat the spontaneous growing of breasts on a male-born person, and the ability of a female-born person to make hir facial hair grow, as minor quirks of life.

We might therefore understand Feinberg's linking of the trans person and the Native American as a form of praxis, rather than an attempt at an accurate historical or ethnographic account, or as a romanticization of the indigenous. First, we have seen that one of the primary understandings of organic transgenderism, as articulated by Feinberg, Cliff, and Mootoo, is the interconnectivity of forms of oppression. These authors do not seek to discount the unique experiences that emerge from different manifestations of oppression, but rather to stress that phenomena as diverse as ecological destruction, workplace inequality, and transphobia are driven by the same hierarchical worldview. Indeed, Jess's connection with Native Americans continues throughout hir adulthood, in ways that acknowledge differences rather than flatten them. At one bindery, where ze works with people of various ethnicities, "About half the women on the line were from the Six Nations. Most were Mohawk or Seneca. What we shared in common was that we worked cooperatively, day in and day out . . . We shared bits of our culture, favorite foods . . . It was just this potential for solidarity the foreman was always looking to sabotage" (78). After the Native American women, led by a woman named Muriel, ask Jess to sing with them as they work, and ze shyly complies, "the foreman called me into his office and handed me a pink slip" (80). Similarly, when ze is out with hir African American butch friend Ed, two policemen assault the pair, and one calls Jess a "fuckin' traitor" as "his boot cracked my rib for punctuation" (57). It is not clear if the officer regards Jess as a traitor to heterosexuality, to gender conformity, to whiteness, or all of the above. But the novel's point is that oppressors fear alliance across any form of difference—and that such alliance is therefore a crucial tool. Thus, even if partly rhetorical, Feinberg's invocation of Native American cultures highlights the importance of respectful encounters that allow each party to gain something from the other, without doing violence to either one.

Moreover, *Stone Butch Blues* does not voice unchecked nostalgia for the Native American—locking him or her in the past, and naively advocating a return to a preindustrial world. Besides including Native American characters such as Jimmy and Muriel, who are integrated into multicultural, post-industrial societies, the novel's characters explicitly articulate their skepticism about returning to an untouched natural world. When Ruth asks Jess, "If we lived in a world where we could be anything we wanted to be, what would you do with your life?" Jess says, "I'd be a gardener in a woods just for children . . . At night I'd sing a song about the way life used to be. It would be such a sad song it would make the grownups nod and the children cry. But I'd sing it every night so that no one would ever confuse nostalgia with wanting to return" (256). After the pair has read up on transgender history, finding that "we haven't always been hated," Ruth observes, "It's changed the way I think. I grew up believing the way things are now is the way they've always been, so why even bother trying to change the world? But just finding out that it was ever different, even if it was long ago, made me feel things could change again" (271). Ruth thus outlines a simultaneously futurist and cyclical vision of history, rather than a teleological or progressive one. In hir vision of history, individuals allow elements of the past to inform the present in order to produce a just future.

Conclusion

The Vine Valley detour that Feinberg added to hir original manuscript takes place just before the novel's conclusion in New York City. En route back to the city, Ruth and Jess meet a dwarf named Carlin at a truck stop. He laments, "I want to get out of here. I want to go to a big city where there's never a dull moment" (293). When Ruth invites him to come visit them, saying, "We'll show you why we love New York," Jess chimes in, "We'll show you why we hate it, too" (293). This conversation, and its placement in the novel, makes clear that the biocentricity of Native and pre-capitalist societies might inform and inspire urban queer existence, but that rurality should not be considered superior to urbanity (or vice versa). *Stone Butch Blues* thus participates in what James L. Machor refers to as "rural–urban synthesis." As he writes, dialectical thinking about nature and culture, the rural and the urban, has "largely obscured the fact that an equally significant strain of thought has conceived of the American scene as a place where that dialectic . . . could be synthesized" (5). Machor analyzes Henry George's 1879 tract *Progress and Poverty*, which envisions a populace in which "labor is [no longer] shut off from nature," with "rural urbanity and homes amongst gardens" (13) as an exemplary vision of rural–urban synthesis. Machor notes that, "unlike the pastoral ideal with its emphasis on individual freedom in a landscape separated from the continuing demands of corporate society, George's vision combines personal fulfillment with cooperative identity. Even as "individual interests [would] be subordinated to general interests," each person would have "leisure, and comfort, and independence . . . Talents now hidden, virtues unsuspected, would come forth to make human life richer, fuller, happier, nobler" (13).

George's vision, like Feinberg's, sounds vaguely socialist, even communist. Perhaps it is no coincidence, then, that the last chapter of *Stone Butch Blues* finds Jess reuniting with hir union organizer friend Duffy at hir first gay-rights rally. Jess asks Duffy if he is a communist, and the novel ends with hir awaiting his answer. Having come to understand the economic dimensions of bodily alienation and subjugation, and having forged the kinds of politicized connections described above, we might assume that Jess's full communist conversion looms on the horizon—perhaps to be even more explicitly integrated with hir environmentalist and queer politics. This stance contrasts starkly with Jess's earlier political apathy; after hir ex-partner Theresa describes how the Second Wave–feminist and anti-war movements have established alliances (while the feminist movement continues to discriminate against butches and femmes), she complains, "You and I never talk about the [Vietnam] war. I don't even know how you feel about it." Jess "shrug[s]," remarking with resignation, "I hate wars. But JFK didn't ask me if I wanted to start one. They're gonna do what they want to do" (126). In this final chapter, Jess demonstrates how ze has moved beyond such resignation, bounding to the stage at the rally to speak publically as a queer/trans person for the first time.

Jess's political/ecological coming-to-consciousness and hir coming-into-her-body are thus achieved simultaneously, though ze clearly still has work to do. In fact, just as *Stone Butch Blues* ends with Jess's question to Duffy, and the suggestion that ze faces a whole new life chapter as an activist, *Cereus Blooms at Night* and *No Telephone to Heaven* leave us with open-ended projects. I want to suggest that, in each case, the open-endedness directly engages readers in the ethical questions at hand and motivates them toward activism of their own. As I have suggested in my introduction, these are notable moves for novels so closely associated with the supposedly apolitical modes of postmodernism and poststructuralism. *Cereus*'s ending harkens back to Tyler's opening, *individualist* declaration that ze is "placing trust in the power of the printed word to reach many people. It is *my* ardent hope that Asha Ramchandin [Mala's long-lost sister] will chance upon this book. . . . If you are not Asha," ze continues, "but know her or someone you suspect might be her or even related to her, please present this and ask that she read it" (3, emphasis mine). The novel ends with the *communal* supplication, "Not a day passes that you are not foremost in *our* minds. *We* await a letter, and better yet, your arrival. She expects you any day soon. You are, to her, the promise of a cereus-scented breeze on a Paradise night" (249, my emphasis). Tyler's direct address throughout the novel hails us as participants and forces us variously to listen on behalf of another (Asha, Mala, and/or Tyler) and to stand in for another (Asha). That is to say, as the entire novel is addressed to Asha and/or her surrogate, in reading it we *are* her surrogate, regardless of whether or not Asha is a "real person"; Tyler's "you" makes us at once someone else and ourselves—and sometimes both indistinguishably.[21] Our very reading is thus premised upon our (metafictional) willingness to accept our moral obligations to others; others we do not know, and who in fact do not occupy the same present reality that we do. Perhaps more bleak, but equally as invested in blurring human/non-human distinctions, is *No Telephone*'s concluding description of a standoff involving Harry/Harriet's guerillas; it is unclear if Clare Savage, Harry/Harriet's best friend and our protagonist, is alive or dead. The novel's last page features the ambiguous statement, "She remembered language. / Then it was gone" (208), and then, before the final statement of "Day broke," we encounter a litany of animal noises, presumably from within the bush: "cuk cuk cuk cuk," "cawak, cawak, cawak," "hoo hoo hoo hoo

hoo hoo hoo hoo hoo hoo hoo," and so on (208). In all three novels, then, the human encounter with the non-human is profoundly transformative. It allows individuals to move beyond dualistic and hierarchical thinking and to find commonality with all manner of living things, in order to oppose all manner of oppression. These novels thus confirm the existence of a complex wholeness that we can only see through an empathetic imagination. And insofar as fiction relies upon, engages, and develops the imagination, we might say that these novels' queer ecological appeals necessarily go far beyond the page.

In offering us a strikingly elaborate ecology—in which the well-being of everything from cacti and eagles to transgender people and colonized populations is interdependent—*Stone Butch Blues*, *Cereus Blooms at Night*, and *No Telephone to Heaven* claim a place for the queer at the pervasive interface of nature and culture. As I have argued throughout this chapter, it is important that the queer characters in these novels are specifically *transgender*. As so-called unnatural, constructed cultural products, trans people have much to gain from seeing themselves as connected to nature. And as entities frequently treated as non-human, they have a uniquely complicated opportunity for empathizing with the non-human world. I want to suggest, then, that an ecological mindset has been crucial in establishing the category of transgender: the ameliorative visions of organic gender transitioning found within these novels constitute some of the earliest articulations of that concept, if not the term. As Siobhan Somerville observes, "a model of 'transgender' identity describes Jess's subjectivity . . . even though this actual term is never used in the novel itself" (171). Likewise, neither *Cereus Blooms at Night* nor *No Telephone to Heaven* use the term. But by outlining somatic and psychic experiences that are ill-fitted, in both medical-social and political-ideological terms, to the earlier sexological model of transsexualism, they begin to create an alternative. This chapter thus shows how new models of gender and sexuality emerge not just out of shifts in areas such as politics, economics, and medicine, but out of shifts in ecological consciousness.

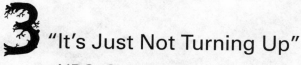

3 "It's Just Not Turning Up"

AIDS, Cinematic Vision, and Environmental Justice in Todd Haynes's *Safe*

To see is to draw a limit beyond which vision becomes barred.
. . . For it is not the closing of one's eyes that determines the
invisible as its empirical result; it is rather the invisible (the
repressed) that predetermines the closing of one's eyes. . . .
Paradoxically enough, however, it is precisely the imposition
of a limit beyond which vision is prohibited which . . . makes
possible the illusion of total mastery over meaning as a whole,
as an unimpaired totality.

—Shoshana Felman, *Writing and Madness*[1]

Released in 1995, writer-director Todd Haynes's *Safe* quickly became associated with the 1990s boom in American independent film and,
more specifically, with what B. Ruby Rich dubbed the "New Queer Cinema":
the "wave of queer films that gained critical acclaim on the festival circuit
in the early 1990s" (Aaron 3). *Safe* falls squarely between two other works
in Haynes's oeuvre that feature the same basic premise: a suburban white
woman suffocates under social and structural pressures. In fact, *Safe*, *Super-
star: The Karen Carpenter Story* (1987), and *Far from Heaven* (2002) evoke 1940s
and 1950s "women's films" such as *Mildred Pierce* (1945) and *All That Heaven
Allows* (1955) to such an extent that Haynes has gained a reputation as a queer
restylist of melodrama.[2] In keeping with that genre, *Safe* has a seemingly
mundane story line: well-to-do housewife Carol White (Julianne Moore) lives
with her husband, Greg (Xander Berkeley), and stepson, Rory (Chauncey
Leopardi), in Southern California's San Fernando Valley. Though notably list-
less, Carol appears otherwise healthy at the film's start. But she soon begins
to experience nosebleeds, vomiting, and seizures, ostensibly because of her
increasing sensitivity to everyday substances such as automobile exhaust and

Figure 2. In Todd Haynes's *Safe*, housewife Carol White enjoys a glass of milk while housepainters ingest a more toxic substance behind her. Columbia Tristar, 1999.

cologne. While her husband is concerned about her illness, he is frustrated by its enigmatic character; though she seeks help from her male doctor and a male psychiatrist, no definitive explanation for her maladies is ever reached. In response to Carol's claim that she has a chemical imbalance, her doctor disdainfully suggests her problems to be psychosomatic, snapping, "It's just not turning up on the tests."

Seeking validation and alternative treatment for her illness, Carol retreats to Wrenwood, a healing center in New Mexico masterminded by a New Age guru named Peter Dunning (Peter Friedman). Although Wrenwood, where *Safe* closes, appears initially to be a more empathetic environment than the hospital or psychiatrist's office, the film indicates that all of these spaces are governed by similar philosophies. As Haynes opines in the 1999 Columbia Tristar DVD liner notes to the film, "New age thought is so big among AIDS and cancer patients . . . because it creates a feeling of comprehension, a way to control the sense of meaninglessness that grips [their] lives. But within that control these doctrines of inner health assign to their sufferers . . . ultimate responsibility . . . [while] society gets off scott [sic] free. This is how new age thought ultimately works in favor of the system while claiming to transcend it." Such machinations, in other words, indirectly blame the victim, and thwart collective action through their privatizing of envirohealth concerns.

I juxtapose Carol's doctor's reaction with Haynes's comment to draw our attention to *Safe*'s abiding interests in visual epistemology and perceptions of bodily risk. I claim that the film's modeling of the interrelationship between the two offers a new way to think about the regimes of visibility—those that underpin both dominant social frameworks and classical film viewership, organizing Carol's world and our world as viewers. Through these regimes, we take the manifest as preeminent, assume that ontology equals visibility, and read the center rather than the margins. But the film cites such behaviors, often quite critically, at multiple points. Taking this fact into account might make us skeptical of the widespread assumption that Carol's story *allegorizes* the experience of AIDS[3]—the assumption, that is, that someone who looks "safe" could never actually *have* AIDS. And, more generally, we might become skeptical of the idea that *Safe* is mainly concerned with the risks faced by Carol White or women like her.

In other words, when we consider that visual epistemology is pointedly held up as a problem in, and by, the film, we might think beyond what's displayed most centrally on the screen. The same holds true for *Safe*'s visual techniques, including the camera's frequent distance from Carol's body, and our concomitant distance from it as viewers; they evoke a sense of a female powerlessness, but they also slacken the viewer's propensity to take Carol as a site of normative identification. In this chapter, I explore what these operations make possible: first, a reconsideration of our criteria for "safe" and "unsafe" bodies and environments, and how those designations become naturalized; and, second, a consideration of the bodies at the literal and figurative margins of the film—bodies that happen to be lower-class and non-white. I argue that the film's queer techniques make possible a consideration of the envirohealth risks to those bodies and the habits of seeing that otherwise obscure them.

Safe thus links the (in)visibilization of envirohealth concerns to dominant racial and class hierarchies, in addition to those of gender and sexuality. And it thereby engages with the complex at the very heart of this book, that of empathy, imagination, interrelationships, and ethics, in a very complicated manner: it checks our empathy for our protagonist precisely at the moments at which she fails to empathize with others, or to recognize her place at the intersection of oppression and privilege. At the same time, it formally models a way of seeing and knowing that acknowledges the interrelationships among gender, class, race, immigration status, health status, sexuality, and environment—a way of seeing and knowing that is empathetically attuned to the experience of the oppressed.

In these ways, *Safe* engages with the concepts of environmental justice and "environmental racism," which we might call prime examples of structural violence. Medical anthropologist Paul Farmer has extended Johan Galtung's definition of "structural violence" in declaring that "rights violations are

... not random in distribution or effect ... [they are], rather, symptoms of deeper pathologies of power and are linked intimately to the social conditions that so often determine who will suffer abuse and who will be shielded from harm" (xiii). Coined in the 1980s by leaders in the U.S. environmental-justice movement, the term "environmental racism" emerged out of this kind of deep structural critique. As Robert D. Bullard explains, "people of color are subjected to a disproportionately large number of health and environmental risks in their neighborhoods ... and on their jobs" (*Confronting* 10). But *Safe* shows us that environmental racism and classism, and the specific gendered/ sexualized dimensions of both, are not relegated to ghettoized communities alone. In focusing on a suburban existence made comfortable by workers who live outside of it, the film suggests that the spheres of enfranchisement and disenfranchisement, of private and public, overlap in more intimate ways than theorists of social justice have imagined.[4] Indeed, the film characterizes the health risks specific to service work in upper-class contexts as particularly insidious, in that these risks are less obvious, less immediate, and frequently naturalized, such that they seem less pressing than those associated with, say, factory labor. The invisibility of such risks at once obfuscates and justifies the operations of environmental injustice.

By engaging with questions of environmental justice as they play out in privileged contexts, *Safe* expands the notion of what constitutes an "environmental crisis." As we explore pollution and toxicity through Carol White's suburban framework, we scrutinize domestic/ interior spaces— those spaces often believed to be constructed in opposition to, or as refuge from, "the environment." I hereby align my work with what Lawrence Buell has identified as the "second wave" of ecocriticism, which holds that "the concentration on 'environment' as 'nature' and on nature writing as the most representative genre [is] too restrictive, and that a mature environmental aesthetics—or ethics, or politics—must take into account the interpenetration of metropolis and outback, of anthropocentric as well as biocentric concerns" (22–23).

Curiously, the film's engagement with environment, and with related concepts such as "nature," has received relatively little attention, despite the fact that it focuses on environmental illness.[5] In fact, perhaps because of the unresolved character of this illness, or because of its perceived status as an AIDS analogue, some critics believe that the film fails to contribute meaningfully to ecocritical discourse.[6] For example, while Laura Christian notes the abjection of racial minorities in *Safe*'s suburban milieu, she calls the film's invocation of deep ecology a "non sequitur interlude" (104). In contrast, this chapter posits *Safe* as a work centrally concerned with environmental issues, and environmental justice in particular, and as one that complicates ecocritical and environmentalist thinking.

In construing Safe as a formal meditation on environmental justice, this chapter seeks to account more fully for its historical and discursive contexts. These include not just "New Queer Cinema," but the iterations of environmentalism that appeared alongside the AIDS crisis. (Indeed, as I will show, Safe is set in a landmark year—1987—for both queer/AIDS activism and environmentalism.) Chief among these environmentalisms is deep ecology, which focuses on the transformation of individual behavior as a solution to environmental crisis—at the risk, its critics would say, of leaving underlying social, economic, and political structures untouched. I also seek to reassess Safe's place in the "woman's film" tradition. I claim that it reworks that genre not only by accounting for intersecting factors such as race, class, and sexuality, as have many post–Second Wave feminist critics, vis-à-vis the film and otherwise,[7] but by showing that those factors make for disparate experiences of bodily risk. Indeed, if we are to believe that a white woman in a "conservative, insular environment" can become ill (Potter 137), then those without the constant advantage of such insularity might be at great risk, indeed. Thus Haynes gives us the melodramatic heroine as a very complicated site of identification: a prism of suffering and privilege, one that both attracts our sympathies and refracts them, such that they extend to those even more invisible than she.

The literal nature of my concerns with visibility cannot be overstated: I argue that the film's formal questioning of the sovereignty of the visible, and how the visible *becomes visible*, is necessarily an invitation to recognize how the spatial logic of racism and classism allows oppression to flourish, unnoticed. As John David Rhodes puts it, "Safe expresses a faith in [the ability of] images—in the cinema—. . . [to] pictur[e] the impossibility of picturing" (74). This invitation to read against dominant tendencies of vision—which coincide with, and even mutually reinforce, the dominant social structures cited by the film—primes us to see what those structures obscure: those whose suffering is not immediately palpable and cannot easily be made manifest; those without access to diagnostic or representational technologies. Those who, to paraphrase Carol's doctor, "just don't show up." This chapter thus offers a specific look at how cinema, dependent as it is on certain habits of seeing, might trouble those habits in the name of social justice and environment. Such a cinema would ask us to recognize not just the *issues* of racism and classism, in addition to sexism, heterosexism, and homophobia, but the structural operations thereof.

I hope to show through this work that Safe is not a queer film that happens to touch on environmental concerns; it is a film that comprehends and articulates environmental concerns in queer terms. This distinction is crucial, as a narrow view of the film as queer might allow us to assume that it uses a suffering white suburban housewife as a point of GLBTQI identification—rather than as grounds for a critical commentary on the interrelationship of race, class, gender, sexuality, immigration status, health status, and environmental injustice and degradation. Likewise, the assumption that the film merely allegorizes AIDS presumes that no pressing connection exists between AIDS and the environment, or between AIDS and concepts of the "natural" or the "unnatural." In providing more expansive readings, then, I seek to combat such limited views of queer texts and to show how all of the above—race, class, gender, sexuality, immigration status, health status, nature, and environment—intersect.

Pathos and Cinematic Vision

Safe employs a battery of distancing and estranging visual techniques. These include poor interior lighting; long, wide-angle shots; static shot compositions; relatively few close-ups; and limited zooms, most of which are so slow as to be almost imperceptible. The film's iconic shot (figure 3) is exemplary: a lone figure in hazmat gear is positioned deep in the shot, dwarfed by the surrounding environment. (This shot was circulated as a promotional still, and a stylized version of it graces the DVD cover. The figure in question is a fellow Wrenwood patient, not Carol, but the latter is positioned similarly at various points in the film.) In an in-depth analysis of the film's camera-work, Roddey Reid concludes that Carol's experience of illness parallels our experience of viewing: "she no more understands herself, her illness, and her world than we do" (38). Indeed, the film catches us in multiple epistemological traps. For example, we do not see Carol's husband's face clearly for the first twenty-two minutes of the film. He becomes potentially monstrous in these few minutes, especially in that the film's beginning moments play much like a horror film.[8] Yet whatever suspicions we might have are never borne out. Greg White is eventually shown to be healthy and human, and his behavior throughout the rest of the film is benign. Such highlighting of vision's failure to offer definitive knowledge[9] allows the film to critique what Reid calls the "populist epistemology of visibility [that] join[s] up with expert vision[,] wherein to see is literally to know" (34). In terms of Safe's critical logic, seeing is certainly not knowing.

The camera's frequent "failure" to get close to Carol's body, and our distance from it as viewers, creates a host of effects. First, this distance is po-

Figure 3. A shot that exemplifies *Safe*'s distancing techniques. Columbia Tristar, 1999.

tentially pathos-inducing. As Mary Ann Doane states, "pathos, the central emotion of melodrama, is reinforced by the disproportion between the weakness of the victim and the seriousness of the danger . . . pathos closely allies itself with the delineation of a lack of social power and effectivity" (4–5). In frequently distancing us from Carol's besieged body, the film enacts some of the very structural inequities that constitute a pathetic state, such as lack of access to the media, lack of tools for self-expression, and lack of attention from the general public. But it also Others the body onscreen. When the camera *does* move in closer to Carol, its pace is often glacial, figuring a deep trepidation. The film's extraordinary last scene, for example, begins with a shot trained on Carol as she sits in a Wrenwood "safe house"; the camera creeps toward her at a rate that is barely perceptible as she looks directly up at the camera and then down again.[10] When she rises, as if to confront the camera (or viewer) up close, the shot cuts away abruptly. Thus, while Carol is in almost every shot of the film, our intimacy with her is troubled on multiple levels. As Susan Potter summarizes, "the potential identificatory effects of closer, more intimate shots are regularly weakened by subsequent extreme long shots emphasizing the space around the human actors" (131); Potter and Reid also claim that those closer shots are "weak" in terms of performance, insofar as Moore plays her role with flat, passive affect and minimal facial expressions. In short, the film does not treat Carol discriminatorily, but it does not treat her in ways that so-called normal bodies, bodies that uncategorically "deserve" attention, are usually treated. In turn, *Safe* prompts the viewer to scrutinize how he or she normally sees, and how those habits might construct what he or she believes.

In terms of pathos, the film's distancing techniques also prompt the viewer to examine the relationship among gender, power, and environment. Specifically, they invoke the neglect of women in health research and treatment, due either to overt sexism or to the "benevolent" discrimination that fails to see them as needing medical intervention. To take a prominent example: Lois Gibbs's whistle-blowing work on the Love Canal disaster of the 1970s—recognized by ecocritics as a crucial moment in the "feminizing" of environmentalism[11]—revealed how androcentricism frames envirohealth crises. Specifically, Susan Buckingham-Hatfield tells us, Love Canal exemplified the disastrous ramifications of "neutral" health data: "inadequate guidelines on the effects of chemical pollutants were given for women and children[,] as the only available estimates were based on the assumption of workplace exposure of forty hours a week on men, who have a heavier body weight" (56). More than suggesting that "gender-neutral" envirohealth data disadvantage female bodies, these facts speak to a deeper problem: the bodies of certain women and certain children are imaginatively sutured into the supposedly safe spaces they occupy, such that any break in that fabric, any experience of bodily illness, cannot be articulated. The only "natural" space for an idealized body, then, is a safe space, and the only "natural" occupant of a safe space is an idealized body—and thus the opposite holds true for non-idealized bodies. Since Carol occupies believed-to-be-safe spaces, the powers that be cannot believe that anything is wrong with her. But *Safe* ironizes this prevailing, and potentially fatal, ideology.

The film's narrative structure echoes these visually established points. First, Carol frustrates narrative conventions by never fully triumphing over her health-related adversities, never reaching enlightenment, and never achieving self-knowledge by the film's end. And the viewer never receives a definitive explanation for her disease. Rather than evincing a clear developmental arc like a conventional character or an ideal person, Carol looks like an incidental flat line. And as an ostensibly conventional film narrative, *Safe* feels rather limp: it has no real point of climax, little drama, and little payoff when things do turn toward the dramatic. Just as many of its long, wide-angle shots are static, we have long stretches of plot with little action of note. But we might recognize these aspects as politicized shiftings of narrative standards, rather than simple failures to meet them.

To begin with, all of the aforementioned narrative features (lack of closure, lack of character development, lack of action) can be described as queer: in addition to flouting Hollywood film conventions, they challenge what Judith Roof, Linda Williams, Susan Winnett, and others have identified as the masculinist heteronormativity of classical narrative dynamics. Consider for a moment the description of plot offered by Peter Brooks: "Plot starts . . . from that moment at which story, or 'life,' is stimulated from quiescence into a state of narratability, into a tension, a kind of irritation, which demands narration . . . [This] narrative desire [is] the arousal that creates the narratable as a condition of tumescence, appetency, ambition, quest, and gives narrative a forward-looking intention" (103). As Roof et al. have observed, such definitions are patriarchal and heterosexist: satisfaction is equated with closure, climax is equated with meaning, and futurity or "forward-looking" is understood as implicitly heterosexual.[12] The "limpness" of a film such as *Safe*, then—its refusal to offer closure, its disinterest in climax—appears particularly queer. But this queerness has even more specific ramifications: Monica Pearl contends that "New Queer Cinema *is* AIDS cinema: not only because the films . . . emerge out of the time of and the preoccupations with AIDS, but because their narratives and also their formal discontinuities and disruptions, are AIDS-related" (23). She explains, for example, that temporal experimentation in New Queer Cinema can be traced to new experiences of time under the threat of AIDS: lifespans cut drastically short, the living of each day as if it might be one's last. We might also note that AIDS spawned in GBLTQI and other alternative communities new ways and means of having sex that did not involve the production or exchange of bodily fluids, thus troubling teleological (ejaculatory/interpersonal) definitions of sex.[13] In this specific way, then, *Safe*'s aesthetic attributes constitute a queer/AIDS-conscious shifting of narrative *and* sexual standards.

Safe's visual and narrative features work together to (re)organize our attention and sympathies toward characters other than Carol—specifically, characters affected by environmental racism and injustice. First, while Carol is undeniably the main character, the aforementioned features prevent her from standing in stark contrast to those racial and class Others included in the film. Second, and relatedly, the film's interrogation of visual epistemology induces a sense of pathos that far exceeds her. Indeed, if our relatively distant protagonist can summon our compassion, then we might ask, what of those who are even further marginalized, visually, narratologically, and within the film's social world? If our indignation is stoked by the fact that no one recognizes Carol's environmental illness, might we not wonder what other experiences of environmental illness are going unrecognized within the diegesis? (At the risk of sounding too cynical, I would say that if we *don't* ask such questions, the point is nonetheless proven: privileged people monopolize attention, sympathy, and other sociopolitical resources.) And if we believe her to be queer in narrative terms, and possibly in terms of being an invisible minority, as I discuss in the next section (a married white woman with AIDS), might we not include within our purview the film's other (in)visible minorities? The film also lets us see racial and class Others in a more literal sense: its visual techniques allow the viewer to scan a wider field, one in which the existence, *but also the absence*, of marginal individuals is occasionally perceptible. In turn, as I will show later in this chapter, these individuals further probe how dominant visual epistemology constructs conceptions of "safe" and "unsafe" bodies and environments. Thus the film does not so much ask us to choose between its more important and less important figures, its more threatened and less threatened bodies, but rather to contemplate how we know the difference.

AIDS as a (Non-)Diagnosis

Safe's 1987 setting, eight years before its actual release, positions it in the thick of the AIDS crisis—and amid other debates that were raging in the United States, around the condition of the nuclear family, the income gap, the role of the Environmental Protection Agency (especially in light of Reagan's unprecedented rollbacks in environmental law), the "War on Drugs," and the criminalization of black/urban youth.[14] Susan Potter maintains that within this historical context, "*Safe* allows AIDS to be easily substituted for Carol's unidentified illness" (147). However, she notes that such a reading "makes it difficult to account for the specific references to people with AIDS" within the narrative (147). More emphatically, John David Rhodes insists that "*Safe* is an allegorical treatment of the AIDS epidemic" (74), noting that "the easy part is seeing that Carol does not have AIDS; the film tells us this itself" (75). I share Rhodes's insistence that we cannot avoid thinking about AIDS when we think about the film. Potter's hesitation is instructive, though; it *is* difficult to sustain a reading of the film as an AIDS allegory when AIDS appears within the diegesis, but not impossible. For one thing, we should note that Carol's self-diagnosis of "environmental illness" does not preclude other maladies. In fact, Peter Dunning, head of the Wrenwood retreat Carol visits, identifies himself as a "chemically sensitive person with AIDS." This self-description makes perfect sense, considering that AIDS destroys the immune system. And all we really know about Carol is that she is likewise "chemically sensitive"; the *cause* of this sensitivity is never identified.

The idea that the film "tells us" that "Carol does not have AIDS" requires particular scrutiny. The film and figures within it tell us all sorts of things that we are then prompted to question, or to recognize as untrue. As we have seen, Carol's doctor insists that there's nothing wrong with her, when clearly *something* is; the film also suggests that sinister things are afoot when, apparently, they are not. As Rhodes himself notes, when we see Carol enter the living room and scream, "Oh my God!" "we might think . . . that Carol might have 'discovered the blood-spattered body of her stepson in the spotless décor'" (Rhodes, quoting Reid, 76–77). The revelation of the black couch, rather than a blood-spattered body, enacts a skeptical hermeneutics whereby we question our ability to perform accurate deductive reasoning, whereby we critically examine frames for what is *not* shown, and whereby we scrutinize appearances for what they *conceal*, and not just what they reveal.

In fact, AIDS figures most prominently in the film when it remains off-screen. In one much-remarked-upon early scene, Carol visits her friend Linda, who mentions that her brother has recently passed away. Carol asks, "It wasn't . . . ?" and Linda replies, "No. Everyone keeps . . . not at all . . . 'cause he wasn't married." This conversation invokes several logical leaps—from Linda's brother being unmarried, to him being gay, to him being HIV-positive, to him being an AIDS patient, to his death from AIDS. The fact that the women barely need articulate these leaps illustrates for us the pervasiveness of sexual-epidemic discourse in the mid-1980s, and the so-called family values that subtend it. Linda Singer argues that "[t]he anxiety . . . mobilized around the connection of sex to death in AIDS . . . is displaced and condensed in the regulation of sexual reproduction and the promotion of the family as the supposedly exclusive site of safe sex" (29). In her clipped response to Carol, Linda intimates how AIDS becomes the occasion for condemning not (just) risky sex or drug use, but something broader: non-heteronormative life. Even in rejecting the aforementioned linkages, Linda reproduces them here for Carol and the viewer. It is not that "AIDS" points back to "unmarried," but that "unmarried" points forward to "AIDS."[15] And considering that "AIDS," in 1987's cultural shorthand, meant "death," the movement described above actually looks much simpler: from "unmarried" to "dead."

Of course, it is not just "unmarried" but everything it connotes—"non-reproductive," "childless," possibly even "sterile"—that leads to the (mis) diagnosis of queerness and AIDS, or queerness *as* AIDS. That is, we can presume that the same suspicions would not have been raised if Linda's brother were, say, a single father, not *just* unmarried. As Singer suggests above, the idealized nuclear family within sexual-epidemic conditions is understood as insulating and literally conservative, capable in and of itself of warding off intruders and disease. By his failure to marry and reproduce, Linda's brother becomes forever diseased within the social imagination. Indeed, his actual life gets overwritten by the ever-generative capacities of gossip—a mode of discourse ironically more viral than his implied human immunodeficiency, and in one sense more lethal, in that it achieves his social death. Carol's halting questioning, and Linda's disjointed explanation, thus represent the difficulty of counterdiscourse in the face of such powerfully infectious suspicions.

To consider the possibility that Carol's ill health is due to AIDS—even if we settle on a different conclusion—forces us to examine these conservative regimes ordering her world and, potentially, ours as viewers. The film suggests that those ensconced in environments considered preventative, insular, and "natural"—the nuclear family, primarily, as well as the suburban home—believe themselves, and their peers, to be immune to such health disasters as HIV infection. And such persons are usually rendered immune from suspicion in the first place. But the film quickly collapses this ideology. Not only is Carol not immune to health disaster, as her illness proves, but her place within the nuclear family is subtly qualified as less than "natural," per normative standards. Most prominently, Haynes makes Carol a stepmother—a non-reproductive woman and non-biological mother—and demonstrates her physical and emotional alienation from her husband. In thus queering her, he denaturalizes the joining-together of particular categories; "woman" and "wife" are decoupled from "mother," just as "AIDS" might be decoupled from "gay man." This work avails Carol to other considerations such as this possibility of AIDS, and, more broadly, forces us to question the automatic contrasts assumed between "obviously" risky bodies and bodies found in conventional social arrangements and spaces. Carol, to put it more simply, might not deserve the mantle of normalcy and purity placed upon her by patriarchal figures of authority.

But they place it nonetheless. Which, I argue, explains why Carol's illness is never investigated to her or our satisfaction. When her doctor snaps that her possible chemical imbalance is "just not turning up on the tests," we might wonder what other tests, literal and figurative, Carol might not have taken, due to her presumed ability to pass them. As suggested above, as a white, married, affluent, suburban woman, she simply does not occupy any of the "classic 4-H 'risk groups'—Homosexuals, Heroin addicts, Hemophiliacs, and Haitians" (Treichler, as quoted in Balsamo 38) for AIDS, as understood in the 1980s. As Paula Treichler explains, because of the early focus on "AIDS as something you get because of who you are, not what you do, women were excluded from the lists of populations believed to be at risk" (as quoted in Balsamo 38)—just as they have been excluded from envirohealth data. Thus we can assume that, of all the possible tests administered to Carol, an HIV test is not one of them.[16]

Whether or not Haynes wants us to believe that Carol as a character "really" has AIDS is actually irrelevant, then. But that does not necessarily render AIDS an external reference point. Within the conservative logic contemporaneous to the film's milieu, Carol will simply never be read as someone with AIDS. Because her doctor, husband, and psychiatrist—along with some viewers, several critics, and she herself, cannot see her white female body as risky or unsafe, and because they *do* believe that seeing is knowing, the possibility of such a diagnosis is never given credence. This is perhaps to her detriment, and certainly to the detriment of more sophisticated medicocultural knowledge about the syndrome. At best, then, the assumption that *Safe* (only) allegorizes AIDS through Carol precludes a critique of the regimes of visibility, and of the regimes of race, class, gender, sexuality, and immigration status, that the film invites. It allows a straight, white, privileged woman to stand in for a (white?) gay male and thus to function primarily as an unchallenging vehicle for sympathy, rather than as the grounds for a radical queer critique of racism, classism, misogyny, heterosexism, xenophobia, and inadequate responses to environmental degradation.[17] But if we take the film's critique of visibility seriously, we can look sympathetically *as well as* critically at Carol White, and we can then look beyond, to see the non-white and lower-class individuals at the film's literal and figurative margins.

The Limits of Sympathy

A brief list will indicate the preponderance of marginalized persons in *Safe*: the African American, white, and possibly Latino movers who transport Carol's new couches to her home; the white customer-service representative who fields her complaints about the couches; her Latina maid Fulvia (Martha Velez-Johnson);[18] her Latina caterers; her friend's Latina maids; the Latino workers who paint her cabinets; her Asian American dry cleaner; the African American medical assistant who comforts her during her allergy test; the nurse of indeterminate race in her hospital room; the white woman who perms her hair and paints her nails; and the white cabdriver who drives her to the Wrenwood retreat in New Mexico. Most criticism on the film ignores these figures in favor of Carol—even though, as Susan Potter notes, many of Haynes's techniques "withhold the identification with character that . . . classical techniques conventionally secure" (126). Of course, such figures would be expected within a film that depicts upper-class life. But as I will describe, these bodies populate the margins and backgrounds of the film even, or especially, when they are not central to the ostensible story—a fact that the film's visual techniques allow us to register. These marginal bodies call into question the hegemonic regimes of visibility I have discussed. Concomitantly, they indict the viewer's willingness to allow the question of sympathy to turn primarily on Carol as a supposed "hostage of her environment" (Doane 6).

Some critics of *Safe* have taken this tack, in the process conflating the existence of the worker with that of the woman of the house. (The term "domestic" for maids and housekeepers does the same.[19]) Besides making "women" into a term encompassing only privileged white women, such criticism furthers the fantasy that all women in the home are part of a cohesive domestic system, untainted by the market or by pesky differences of race and class. For instance, Mary Ann Doane claims that "Carol's struggle with the color of the couches testifies to the heavy weight of the minutiae of everyday life, of the constant effort to keep up the home" (7). This claim collapses Fulvia's position into Carol's—Carol makes virtually *no* efforts to keep up the home—and glosses over the fact that these "minutiae" are actually contracted out to workers who do not permanently live in "the home." Potter's work on the film is much more critically attuned to these relations, but she nonetheless categorizes the Whites' home as a "gendered space" and asserts that "the distantly perceived figure of a woman [Carol] becomes another ornament within a frame filled with furniture and decorative objects such as lamps, vases . . . [and] prints" (130, 135). The Whites' home, as that loaded name suggests, is a *raced, and classed,* gendered space—unless Carol's maid does not count as a woman. And the positioning Potter refers to thus holds true only for the white, upper-class woman.[20] The "distantly perceived" figures of women such as maids and nurses, in addition to other service workers, are not "decorative" in this sense, and they show up onscreen much less frequently. But what I find most problematic is the insistence on Carol's position as a restrictive one—as a kind of danger to her, instead of a means of *avoiding* danger. Better an ornament, some would say, than the one who has to polish it.

Carol herself blithely glosses over the actual dimensions of her position. We watch, for example, as she attempts to interpellate Fulvia while lodging a telephone complaint about the mistaken couch delivery—an event she did not witness, having previously briefed the deliverymen on their duties. (Indeed, it seems as if it is her *lack* of labor, her delegations, that create many of her "struggle[s].") Looking directly at the maid standing in the doorway, a seated Carol shakes her head in frustration and says, "I don't believe this." Fulvia, wearing rubber gloves and holding a trashcan, is unresponsive save for a skeptical expression. Interestingly, we find a similar scene in Haynes's *Far from Heaven*, set thirty years earlier: Cathy Whitaker (also played by Julianne Moore) asks her black maid Sybil (Viola Davis) if her husband phoned while she was out grocery shopping. When Sybil, laden with the grocery bags she came outside to collect, responds in the negative, a cheerful but perturbed Cathy says, "How do you like that guy?" Sybil smiles politely and returns to the house. In both films, the posture of the maid of color, her silence, and the trappings of labor she bears put the white female protagonist's frustrations into critical perspective. The latter's attempts at establishing grounds for commiseration are rendered disingenuous, even laughable, by the maid's prominent disinterest. Whether we then begin to identify more with the maid, or simply to conceive more fully of our protagonist's position vis-à-vis such others, sympathy for that protagonist has been delimited.

I do not want to suggest that *Safe* never courts the kind of liberal-feminist reading that would conceive of Carol as a victim. As noted, the film's camerawork, and its evocation of the gendered dimensions of envirohealth crises, elicits sympathy. Content-wise, moreover, *Safe* does hold out possibilities for Carol as the face of the oppressed.[21] But these possibilities are frequently foreclosed by the film's visual features and narrative, sometimes immediately after being raised. For example, after Carol's doctor informs her that the tests do not show conclusive results, we hear an inexplicable hissing sound. The camera cuts to a shot of a nurse spraying cleaning fluid in a corner of the room, then back to Carol, who screams, "Please don't do that!" from her hospital bed. The doctor then reprimands the nurse. (See figures 4 and 5.) The regimes of visibility—those which refute her health complaints on the grounds that no concrete causes are appearing "on the [medical] tests"—have just victimized Carol. And yet she, in turn, victimizes the nurse; we might find Carol's rebuke upsetting not for its very utterance, but for its blindness to the nurse's physical well-being and to the demands of her job.

But an even more pressing point obtains. Whether Haynes intends it or not, the *camera* and consequently we, as viewers, are also blind to the nurse's experience—*until we become momentarily aware of our own blindness.* That is, the film registers, rather than letting pass, the gaps that dominant epistemology allows for. The initial frame in which the nurse does *not* appear constitutes the mindset that allows a viewer to not see certain bodies, or to not conceive of their existence outside of the field of more important

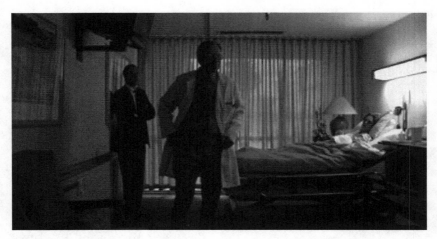

Figure 4. Carol in her hospital bed with her doctor and husband attending, in Haynes's *Safe*. Columbia Tristar, 1999.

Figure 5. A reverse shot from the hospital bed in *Safe* reveals a nurse spraying cleaning fluid. Columbia Tristar, 1999.

bodies. The nurse's subsequent appearance thus draws attention to, and briefly rectifies, her prior absence. Moreover, in presenting the sound of the chemical spray before presenting the body of the nurse who is spraying, the film cites the subordination of the latter to the former. The implication is that the functions lower-status bodies serve, whether good or bad, are in the dominant framework considered more pertinent than the bodies themselves. Such thinking dovetails not just with normative social patterns but with normative viewing ones: *If I don't see it, it doesn't matter. If I can't read it, it isn't there.* Such thinking, of course, is precisely what allows us the illusion of omniscience as film viewers.[22] But Haynes's camera (or, as it were, cinematographer Alex Nepomniaschy's) pointedly dismantles this thinking, and its ability to normalize certain social arrangements.

Such scenes have deep overtones of class domination: Carol is ignorant about the status of lower-class workers, even as she benefits from their work. Instances such as the nurse's delayed entrance into the frame, then, constitute a return of the socioeconomically repressed, of the hidden means of privilege. Various other shots, such as the one that opens on Carol's empty living room, advance these same critical ideas. There, we can hear a radio and vacuum cleaner, but see no people, until Carol enters the frame and calls, "Fulvia? Fulvia?" to the offscreen maid. The underappreciated, underpaid labor of workers of color is "invisible" to people like the Whites, and largely invisible to the camera as well. The difference in the latter case, though, is that this invisibility becomes painfully obvious to the spectator. In fact, this is just one of many exaggeratedly long, empty shots that give the viewer the time and space to wonder what's happening outside of the frame. Relatedly, we might note that Carol invokes Fulvia's name more than anyone else's, here even calling out to her *before* she calls out to her husband. At such moments, the film clearly goes beyond critiquing Carol's subordination within a patriarchal system: Fulvia is at Carol's beck and call as a matter of upper-class domination, not (just) male domination.[23]

But perhaps more interesting is how the film shows Fulvia to be more closely associated with Carol's home and its operations than is Carol herself. In one early scene, Carol asks Fulvia where to find her phone book. Again, this scene prefigures one in *Far from Heaven*: Cathy Whitaker descends the staircase, calling, "Sybil, did I leave my gloves on the hall table?" The maid responds, "Yes, I see them" from out of frame. While Sybil has spotted the gloves, we have yet to spot *her*. In the case of *Safe*, the everyday objects handled by the service worker have become notably more hazardous than gloves, and they are almost exclusively that worker's province. (Comparing the two films, we see how environmental degradation has become a pressing concern over the past thirty years—and how it is compounded by the still-pervasive forces of racism.) The maid comes in closer contact with all manner of household pollution, from the noise pollution of the vacuum cleaner to the chemicals in the cleaning fluids she uses. And yet the housewife is the one who seeks treatment for toxic exposure. Carol's call to Fulvia, like Cathy's to Sybil, thus constitutes an ironic invocation of the maid's supposed domestic sovereignty, one that simultaneously calls attention to hidden structural inequities.

Whereas social-justice scholars such as Robert Bullard and Paul Farmer detail the ghettoizing effects of environmental racism and injustice, we see here the ghettoization of people of color and lower class *within* spheres of entitlement. The suffering housewife's ability to employ service people asserts her place of dominance in those spheres. Thus when critics speak of how *Safe* exemplifies the "dreary emptiness of women's lives" (Davis 185), of how "the alienating architecture of Carol's suburban manse" (Rhodes 71) "constantly restricts her movements" (Potter 130), or of Carol's "unbearably restrictive social role" (Naismith 368), we might object on several counts. Only a very specific type of woman within this film, and outside of it, has the *advantage* of an empty life. And those who help make that life empty are restricted in multiple ways. So, while many have argued that the film's wide-angle shots indicate that Carol White is overwhelmed by the vastness of her house,[24] we might also consider that those shots ask us to imagine the overwhelming task of *maintaining* such a vast space, and how cruelly ironic it is that one's familiarity with such a space is precisely what marks one's social and economic alienation from it. Fulvia's job requires her to master the intricacies of a domain to which she has no claim and which dominates her with its size and its health-threatening "needs." Considering the ways in which *Safe* qualifies Carol's centrality, and considering that its wide-angle shots can thus also be read as indexing Fulvia's dread, any courting of liberal feminist sympathies for Carol on the part of the film thus seems at least somewhat wry.

The staging of bodies in one particular scene further ironizes the kind of feminist readings some critics have offered and that the "woman's film" designation might imply. Halfway through the film, Carol attends a baby shower at a friend's house. Notably, Carol's friend's Latina maid is the one truly restricted and overwhelmed by domestic space here. While the guests move about freely, she is relegated to the kitchen. The white women who move across the frame also frequently block our visual access to her. Moreover, the maid is dwarfed by the vastness of the shot's scope, which keeps her at the farthest reaches of the eye (see figure 6). Carol then emerges from the back of the frame on the left and is, momentarily, geometrically parallel with the maid (see figure 7). But this is a sardonic, symbolic paralleling: Carol's status, at this moment and otherwise, is not at all parallel to this woman's. The fact that Carol's friend Linda is ministering to her, and the obvious fact that one body is a guest and the other a servant, suggests inequality. Moreover, the maid's face is obscured here, while Carol faces forward toward the camera. The same kind of sardonic paralleling is achieved elsewhere with objects, such as in the scene captured in figure 2.

There, Carol drinks a glass of white milk while laborers paint milky-white cabinets far behind her, without safety masks. Nonetheless, for many a viewer, it is only Carol's body that allows for a view of the maid and the painters; few are accustomed to reading that deeply into a shot unless otherwise prompted. (In the case of the baby-shower scene, it may be the direct address to Carol by her friend that initially draws the viewer into that deep background.) But these facts further lay bare the normative operations of

Figure 6. In Haynes's *Safe*, Carol is lost in the crowd at a baby shower. Columbia Tristar, 1999.

Figure 7. Bodies shift to reveal an ironic paralleling of Carol and a maid in Todd Haynes's *Safe*. Columbia Tristar, 1999.

both cinematic and social vision. Not only are certain bodies prominent, but the recognition of them *as such* can render other bodies marginal.

Like the novels in Chapter 1, then, *Safe* enacts an ethical interconnected ecology, but in a rather different manner. While Cliff, Feinberg, and Mootoo valorize queer humans' empathy for, and connectivity to, the non-human, Haynes warns us to be judicious in answering appeals for sympathy and in recognizing connections between different entities. After all, as I have just described, the kind of imagination that would parallel Carol White to a non-white maid is not a *response to* oppression, but a *form of* oppression. And, by extension, *Safe* suggests that it is devastatingly shortsighted, if it is possible at all, for a human to truly care about a toxic or otherwise de-graded environment if s/he cannot care about those humans affected by that environment. Again, this is not to say that *Safe*'s protagonist should invoke no fellow-feeling in viewers whatsoever, but, rather, that we must be able to recognize different forms of privilege and how they make for different experiences of environment. Being able to do so, I maintain, is a crucial "real world" skill: it can allow us to build political coalitions that can function across divides such as race, sexuality, and species, in ways that are not superficial or fallacious and that do not replicate the oppressions that necessitate coalition in the first place.

Toxic Bodies?

While *Safe*'s literally marginal figures allow the film to critique the sociocul-tural standards of visibility, they more specifically play a role in the film's exploration of environmental illness. The crisis driving the film, of course, is Carol's increasingly acute sensitivity to chemicals and pollutants. But there is another commentary on toxicity being tendered here: every time Carol's body comes into contact with chemicals or pollutants, we see a person who maintains even more direct and sustained contact with such elements. For example, her first attack reaches a climax as her Mercedes passes a polluting dump truck, sending her swerving off the road into an underground parking garage. The face of the truck driver—who, unlike Carol, remains close to the pollution—is never seen. Interestingly, this scene is titled "Exhaustion" on the Columbia Tristar DVD menu. This pun illuminates the role of privilege in the articulation of envirohealth concerns: while the truck driver is sur-rounded by exhaust, the only person who exhibits exhaustion is Carol, who regularly complains of fatigue and at one point falls asleep during a dinner party. Another scene shows Carol breezing in and out of the dry cleaner's, the place where she will later collapse from fumes. The breeziness of this first encounter almost allows the viewer to ignore the person who works at the dry cleaner's on a daily basis: a middle-aged Asian American woman. In yet another scene, Carol visits a hair salon. While the white hairdresser is tending to her works with chemicals all day long, it is Carol whose nose starts bleeding. In each of these cases, we as viewers are prevented from exploring the lower-status experience of toxic exposure, because in each one the camerawork mimics the experience of white, upper-class existence: it confers mobility, it offers the option of leaving the scene of risk and degradation. It cuts short our access to evidence of racial and class inequality, and to the *effects* of that inequality on individual bodies. In short, while the spheres of advantage and disadvantage overlap to the degree that Carol does encounter toxic workplace ghettos, and workers encounter her, an important differential obtains: neither she nor we sustain contact with the toxins or the workers associated with them.

But we cannot forget that Carol *does* become ill. Apropos of its reluctance to offer definitive answers, the film offers several other explanations, and then holds these up for critical examination. Midway through the film, we hear a voiceover on TV mention deep ecology. (This is the voiceover that Laura Christian has dubbed a "non sequitur.") Deep ecology is the radical philosophy developed in the 1980s that advocates a transformation in humans' relationship to the earth, such that biocentrism replaces anthropocentrism. According to social philosopher Murray Bookchin, "implicit in deep ecology is the notion that a 'humanity' exists that accurses the natural world; that individual selfhood must be transformed into a cosmic 'Selfhood' that essentially transcends the person and his or her uniqueness" ("Social Ecology" 291). Perhaps not surprisingly, this philosophy has been criticized for being elitist, naively universalist, and/ or misanthropic—which many of its followers readily admit, in musing about the depopulation benefits of global crises such as AIDS. According to Bookchin, deep ecology "ignore[s] class, ethnic difference, imperialism, and oppression by creating a grab bag called Humanity that is placed in opposition to a mystified Nature, divested of all development" (299). This description sounds strikingly similar to the privatizing mantras of the Wrenwood Center, where Carol retreats—including "What you're seeing outside is a reflection of what you're feeling inside," "The only person that can make you get sick is you," and "If our immune system is damaged, it's because we have allowed it to be." Envirohealth problems, in both cases, are reduced to individual deficiencies.

The film frames this ideology as both hegemonic and oppressive. In one shot, we watch Carol listening to a tape recorder with headphones, as a woman's voice intones, "Safe bodies need safe environments in which to live." The shot then changes to the outside of the dry cleaner's, while the self-help narration continues; the woman purrs matter-of-factly, "There are healthy alternatives that exist for just about every toxic product, gas, or ventilation system out there. But it's up to *you* to find them." I contend that the move here from captured speech to film voiceover, from diegetic to non-diegetic sound, indicates that this statement is a dominant kind of discourse—the kind that organizes readerly/viewerly tendencies at large, not just those of Carol herself. Haynes has already primed us to consider that the supposedly self-evident concept of "safe" is actually a constructed, contingent one. By maintaining this discourse while moving us from Carol White's palatial house to the Asian American dry cleaner's toxic workplace, then, he asks us to think about how that discourse affects those non-white and lower-class individuals I have been concerned with here. First, we might say that this discourse takes attention away from structural inequalities. If it's "up [to each of] them" to achieve their own environmental health, then the fact that wealthy Carol White enjoys multiple privileges, while the lower-class woman of color faces various challenges and barriers, becomes irrelevant—as does the fact that it is exponentially easier for someone like Carol to find and implement healthy alternatives, compared to her maid, dry cleaner, or housepainter. This discourse of privatization and personal responsibility also lets corporations, governments, patriarchal family structures, and other larger forces off the hook. It fantasizes that we live in a world in which, say, a poor worker of color employed in a toxic or otherwise dangerous workplace has all the power in the world to fight "the Man," or to select a new job from a wide pool of safe, well-paying options.

I want to return for a moment to the aforementioned appearance of AIDS in deep-ecology discourse. I suggest that we consider this appearance to be more than a passing coincidence—and, in turn, consider *Safe*'s commentaries on AIDS and environmental justice to be meaningfully entangled. Writing in the *Earth First!* journal under the pseudonym "Miss Ann Thropy" in 1987, the year in which *Safe* is set, former Earth First! activist Christopher Manes declared, "As radical environmentalists, we can see AIDS not as a problem, but a necessary solution" (32). In his dialogue with Dave Foreman, a prominent deep ecologist who has spoken out against immigration and "overpopulation," Murray Bookchin recounts searingly, "It is a strictly political fact that 'Miss Ann Thropy' . . . welcomed the AIDS epidemic . . . (generously including 'war, famine, [and] humiliating poverty' along with AIDS) and wrote: 'To paraphrase Voltaire: if the AIDS epidemic didn't exist, radical environmentalists would have to invent one.' It is also a strictly political fact that Dave himself declared . . . that 'the worst thing we could do in Ethiopia is to give aid—the best thing would be to just let *nature* seek its own balance, to let the people there just starve'" (124, my emphasis).

Queers, poor people, and people of color are thus treated in the same manner under some environmentalisms as they are under the conservative regimes cited in the film: their experiences of suffering are framed as "natural" occurrences, occurrences that may in fact serve the natural world, which then allows that suffering to go unlamented or even celebrated. In contrast, the *lack* of suffering experienced by the privileged is, apparently, just as it should be. As Bookchin puts it, these perspectives "presen[t] no explanation of—indeed, . . . little interest in—. . . the highly graded social as well as ideological developments which are at the roots of the ecological problem" (96).

This assessment speaks to the need for a queer ecological perspective attuned to social justice—one that is willing to probe "nature" as an often oppressive heuristic, but not to dismiss the non-human natural world. But his assessment speaks, more specifically, to the need for queer reconfigurations of "nature." Allan Bérubé's complex understanding of AIDS offers us some innovative possibilities in this regard: "Like many other disasters, this epidemic is a part of nature that devastates our lives and makes us wonder why. Yet AIDS is nothing more or less than a disease that is killing human beings. It is a natural event that exists because it exists. While HIV itself may have no inherent meaning or purpose, the ways that [his late partner] Brian and I responded to its presence in his body made all the difference in the world" (150–51).

Whether intentionally or not, Bérubé has delivered a perfect definition of environmental-justice work: to determine where nature ends and the sociocultural begins. We could, for instance, paraphrase him to say that while Hurricane Katrina itself may have had no inherent meaning or purpose, the ways that the government responded to its presence made all the difference in the world.[25] Bérubé's understanding of AIDS as "natural" is the complete opposite of Manes's understanding of AIDS as "natural": the former does not seize upon it to naturalize or otherwise conjecture about any experience of suffering, but rather to empty it of all meaning, an emptying that is anything but meaningless. Thus we see that there are moments at which it may be ethical to invoke nature—when it comes to those things over which we have no control, when it comes to those things that strike indiscriminately—and moments at which it is ethical to disavow it—when it comes to excusing human-made problems, when it comes to suffering and social discrimination. The lesson for queer theory, queer activism, and queer ecology is plain: "nature" is not a dirty word, but it can be used in plenty of dirty ways.

In addition to "nature," the concept of "toxicity" also ties the experience of those who live under environmental injustice to the experiences of those with AIDS—or those who experience AIDS-phobia, or homophobia more broadly. (As I have suggested, Carol could be both a beneficiary and a victim of AIDS-phobia: the image of the AIDS patient constructed in the cultural imagination does not apply to her, leaving her potentially undiagnosed and untreated.) As Beth Berila observes from a queer ecology perspective, the U.S. AIDS activist group ACT UP "battle[d] mainstream public perception that people living with AIDS are somehow toxic to public health, at both the individual and national levels" (128). ACT UP formed in New York in, you guessed it, 1987 and, not surprisingly to us now, counted Todd Haynes among its members. Berila elaborates, "Environmental dangers, like AIDS, are . . . seen as invisible 'intruders' that can have lasting and unforeseen consequences. . . . Rhetoric of AIDS phobia, as well as much mainstream discourse around toxicity, reflects fears that 'contamination' will 'seep into' the heterogeneous and contained nation. Environmental discourse is thus appropriated in ways that uphold narrow constructs of the heteronormative—and thus 'pure'— national body" (130).

It might seem at first as if Berila's argument separates those who live under environmental injustice from those with AIDS. After all, while a social-justice perspective would likely find it "bad" that AIDS is perceived phobically, wouldn't the same perspective find it somewhat "good" that environmental dangers are perceived phobically? Not exactly. First, as I explain in greater depth below, environmental dangers are rarely taken seriously—or seen as dangers at all—unless they affect those who are part of the pure national body (i.e., white, heterosexual, and affluent). This mindset allows such dangers to run rampant in marginal communities. Moreover, the toxification of such communities is in part made possible by the perception that they *deserve* their toxic environments—just as homosexuals "deserve" AIDS—and that they are *naturally* suited to certain types of labor or environments, and/or that they *are* toxic. If you're looking to dump toxic waste in a landfill, to be more blunt, you have to be able to conflate that landfill with the underachieving black kid who lives next to it. In fact, you have to think of that kid's body, if you think of him at all, *as* a landfill. Again, we see how a queer ecological perspective attuned to social justice can allow us to trace the common sources of oppressions that seem otherwise unrelated.

We can also see additional connections between the experiences of those who live under environmental injustice and the experiences of those with AIDS when we consider that both groups have had little access to representational technologies and public attention, especially in 1987. The dominant logic that invisibilizes the people of color and of lower class in the film, and that invisibilizes environmental concerns more generally, also invisibilizes queers. As Berila observes of ACT UP, "th[eir] focus on *representation* and interpretation is crucial, both for AIDS issues and for environmental justice movements, since who and what counts as toxic depends on the political perspective one holds" (129, my emphasis). Haynes's film thus constitutes an ameliorative representation of both the AIDS experience and the environmental-injustice experience by, paradoxically, showing how both experiences disappear from view.

Not in My Backyard: Privatization and the Failure of Empathy

Safe references the kinds of social Darwinist arguments made by some deep ecologists, as well as by many in the dominant culture, framing them as ludicrous. It acknowledges that privileged groups fear the dangers of racial and economic Others, but counters with the concrete and ideological dangers to those Others. In one scene, for example, Carol's stepson Rory reads a school essay on "black and Chicano gangs," gleefully detailing how "slashing throats, arms and legs being dissected . . . were all common sights in the black ghettos of L.A." But "today," he continues, "black and Chicano gangs are coming into the valleys . . . in mostly white areas." Those "common sights" are little cause for concern for people like the Whites. Indeed, Carol's only concern after hearing the description of the black ghettos is an aesthetic one: "Why does it have to be so gory?" The essay even seems to suggest minority-on-minority violence as an organic solution to the problems of poverty—social Darwinism and race suicide in action. It is only when the common sights of the black ghetto become the uncommon sights (or nightmares, as it were) of the white suburb that the issue of bodily risk takes on narrative urgency. This kind of mindset underwrites environmental injustice; the idea that lower-status bodies might themselves be suffering is irrelevant within dominant visual/social reasoning. If such suffering was believed to exist, or was made visible, it would simply be understood as predetermined, even deserved—a private issue of incurred risk rather than a public problem of violated rights.

While Carol frets over the graphic nature of Rory's essay, her husband, Greg, heartily congratulates him. This scene is echoed, yet again, in Haynes's *Far from Heaven*. When the Whitakers' son reports that some of his school-mates were expelled "for throwing a rock at a girl's head," Cathy exclaims, "That's terrible! A little girl at school?" The son replies, "No. She was a Negro." When Cathy asks, "What on earth has gotten into this town?" her husband replies, "It was just a couple of foolish kids." The son, perhaps more disturbingly, enthuses, "Yeah. Hutch said that they were just trying to teach her a lesson." Frank then asks the boy to switch on the television for his "pop." While Cathy is concerned, she fails to oppose the white male supremacy being reproduced before her very eyes. And she cannot recognize this incident as part of the larger structure of white supremacy within which she lives, rather than an aberration in an otherwise harmonious town. Moreover, Cathy is not truly distraught until she realizes that the child in question is the daughter of her lover, the family's gardener.

This disastrous failure of empathy on the part of both adults in both films speaks to the importance of an intersectional, wide-ranging queer ecological ethics, the kind that *Safe* ultimately enacts. I have described how the otherwise passive Carol takes the potentially toxified status of Others as grounds for vitriol rather than compassion—corroborating the idea that not all bodies are "safe" bodies, and that some therefore deserve "safe" environments more than others. But more than (just) discriminating against people of lower status, that dominant discourse also invisibilizes potential connections among disparate groups of people—leaving Carol White unable to imagine or care that others might be vulnerable to toxic substances just like she is (and sometimes at her own behest), and Cathy Whitaker unable to concern herself with blacks other than those with whom she's romantically involved. Indeed, Carol never successfully connects with any of her *peers*, much less with those lower-status persons who serve her.

But perhaps even more disturbing than the discrimination and discon-nection occasioned by these failures of empathy is the cool complacency that accompanies them. Returning to Bookchin's claim that deep ecology, "despite all its social rhetoric, has virtually no real sense that our ecological problems have their ultimate roots in society and in social problems" (3), we realize that social awareness is precisely what Carol never achieves. She fails to see the whole of her society's structure, something that Cathy Whitaker of *Far from Heaven* at least attempts, in exploring the side of town where her black employees live. And she implicitly embraces the "NIMBY," or "not in my backyard" principle: a privatizing, short-sighted mantra that, as environmental justice advocates have shown, ignores the question, "Then whose?"[26]

"Unsafety" can be allowed to run rampant in those people's backyards, as Rory White informs us, but not in those of upper-class whites. Similarly, if we return to Manes, we see that his dispassion is actually what's most appalling: by his account, acts such as having children when you're poor, or having gay sex, are not immoral, per se, and nor are they informed by any particular historical or political context. They're just terrible personal choices. By extension, being born Native American, or black, or Chicano, or near a landfill, or downstream from a chemical factory is just a raw deal about which one can only be complacent. And it's cause for no one else's concern.

But we should note that, as Carol White retreats further and further from society through the course of *Safe*, she becomes sicker and sicker. We could then say that her empathetic failures are connected to her ill health, whether in an auxiliary or causal way—perhaps even as a kind of twisted poetic justice. In critiquing her affective and ideological tendencies, Haynes calls for a non-identitarian ethical position that would allow for the building of solidarity with others—and that would demand justice as a matter of course, rather than in response to personal affronts. Thus *Safe*'s "non sequitur" moments—the TV segment on deep ecology, the reference to gang warfare—actually constitute important sites for discursive engagement. They ask the viewer to consider how moral and political judgments construct conceptions of who is at risk and whose risk matters; how certain experiences are naturalized and/or pathologized; and how institutions and individuals justify their treatment of certain bodies. In short, they ask us to possess a consciousness around social injustice in general, and environmental injustice in particular, and to see it as "our problem," not "my problem" or "their problem."

Now, it must be noted that the Othered bodies in the film do not display symptoms of toxicity like Carol does. They do not bleed, vomit, or seize. How to explain this difference? And, more pressingly for my argument in this chapter, why read them as equally, or even more, threatened than Carol? We can find some explanations in returning to the regimes of visibility cited in *Safe*. For one thing, the film's undermining of normative epistemologies should make us wary of equating the lack of *evidence* for suffering with the lack of suffering. This point has material as well as theoretical implications: lower-status bodies are often prohibited from exhibiting pain and suffering when on the job. In fact, research has shown that displays of physical vulnerability can threaten one's already-precarious job security, especially in an employment situation with few or no health benefits.[27] In turn, many lower-status workers forego filing claims or seeking medical attention, often with disastrous results. In juxtaposing workers' bodies with Carol's body, then, Haynes's film gestures toward the factors that circumscribe our ability and our willingness to recognize pain and suffering.

Scholars such as David B. Morris have found that race has long played a role in constructing conceptions of pain. As he notes, "Enlightenment thinkers on primitivism celebrated the pain-free state of the natural savage, who supposedly did not suffer the debilitating illnesses and nervous disorders of the 'hypersensitive' European races" (39). But the treatment of such Othered groups has hardly been celebratory. Morris quotes the writings of Dr. J. Marion Sims, "America's most distinguished gynecological surgeon," on his appalling 1817 experiments on slave women: "Negresses . . . will bear cutting with nearly, if not quite, as much impunity as dogs and rabbits" (40). Contemporary studies indicate that pain and suffering are still disproportionately recognized. For example, researchers from Georgetown and Duke have found that, when presenting with the same symptoms as white patients, black patients are less likely to be referred for certain cardiac procedures.[28] It is clear, then, that racial hierarchies have allowed those in power to discount the suffering of those deemed "Other," often by figuring those Othered bodies as hardier and thus more suited to labor and other physical challenges. It is then the process of naturalizing difference ("Negresses . . . bear cutting" or "Mexicans are well-suited to field labor") that prevents those in power from comprehending, or, as with the film, from literally *seeing*, how "unsafe" bodies might experience pain and suffering just as "safe" bodies do.

Safe's brand of environmental justice, then, is queer at its core: it is antiessentialist and attuned to social construction and the contingency of meaning. It is opposed to the naturalization of oppressive experiences of race, class, gender, and sexuality, and, in suggesting that empathetic connections across differences are necessary, to ethics premised solely on identity. We might go even further, to say that the film asks us to look at the experiences of the workers shown briefly on film as "queer." Doing so opposes two converging epistemologies: that their work with dangerous chemicals and pollutants is "natural," and thus its negative outcomes "natural"; and that these people do not merit recognition in the first place. To consider them queer is not to Other them further, then, but to refuse to accept their invisibilized suffering—to look from the standpoint of environmental justice and find them just as threatened, if not more so, than the privileged white bodies we might otherwise focus our attentions on. *Safe* thus allows us to see the "natural" as a shifting designation that often underwrites the exploitation of certain humans and, ironically, non-human nature, as well. This complex understanding of the "natural," as I have suggested in my introduction, is what has been missing from queer theory.

In the case I have made above, the visual marginalization of the poor and of people of color can be understood as an invocation of their *socioeconomic* marginalization within the film's world and, we might say, "the real world." Of course, our familiarity with classical narrative cinema can produce formally conservative readings of the film, despite its non-normative techniques. For example, despite the flatness of her character, the spectacle of Carol's suffering body threatens to overshadow the marginal body's experience of routine exposure—leaving intact, though partially unmasked, the logic that finds such oppression to be unremarkable in narrative or any other terms. Indeed, the development of, say, cancer due to workplace pollutants, or the experience of chronic pain due to physical labor, cannot be represented within the space of a conventional narrative feature film—not to mention the fact that labor, in its repetitive, static character, is not generally conducive to storytelling. But we must remember that *Safe*, as a New Queer Cinema text, cites, critiques, and sometimes fails to meet the visual and narrative standards of classical cinema. Thus what I have identified as its gestures toward the unrepresentability of lower-status experiences of labor, envirohealth risks, and physical suffering appear to the viewer not as endorsements, but as indictments thereof. More specifically, we might consider that *Safe*'s lack of climaxes and general monotony mimic both working-class labor and environmental degradation—the everyday toxins, the prolonged exposures, the slow degradation of natural landscape and resources that goes unrecognized until, often, it's too late. (Here, we might think of Ralph Nader's claim that pollution is "a cumulative form of violence that is different from street crime only in that the cause and effect is not immediate . . . it is deferred battery" [as quoted in Shabecoff 98].) The film thus critiques the kind of mindset that finds only visible degradation and dramatic catastrophes—things that matter to people who matter—worth noticing. Put most simply, the film suggests that laboring bodies and their envirohealth risks are invisible not because they don't exist, or don't matter, but because they are unrepresentable within dominant frameworks.

"Where Am I? Right Now?": House as Environment

The house, where much of *Safe*'s action takes place, is crucial to these discussions of visibility and invisibility, safety and risk, and the ecocritical implications thereof. In contemporary U.S. society, the house has been idealized as the opposite of how we tend to perceive nature. The house is rational, safe, and just, whereas nature is irrational, threatening, and cruel. Houses are understood as "inside," and the outside is then "the environment," or "nature." Difference is constituted by disavowal: human superiority is established through the identification with the house (culture) against its outside (nature). As Gaston Bachelard notes, rather bemusedly, in his exploration of poetic archetypes of inside–outside, "we feel warm *because* it is cold out-of-doors" (39, emphasis original). Thus the ideal Western home is defined by its insularity; this is the spatial equivalent, as it were, of the social/political/sexual insularity of the nuclear family.[29] But the problem is that "inside" can never be fully inside, and "outside" can never be fully outside. As Laura Christian notes, "it is precisely the boundary between 'inside' and 'outside' that the abject destabilizes" (107). Drawing on Julia Kristeva's *Powers of Horror* in reading *Safe*, Christian observes that, as the outside is constitutive of the inside, abjection is a process that must be repeated endlessly. This compulsion can be found, among other behaviors, in Carol's obsession with "the upkeep and renovation of her home" (108).

We might consider this kind of obsessiveness to be a pathos-generating mechanism. But we can also see *Safe* delighting in abjection's failures, and in how these failures highlight the discriminatory procedures of abjection—the maniacal repetition of "Self–Other" that validates the self by subordinating the non-human, as well as certain human beings, and by denying the interrelationships thereof. For one thing, if Fulvia is abject by virtue of her class status, her ethnicity, and nationality, as well as her potential toxicity, it is ironic that she is a fixture in the White home. When Carol's stepson, Rory, reads his essay about black and Chicano gangs at the table, Fulvia, herself Latina and maybe Chicana, reaches past him to clear the dinner plates. Rory's childish racism is not merely ignorant of Fulvia's feelings, it is blind to the fact that "foreigners" have already invaded his space. Moreover, they move throughout it with greater facility than the W/whites, locating objects, fixing meals, painting cabinets, and receiving money for doing so. *Far from Heaven* stages such ironies even more explicitly. At a dinner party, a white guest proclaims, "There are no Negroes [in Hartford]"; the film then cuts to a shot of a black waiter holding a tray of hors d'oeuvres. Both films gesture toward that which the privileged do not see in their own homes. But whereas the latter film also grants us some access to the world of the non-privileged, *Safe* imposes limits on our vision and then draws attention to those limits.

Carol's fixity within the home is also frequently thrown into question, again suggesting the untenability of insider–outsider, culture–nature schemas. Near the beginning of the film, we see her stumble around her own living room as she looks for her phone book. Later, Greg approaches Carol while she sits in bed, and she suddenly becomes bewildered, crying, "Where am I? Right now?" Carol's question expresses disorientation, but also de-naturalization. The space thought to be, by definition, the familiar and the safe has proved otherwise. In such moments, the film militates against the naturalization of certain experiences, such that certain bodies are believed to be extensions of the environs in which they appear. Carol no more "be-longs" in her house than Fulvia "deserves" to be the one to clean it.

Through its presentation of these ideological failures, the film explicates traditional concepts of public and private, and their racial and class politics. As Linda Kerber tells us, "one of our culture's presuppositions has been that men and women live in separate spheres" (31)—respectively, the public/economic and the private/domestic. But she and other feminist critics have drawn attention to the over-totalizing character of these divisions. To begin with, defining the home as the private, domestic realm of women, as opposed to the male realm of the market and labor, obfuscates the ideological and physical labor behind the concept of home. As Susan Buckingham-Hatfield explains, "the *traditional family* . . . is a socially constructed response to [his-torical] conditions . . . and is as much an ideal as a reality[,] as a percentage of women have continued to work outside the home throughout the twen-tieth century" (65, emphasis original). But more specifically, upper-class women have long hired lower-class women and women of color from *outside* the home in order to, ironically, fulfill the adage that "a woman's place is in the home." Thus the notion of public versus private not only maintains a cultural ignorance, it ensures that "women" denotes only "privileged white women." As Kerber remarks, the "language of separate spheres [has] helped historians avoid thinking about race; virtually all discussion of the subject until very recently has focused on the experience of white women, mostly of the middle class" (37). *Safe* invites the viewer to both shift that focus and consider the points at which those spheres overlap.

The film also brings to light the gendered dimensions of environmental racism and classism, a consideration not often made in work on the subject. First, it suggests that a seemingly benign, "feminine" work environment such as the home can have detrimental effects on a worker's health, just as obviously malignant environments such as factories and fields do. If, as Buckingham-Hatfield tells us, "poor women . . . are particularly dis-advantaged by environmental degradation[,] as they are not usually in a position to delegate the household chores which expose them to environ-mental vulnerability" (80), it is certainly notable that a character such as Fulvia also does household chores *for a living*. (Re)defining the home as a work environment for women like Fulvia, then, critiques the general fan-tasy that "home" stands in contrast to "environment"—and that "inside" stands neatly in opposition to "outside." Moreover, it puts the lie to the fantasies of privatization that so often accompany domestic employment. The "pleasant" work atmosphere and the idea, whether fallacious or not, that a domestic servant is part of the family are often thought of as partial compensation. And this familiality is precisely what allows service work to not seem like work in the first place—when, in fact, the so-called second shift for middle-to-upper-class women has become these workers' primary shift.[30] These fantasies are particularly troubling, considering that the "pink-collar ghetto" has grown less white and less affluent over time.[31]

This analysis demonstrates how racism, classism, sexism, and heterosexism operate interdependently, but in complicated ways. I have already noted that pink-collar work is inconsistently recognized as "real work" by critics of *Safe*, by real-world policymakers, and by other cultural arbiters. The *gendered* terms of that fantasy—it's simply "women's work," writ large—obfuscate the particular *race and class* lines along which such work falls. Such coding further naturalizes envirohealth outcomes such as toxification. That is, the particular risks of lower-status jobs, and their bases in systems of inequality, are invisibilized by how they "match" the gendered body of the worker. For instance: hairdressers are straight women or gay men naturally skilled in the ways of femininity, and they are obligated to suffer the risks of exposure to chemicals. Notably, almost all of the service occupations depicted in the film are, like the latter two examples, strongly gender-coded. Through its contrary visual and narrative moves, however, *Safe* shows these operations and their fallout to be rooted in socially unjust ideology rather than natural facts.

Finally, then, the fact that marginal bodies within the film do not perceptibly react to chemicals or pollutants is particularly meaningful. Whether the marginalized body is imagined as always already containing these substances, as immune to them, or as able to withstand them, these imaginings parallel how their raced, classed, and gendered attributes are characterized as natural within the milieu the film depicts. *Safe* indicates yet again the lethalness of such characterizations: the fact that these bodies are immediately written off as unsafe means that their experiences of unsafety do not constitute a worthy story. They cannot grab the viewer's attention through the frame of dramatic irony the way Carol might, because there is nothing dramatic, or ironic, about their experiences of environmental risk. Narrative logic thus intertwines with the visual epistemologies and social prejudices that *Safe* critically reifies. Just like Carol's doctor's methodology, these interrelated ways of knowing come with predeterminations intact and show only what they have been calculated to show.

Conclusion

Through this chapter, I have claimed Todd Haynes's New Queer Cinema film *Safe* as a formal ethical response to AIDS and homophobia on the one hand, and environmental degradation and injustice on the other—a response that illuminates the interrelationship of the two sets of concerns. By these criteria, we might extend Monica Pearl's assertion that "New Queer Cinema is AIDS cinema" (23): AIDS cinema, in turn, might be New Environmental Cinema. I hope to have shown that what we recognize as queer stylistic and discursive techniques can and do work toward anti-racist, anti-classist environmentalist agendas. In this particular example, non-normative narrative/visual features, and the denaturalization of identity categories, constitute not just a queer stance or an ecological stance, but a queer ecological stance. More generally, I hope to have shown that it is not just possible, but crucial, to enact through art and activism a committed environmentalism that does not discount "special-interest" concerns such as heterosexism and homophobia. *Safe*'s environmentalism, in fact, in large part *emerges from* a queer consideration of sexuality, alongside its queer considerations of race, class, and gender and the intersections thereof. That is, it emerges from a truly ecological imagination. Of course, *Safe* does not actually *depict* the harmonious relationships it gestures toward. But it laments the ways of seeing and knowing that prevent them and points toward the ways of seeing and knowing that might produce them.

I want to stress that these efforts have real-world implications. I have suggested that much of the film's work is rhetorical: it offers us a model for grappling with contradictory deployments of the natural from a queer, ecological, and anti-racist and -classist perspective—such that we can, say, argue against the naturalization of environmental injustice while still articulating concern for the natural qua the non-human. But the film's work also takes place at the most basic and mechanical of levels. Simply put, *Safe* teaches us to read the margins. It encourages us to ask what the media is *not* showing us or *not* telling us. It asks us to think about the connection between forms of representation and real-world problems—what gets lost in certain representations and what rises to the top. These efforts are unique to the visual art that is film: while the specific story *Safe* tells us is of course fictional, its use of our vision is quite real and quite visceral. The kind of seeing that it curates can affect how we read multiple kinds of texts and what we notice in the world around us.

It must be said that the limitations *Safe* reifies do not always feel like limitations. As film theory has long held, the vantage point of the viewer is one of apparent omniscience, of epistemological privilege. This fact may interfere with the film's own concern with those at the farthest distance and at the farthest margins; those who are more obscure in both senses of the word, barely readable to the cinematic and human eye, and darker—and thus, to some, *unworthy* of being read. The film thus poses a major challenge to us as viewers: to work against the machinations of the very apparatus that offers us authority—and, thereby, to become attuned to oppression's environmental and spatial manifestations. But even if we fail to meet that challenge, our failures do not go "unpunished": we never *do* reach a resolution. In short, then, *Safe* courts a reading that is resistant to classical film-viewing habits and dominant social habits, and that disappoints those who still insist upon those habits.

Perhaps more importantly, though, even if we take up the challenge of reading the margins of the film along with its center, the obscure along with the manifest, there is a limit to our undertakings. Our paths to knowledge have already been set for us, the camerawork and narrative ultimately keeping us from fully entering a world beyond Carol White's upper-class suburban existence. Such a realization exposes the viewer's agential position as a mere effect of film itself—an *illusion* of agency. That is to say, if we strain to see those obscure, distant, and literally/figuratively marginal bodies, or even to better see our strange and sometimes-estranged heroine, we are straining to see beyond the work of Haynes's camera. And we then encounter very real barriers: we are still largely barred from seeing, or dwelling on, the lives, bodies, and faces of toxified Others. As thinkers from Ludwig Wittgenstein to Elaine Scarry have noted, the human body, and the face in particular, is the central register for pain and suffering—and, therefore, the central site for empathizing. Thus, in so often refusing the viewer full access to these registers and sites, while simultaneously raising our consciousness about pain and suffering, *Safe* enacts a frustration about the limitations of dominant perspectives, including representative media. Carol White never discerns these limitations. And nor can she imagine the kind of coalitional, communal responses to structural subjugation that environmental-justice movements have offered. But perhaps, Haynes suggests, we can.

"Ranch Stiffs" and "Beach Cowboys" in the Shrinking Public Sphere

Sexual Domestication in *Brokeback Mountain* and *Surf Party*

They paved paradise and put up a parking lot.
—Joni Mitchell

They'll take away Brokeback Mountain, but they'll give you
a gay bar.
—Alex Sugzda

Director Ang Lee's 2002 film *Brokeback Mountain* offers a rather
unglamorous conclusion to its lovers' initial dalliances. Having parted ways
with Jack Twist (Jake Gyllenhaal) after meeting him on a seasonal sheepherd-
ing gig in rural Wyoming, Ennis del Mar (Heath Ledger) darts into an alleyway
and begins to vomit. We might read his reaction as a sign of lovesickness,
as disgust over his recent same-sex encounters, or as anxiety over the prospect of reentering town and getting married to his fiancée Alma (Michelle
Williams)—or all of the above. In any case, our attention soon shifts from this
individual's private torment to its public witnessing: as we watch Ennis in the
foreground, framed between the two walls of the alley, a cowboy passes in
the background and stops to stare. Ennis snarls, "What the fuck you lookin'
at?" and the cowboy ambles on.

This scene is just one of many in the film centered around surveillance,
visually and/or thematically. In fact, the scene just preceding shows Jack
driving away from Ennis in his truck, then cuts to Jack's view of Ennis walking in the truck's side mirror. The latter scene complements an even earlier
one in which Jack sizes up Ennis through his side mirror as the two wait to
meet their prospective boss. Making the trope of surveillance explicit later

in the film, Ennis asks Jack, "You ever get the feelin,' I don't know, when you're in town, and someone looks at you, suspicious, like he knows. And then you go out on the pavement and everyone's looking at you like they all know, too?"

It is tempting to ascribe Ennis's paranoia, and the aggression that so frequently attends it, to internalized gay panic. But I propose that something more complicated is at work in the film, which was adapted by Larry McMurtry and Diana Ossana from Annie Proulx's 1997 short story. Consider two scenes in which Jack, and same-sex desire more generally, is absent from the frame: Ennis and Alma's outing to the drive-in after their wedding, and their visit to a Fourth of July fireworks show with their two young daughters. In the first, the couple watches the 1964 film *Surf Party* (directed by Maury Dexter), which depicts a group of amorous teenagers who come under the scrutiny of the authorities who police the local beach. In the second, Ennis explodes in anger as a group of bikers engages in lewd banter in earshot of his daughters. Reading these scenes against those with which I began, we see that the film's depiction of surveillance is part of a broader depiction of the collision of the public and the private when it comes to sexuality—and, more pointedly, of the violence of public–private divisions that privilege reproductive heteronormativity and punish anything that falls outside it.

But these public–private divisions and their regulation are not unique to the realm of human sexuality, or even the realm of the human. As the film makes plain, natural landscapes pose ontological quandaries on the same order: Is nature inherently public? Can nature be owned? If so, by whom? What happens when natural spaces are privatized? I argue that the film demonstrates that these two sets of concerns, over the regulation of desire and

Figure 8.
Maury Dexter's *Surf
Party* onscreen in
Ang Lee's *Brokeback
Mountain*. Universal
Home Entertainment,
2006.

over the regulation of the natural world, are intertwined. Indeed, the question at the center of Brokeback Mountain is not what happens when two men love each other, but *in what physical context*—the private domestic realm; the urban public realm; the rural public realm, et cetera—they could possibly do so. Similarly, the question at the center of the film Brokeback Mountain excerpts, Surf Party, is what sorts of activities can be construed as "natural" in a given natural context, and which must be either banned outright or confined to the private, domestic home. Thus Brokeback Mountain engages in three complementary tasks. First, it asks us to consider the structural similarities between the position of the "unnatural" queer and the position of the natural landscape, in opposition to the prevailing social rhetoric. Second, it tracks the physical interaction between, and the simultaneous exploitation of, human queers and non-human nature—making clear that the queer and the natural are interconnected not just in theory, but in practice. Finally, it asks us to see how the privatization and domestication of queer sexuality and that of the natural landscape are interrelated, and objectionable, processes.

Through those processes of privatization and domestication, I argue, queerness becomes abjected from what counts as "nature," and what counts as nature in turn comes under the auspices of the bourgeois family. Specifically, Brokeback Mountain frames homophobia as a function of a capitalist system bent on rendering public, natural spaces "useful," and on ghettoizing minorities into for-profit spaces at the edges of the map. The exploitation of landscape for private, capitalist, and/or heterosexist ends is thereby, paradoxically, naturalized along with heterosexuality itself. Thus, whereas my previous chapters have problematized the dissociation of the queer and the natural, this chapter offers a look at how that dissociation occurs in the first place. As I will discuss in greater depth later, Surf Party actively engages in this dissociation, while Brokeback Mountain resists it. I therefore propose Surf Party as a crucial intertext, rather than an incidental inclusion: it gives us a glimpse of how queerness and the natural world are constructed as opposites in the postwar period, while Brokeback Mountain opposes that construction. In thus historicizing and decoupling the queer/unnatural dyad, Lee's film frees us to think in more complicated ways about sexuality and, more specifically, to think of the natural from a queer standpoint.

This chapter seeks to move us away from the general definition of "homophobia" as "non-inclusion," as the crushing of domestic/assimilationist aspirations. This seems to be what critics see in the film when they deride it as "a neoliberal story of gay love" (Manalansan) or designate it as simply "gay," or even coercively normative, rather than queer.[1] I also seek to move us away from the slightly more positive, but equally problematic, readings of the film as an ahistorical pastoral. Dwight A. McBride, for instance, claims that the film tries to "represen[t] universal gay male experience" (96), while William Leung adds that it "achieves . . . [this] universality . . . by deploying the macrocosmic visual metaphor of nature" (34). B. Ruby Rich, in a more adulatory spirit, claims that the film "queers the Wyoming landscape as a playground of sexuality freed from judgment, an Eden poised to restore prelapsarian innocence to a sexuality long sullied by social shame"[2]—a claim that ignores how the land depicted in *Brokeback Mountain* is under as much threat of violence and/or capitalist domestication as are the queers who occupy it. Such readings, ironically, detach queerness from nature by making the first the "real" issue and the latter a symbolic backdrop. They allow the questions of empathy and identification to turn solely on humans and human sexuality—the same way that readings of *Safe* have focused on Carol White at the expense of figures of color and environmental-justice issues. This is a particularly problematic critical tendency, I argue, because the literal and figurative separation of the queer from the natural is what informs the oppression of people like Ennis del Mar and Jack Twist in the first place.

Indeed, such critics have paid little attention to *Brokeback Mountain*'s historical specificities when it comes to both sexuality and landscape. The diegesis of the film spans the 1960s to the 1980s, a time that sees (among other things) gay liberation and the consolidation of "gay" and "lesbian" as coherent political identities, and the advanced development of the American West through a series of Reclamation projects that made land suitable for "homemaking."[3] This period of Reclamation, a loaded term that posits non-indigenous humans as the true owners of the natural landscape, was met with furor from environmental groups—a reaction that, interestingly enough, equates environmentalism with anti-domesticity. This equation suggests that the rhetorics that undergird the development of the natural landscape are more often than not those that champion normative, stable family life.

The 1960s–1980s also sees the rise of late capitalism, postmodernism, and poststructuralism. This is a period, then, when "nature" was a major site of contestation, with dominant forces seeking to transform, control, and narrowly define it—just as mass production and postmodern/poststructural thought threw anything as authentic as "nature" into question. This chapter traces the influence of such thought on *Brokeback Mountain*, in contrast to those critics who consider Lee's work to be "conspicuously unpostmodernist . . . character-plot oriented rather than style-polemic oriented" (Leung 24). I argue that the film undertakes the queer ecological venture of "interrogat[ing] the co-relations between the social organization of sexuality and ecology" (Sandilands, "Sexual Politics" 110) in ways that only a postmodern, poststructuralist awareness of social constructionism could allow. Further, I maintain that it is *Brokeback Mountain*'s self-conscious inclusion of its own filmic intertext, *Surf Party*, that makes its critique of sexual-environmental privatization most clear.

The historical conditions of late capitalism, postmodernism, and post-structuralism have a slightly different resonance within Jack and Ennis's diegetic world than they do for Lee as a filmmaker, however. To varying degrees, both men cling to an older model of relating to the natural world, one that is less alienating, and less commodified. As this older model becomes obsolete, though, we see that Jack and Ennis are prevented the option of relating to the natural world in any capacity other than a domestic, bourgeois-familial one—and that even that option is heavily circumscribed. We might then say that if "nature" is up for grabs, conceptually and actually, in the era depicted by *Brokeback Mountain*, then dominant homophobic forces have been quite successful in grabbing it. But the film does not merely lament this turn of events. It refuses to view capitalist domesticity as a viable means for queers to achieve equality, or to agree that queerness is neither natural nor public in character.

The film thereby speaks to additional historical conditions that were emerging at the end of its depicted time frame: the neoliberal shrinking of the public sphere, and debates over issues such as same-sex marriage and public indecency. That is, I argue that the film portrays the trend toward privatization in GLBTQI life, and the concomitant shrinking of the public sphere witnessed in the United States in the last several decades, through a portrayal of the development and privatization of the landscape of the American West. That landscape does not become a mere metaphor, though. As I have argued throughout *Strange Natures*, the status of the environment is not just *like* the status of queers, or vice versa; the two are deeply imbricated, physically and ideologically. Thus this chapter shows that mainstream gay identity emerges not just alongside, but through the privatization of public and natural spaces. (If it is the *rejection* of nature that, at least in part, makes for mainstream gay identity, then we might say that queer theory is all the more remiss in embracing that rejection.) I show, alternately, how queer identity can and does emerge from a rejection of privatization, and through an environmental ethics that refuses to see land as something to be owned.

Biosurveillance and the
Taming of (Queer) Nature

Understanding *Brokeback*'s ecologically minded critique of what R. Anthony Slagle calls "the 'heterosexist' dichotomies of public and private space" (Ingram 30–31) requires a reconstruction of the film's expository details. First, the land that encompasses the fictional Brokeback Mountain is, paradoxically, both public and private space: it is under the jurisdiction of the U.S. Forest Service but has been parceled out to individual businessmen for raising livestock. As Jack and Ennis's boss, Joe Aguirre (Randy Quaid), explains,

> The Forest Service has got designated campsites on the allotments. Them camps can be 3, 4 miles from where we pasture the [sheep]. Bad predator loss if there's nobody lookin' after 'em at night. Now, what I want is a camp tender to stay in the main camp, where the Forest Service says. But the herder, he's gonna pitch a pup tent on the Q.T. [that is, surreptitiously] with the sheep and he's gonna sleep there. You eat your supper and breakfast at camp, but you sleep with the sheep 100%. No fire, don't leave no sign. You roll up that tent every mornin' in case the Forest Service snoops around.

Jack and Ennis's work on Brokeback Mountain is thus explicitly framed as a violation of both public and ecological interests, or at least of what the Forest Service has designated as such.

But soon, Jack and Ennis are refusing to go along with Aguirre's plan. They begin sleeping with each other instead of with the sheep and begin to enjoy their surroundings in a leisure, not labor, capacity—wrestling, drinking, singing, and generally horsing around. In so doing, they expose the sheep to predators. From Aguirre's perspective, this is an economic disaster. But from an ecological standpoint, it's a natural function of the food chain. Perhaps more interestingly, though, Jack and Ennis's neglect results in the sheep they are overseeing becoming entangled with those of some Chilean herders—an image redolent of miscegenation, transnational interaction, and other forms of "abnormal" congress. At the same time that Jack and Ennis violate the social rules prohibiting same-sex sexuality, then, they also violate the rules of private enterprise, and more abstract socioeconomic rules against "mixing." In fact, the problem with what Joe Aguirre eventually spies on Brokeback Mountain—the two men frolicking rather than working—is not just that it is queer. At least equally, if not more, problematic is the fact that the men are not doing their job, which is to maximize the profits of the private businessmen using the public land.

The queerness of their actions, in other words, lies in how they disregard private, capitalist designs on public, natural space.

In fact, when Aguirre lets the men go with docked pay, he is undeniably hostile, but not explicitly homophobic. Later, when Jack protests Aguirre's decision not to rehire them, Aguirre snaps, "You guys wasn't gettin' paid to leave the dogs babysittin' the sheep while you stem the rose"—an ambiguous turn of phrase that seems to have originated with Proulx's short story.[4] Aguirre's statement invokes prominent stereotypes of queer sexuality as "wasteful," "indulgent," and "non-[re]productive," but also happens to draw on classist stereotypes of the poor as lazy and unmotivated. As he concludes, "You ranch stiffs, you ain't never no good." The pair's sexual status, in other words, is intimately intertwined with their economic status. (We should note that Aguirre's namesake, the Spanish conquistador whose surname means "open pasture," famously plundered the Americas in search of El Dorado, the City of Gold—a quest captured in Werner Herzog's 1972 film *Aguirre, the Wrath of God*.) In sympathetically staging Jack and Ennis's experience as two men whose first taste of queer pleasure coincides with both a rare taste of freedom from lower-class drudgery and the enjoyment of the natural world, *Brokeback* suggests that these stereotypes are less objective realities than concepts that emerge from the capitalist management of natural resources. In other words, per the film, (poor) queers are "against nature" only to the extent that they oppose its exploitation.

What appears to be surveillance of queer sexuality in the filmstory, then, might be more properly construed as the management of the unruly and the *potentially* (re)productive—which includes both queer individuals and the non-human natural world. In one scene, this connection is physically enacted, as Jack and Ennis stand awkwardly near Aguirre while one of the Chilean shepherds counts the sheep. Both the queers and the animals are under scrutiny by those invested in the management of nature (as capital). Lee also establishes this connection by juxtaposing two scenes of surveillance. The first shows us Jack and Ennis frolicking on the mountainside (figure 9), then abruptly cuts to a shot of Aguirre, watching the two through his binoculars (figure 10). Shortly thereafter, we see a shot of sheep grazing. This time, because of the prior revelation of Aguirre's presence, as well as the shaky quality of the shot, we recognize almost immediately that we are seeing through his perspective. The binocular shot trails up until it locates Ennis within the same scope as the sheep. Again, the queer human is positioned in relationship to capitalist (re)production as an unruly creature who must be monitored and managed, just like the land and the sheep. In asking for our sympathy for the former, then, the film necessarily asks for our sympathies for the latter.

We can see here how queerness gets positioned in dominant frameworks as against nature, despite its (sometimes) originary relationship therewith. Jack and Ennis have worked with animals and the natural landscape their entire lives, but they are marked as unnatural for failing to properly effect the capitalist development of those entities; it is not just their biological and social non-reproductivity, but their *economic* non-reproductivity that renders them abject. Not only are they unwilling to manage their own natures, and to be "useful" and productive, they seem unwilling to manage nature, to render it "useful" or productive. Their failure on both ends effects their rejection *from* nature; Aguirre, like that wrathful God he invokes, casts the men out

Figures 9–10. Jack and Ennis frolic on Brokeback Mountain in what seems at first to be an objective shot; the shot's subjectiveness is then revealed. Universal Home Entertainment, 2006.

of Brokeback forever. Jack and Ennis's encounter troubles him not just because it is queer, but because it suggests that nature might have intrinsic or use value, rather than exchange value, that it might exist for pleasure rather than profit. Lee's film thus references how capitalist interests become the supreme representative, and measure, of what counts as natural.

Brokeback Mountain's citation of *Surf Party* invites us to consider how such beliefs circulated in cultural texts contemporaneous with its diegesis. Now long out of print, *Surf Party* initially appeared in the wave of teenage party movies that included 1963's *Palm Springs Weekend* and 1965's *Beach Blanket Bingo*. The section of the film that we see Ennis and Alma watch has surprising resonance with the surveillance scenes in *Brokeback*. On the drive-in screen watched by the couple (see figure 7), we first see a young white woman stick her head outside of a trailer door. The camera cuts to the clean-cut young white man outside who has just knocked. He asks, "Pulled in last night? . . . I thought I'd tell you before the Sergeant showed up. Parking this trailer on the beach is illegal." In the full film, this goody-two-shoes surfer, Len Marshal (Bobby Vinton), continues, "Subject to fine and/or imprisonment." The young woman, Terry (Patricia Morrow), asks, "Well, where can we put it? We wanna be near the beach." Len responds, "A block up the highway there's a trailer park. Tell 'em I sent ya."

Like the binoculars scene, this scene from *Surf Party* references an open, public, and natural space that has become exclusive and restricted under the watchful eyes of a patriarchal authority figure. Moreover, both scenes capture cultural anxieties around idle, lustful youth; while Jack and Ennis have been wrestling, drinking, and "stemming the rose" instead of doing their job, Terry and her girlfriends have arrived from Phoenix on a mission to party with some Malibu "Beach Cowboys"—as the movie trailer dubs surfers, in another interesting resonance with *Brokeback*—including her older brother, Skeet. Indeed, *Surf Party* features many stock juvenile-delinquent sequences, including a wild house party with dancing and a rock-and-roll band. While Joe Aguirre monitors the actions of Jack and Ennis in *Brokeback Mountain*, one Sergeant Neal (Richard Crane) monitors those of the local kids in *Surf Party*—and threatens to close the beach to surfing altogether.

But the differences between these two scenes are perhaps even more instructive than their similarities. Most importantly, there is no correlating subjective shot in *Surf Party*, no instance where our watching of the characters coincides with their being watched by outside forces. Moreover, while Aguirre spies on Jack and Ennis, Ennis and Alma are merely *watching* Terry and Len—with, of course, the added mediation of film. We can relate these differences to some basic facts: the watched couple is male and female, while the surveilled couple is male and male. That is, while both films suggest that unruly desire cannot be freely expressed in natural, public space, Brokeback Mountain reminds us that queer desire is under particularly severe scrutiny. Moreover, as I have suggested above, queers do not just experience homophobia as the crushing of domestic/assimilationist aspirations. In fact, I am attempting to define the separation of the queer from the natural, with the "compensation" of domesticity, as an often-unrecognized form of anti-queer violence (not to mention classism). These processes entail a paradoxical treatment of queerness. First, queerness is deemed inherently private, and therefore unacceptable for public appearance. Recourse is then limited to middle- and upper-class behaviors of consumption: ghettoization into gay bars, "gayborhoods," and gay marriages.

We should also note that even the most private expressions of queerness are construed as inherently public and subjected to further surveillance and discipline—thus indicating that the capitulation to the demand for gay privatization is something of a Pyrrhic victory. We might recall, for example, the landmark 1986 case Bowers v. Hardwicke, in which the U.S. Supreme Court decided that consensual sodomy, even in one's own home, was not covered under the right to privacy and thus was prosecutable under existing state laws. (The case was not overturned until 2003, with the decision in Lawrence v. Texas.) Or we might think of the group of black lesbians whose act of self-defense against street harassment in 2007 prompted conservative commentator Bill O'Reilly to claim that lesbian gangs were prowling the streets "all over the country."[5] These real-life examples suggest that the era traced by Brokeback Mountain is one in which GLBTQI expression is delimited to sites of gay consumption, in which queer desire in the home is considered a matter of public concern and in which the *victimization* of queers and women of color can be seen as a threat not to such groups but to (heterosexual) public safety.[6]

But this is also the era of gay liberation, not to mention an unprecedented push in environmental activism. So what are two illicit lovers in such an era to do? In Brokeback Mountain, as we will see, at least one ultimately refuses to accept the domestication and privatization of either sexuality or land, while in Surf Party all the characters ultimately agree to it, with great enthusiasm. Not surprisingly, the results for the poor and queer are much worse than for the middle-class and straight. Jack and Ennis are left with literally no place to go, while the girls of Surf Party are never without a home, despite their censure by the sergeant. (He gives them a ticket for parking on the beach.) Once they park their trailer a block away, as Len instructs them, they circulate freely on the beach. We might note that the characters in Brokeback

Mountain have trailers, as well—but whereas in *Surf Party* the trailer represents privilege and mobility, in the other film it speaks to the protagonists' poverty and lack of mobility. When the *Surf Party* girls first roll into town with their trailer hitched to their convertible, they track down the address of Terry's brother, Skeet, and she declares, "Well, we know where his house is. Guess we find a place to put ours." It's worth noting here that Catriona Mortimer-Sandilands and Bruce Erickson have argued that "the postwar rise of family camping"—enabled not just by an expanding *automobile* culture, but by the *trailer* in particular—has contributed to a U.S. landscape in which "wilderness areas are highly heterosexualized" (*Queer Ecologies* 4). Drawing on Joe Hermer's work, Mortimer-Sandilands and Erickson observe that "[m]any camping facilities were created with an intentional design to resemble suburban cul-de-sacs—each campsite clearly designed for one nuclear family—and all camping occurring in designated 'private' spaces away from 'public' recreational activities such as swimming" (19). Both Terry and Ennis's trailers position them, literally, outside the realm of the white suburban leisure class, pointing instead to the paradoxical, abhorrent combination of transience and lack of social/physical mobility. However, Terry's status can be recuperated through a move of just a couple of blocks.

Through its invocation of such a surprisingly comparable film, *Brokeback Mountain* uncovers similarities between the status of human queerness and that of non-human nature, while also offering insight into the simultaneous exploitation of each. As Greta Gaard has observed, the homophobic claim that queers are "against nature" suggests that the dominant culture values nature—when, in fact, it does not. The dominant culture positions queer eroticism as excessive and in need of taming, just like non-human nature. Gaard therefore suggests that we revise the ecofeminist list of oppressive structuring dualisms—such as "culture/nature" and "male/female"—to include the "reason/erotic dualism" ("Toward" 118).[7] Her points help us see that the impulse to manage non-human nature is inseparable from the impulse to manage human eroticism, as two central forces that threaten to break down the social order. And indeed, Jack and Ennis's first sexual encounter is nothing if not "animalistic": after horsing around with Jack, Ennis spits on his hand and penetrates him "doggie-style" in a flimsy pup tent.

I belabor this point for a reason: recognizing connections between the queer and the non-human can allow us to challenge the interrelated oppression of queers and the natural world in ways that do not disavow that world. (In the case of the transgender novels in my archive, such a disavowal would take the form of, say, insisting that the trans person is human and thus deserves respect; in the world of *Brokeback Mountain*, it might take the form of, say, insisting that gay people can have non-animalistic sex, whatever that might look like.) And of course, recognizing such connections can allow us to read with greater nuance texts that deal with both human sexuality and the environment. For example, the recognition that queerness and the natural world have been similarly conceived by the dominant culture would force us to reconsider the idea that Brokeback Mountain's lovers are "construct[ed] . . . as classically tragic—virtually alone in their own pristine temporal and cultural space" (Manalansan 99), that Brokeback Mountain is an "idyllic" space (Rich), and that the film "tries . . . hard not to acknowledge" historical contexts such as "recent U.S. sex panics" (Herring, "Brokeback Mountain Dossier" 94). While the film is certainly subtle on these counts, it is difficult to believe that its depiction of surveillance and internalized queer paranoia has no relationship to the history of sex panics. Moreover, not only are the men definitely not alone—they are under Aguirre's watchful eye and under their own personal panopticons—they are located in a very particular time and place, one that is not exactly pristine. Theirs is the era of a notable developmental push in the American West, and a time at which private interests increasingly encroach upon both public landscapes and public sexualities.

Technologies of Homophobia

Brokeback Mountain cites not just the oppressive surveillance of queers and nature, but their interrelated surveillance through technology. The film thus speaks against the progress narrative that assumes that social and technological advancements, which so often separate the human from the nonhuman, benefit the queer. (We might say that this narrative contributes to the general perception of queers as urban and/or "unnatural.") The most representative scene in this sense is, of course, the binoculars scene. But the film itself arguably constitutes a technological mode of surveillance. That is, it offers us as viewers access to sexual acts otherwise private to Jack and Ennis, and to ecological sites otherwise inaccessible to the average viewer. But, as I discuss below, the film self-reflexively calls attention to, and problematizes, its proffering of these possibilities. It asks us to consider how visibility and publicness need not be problematic in and of themselves—to consider, that is, how the values of homophobia and privatization turn the act of *watching* into *surveillance*, and how they render certain acts of desire shameful and "unnatural" in the public eye, while naturalizing others.

The film's treatment of technologized surveillance both enacts and critiques what Tim Davis has termed "the panoptic gaze of heterosexism" (as quoted in Ingram, Bouthillette, and Retter, "Strategies for (Re)constructing Queer Communities" 108). In this sense, the film invokes Foucauldian and Marxist claims about minority visibility as an effect of management, and as therefore ill-suited to effecting liberation;[8] Brokeback Mountain insists that queer visibility and presence in natural/public space is insufficient if it is not critical of those dichotomies of public and private space, and of the fact that visibility is so often achieved and validated through capitalist means.[9] But in addition to referencing sexual surveillance, the film references what David Mazel calls "global biosurveillance." As he observes,

> it is not merely that we moderns know more about nature, but that, because we read at this particular historical moment, we behold nature in a particular way: as the object of the sort of panoptic gaze that for the ancient reader was the sole prerogative of God. Our perspective has been decisively shaped by *global biosurveillance*, a term I use to denote the vast and growing complex of activities that enable us, first, to understand living nature as a biological whole—as the biosphere—and, second, to strip it of layer after layer of what used to be spoken of as its "mystery" (and thereby render it increasingly amenable to human ends). ("Annie Dillard" 186)

While I do not share Mazel's concern with the waning of "mystery," the fact remains that the landscape as rendered in Brokeback Mountain is clearly under such surveillance. We can see this in several places in the film: in Aguirre's strict tracking of the sheep; in his references to the U.S. Forest Service's "snooping"; and in Jack's quip, after he and Ennis kill an elk to eat, that they "[d]on't want the Game and Fish to catch us." Of course, the Fish and Game Department and the U.S. Forest Service are charged with overseeing the sustainable use of natural resources. But the point is that the film treats the surveillance of the natural world with the same frequency as it treats the surveillance of (queer) human activity—and, in fact, it often treats them together.

As I have suggested, we can also recognize biosurveillance in the film's own production of scenes of nature, over which countless critics and reviewers have marveled. Many of these scenes are composed of sweeping tracking shots and aerial shots, views not normally available to the naked human eye, and certainly not available to Jack and Ennis to the degree that they are to us. The film's gaze also literally reflects the processes of globalization: while the extended nature scenes purportedly show us Wyoming, most viewers know, or can easily learn, that we are actually seeing Canada. Technology meets the demands of global capital, in the process (re)mastering the Canadian landscape as the American West. In thematizing global biosurveillance, however, the film probes its own complicity in this phenomenon. Moreover, as I show later, it distinguishes between a discriminatory looking *at* and an empathetic looking *with*.

Beyond surveillance specifically, the film's basic plot points highlight the operations of technological development and global capital. For one thing, Ennis initially resists his wife's pleas to move closer to town. Once she convinces him, she begins working at a grocery store—a clear sign of the town's relative development. A pivotal scene in the store finds Alma arguing with Ennis when one of their daughters sends a carefully constructed display of mass-produced glass food jars crashing down. Later, after Alma learns about Jack and divorces Ennis, she marries the grocery-store manager, Monroe. The couple eventually moves to a home in the suburbs, while Ennis moves to a trailer in an unpopulated area—Alma's move away from her and Ennis's initial ruralism complete, and Ennis's distaste for domesticity and "civilization" taken to its logical extreme.

These small details—the move away from rural life, the evidence of mass production and consumption of processed foods—invoke the larger historical shifts that are happening during the film's milieu. But they also underline the place of the queer in those shifts. For instance, Ennis appears ignorant of many aspects of so-called "civilized" life. When he stops into the grocery store to ask Monroe where to find Alma and Monroe replies, "she's in the condiments aisle," Ennis blurts, "The what?" "Uh, ketchup," Monroe offers. Monroe, the figure in the film most closely aligned with capital accumulation and mass consumption, and a figure both alienated from the natural landscape and in possession of the technology to master it, subsequently replaces Ennis as head of the family. This link, between the mastery of unruly nature and the mastery of unruly sexuality, is made plain by a well-orchestrated juxtaposition of shots: first, after standing up to his bullying, wealthy patriarch of a father-in-law at Thanksgiving dinner, Jack starts to carve the turkey with a knife; the shot then cuts to an electric knife that Monroe uses to carve the turkey at his new home with Alma and the kids, with Ennis as the awkward dinner guest in the background. This set of shots also alerts us to the possibility that Ennis and Jack's main struggle might not be with their queer desires, per se, but rather with the fact that their way of life is becoming obsolete. The mastery over nature that Monroe represents has, ironically, become the new natural, the new status quo.

The film thus reworks the normative schema in which the heterosexual family stands as the more traditional formation—associated with a time that is supposedly simpler and more natural—and the queer stands as the new disruption to that formation. It refuses what Noël Sturgeon has identified as a disturbing paradigm in popular culture: "equating the restoration of natural harmony with the restoration of the two-parent, suburban family," thereby "naturaliz[ing] the nuclear family" ("'The Power Is Yours, Planeteers!'" 267). In fact, the characters more closely associated with "natural harmony" in this film are the queers. We might even go further, to claim that the film highlights the ways in which heterosexual life can be "unnatural." For instance, after Jack's wife Lureen (Anne Hathaway) gives birth to their son, Lureen's mother enthusiastically delivers "two whole boxes of formula" to her in the hospital. This is not to say that *Brokeback Mountain* simply reverses the dominant binary in question, framing *heterosexuality* as unnatural—but, rather, that it disarticulates the terms "queer," "unnatural," "straight," and "natural," thus fostering a more critical view of how they usually come together.

No Home on the Range:
Class Status and Access to Natural Space

An examination of the class statuses of Jack and Ennis will clarify how the film resists the idea that equality for queers can be achieved through commodification—and how it speaks to the role of economic imperatives in organizing both nature and desire. To begin with, Jack and Ennis are aligned as poor country folk. Early on, Jack asks Ennis, "Are you from ranch people?" and Ennis replies, "Yeah, I was"; orphaned as a child, his sister and then his brother married off, leaving "no more room for me." Notably, then, Ennis is ejected from the nuclear family very early on. He remains poor through the next few decades that the film tracks, and presumably for the rest of his life, piecing together a living through occasional ranch work and road paving gigs. Jack, on the other hand, gains some financial stability through his marriage. But notably, neither man ever has any land to call his own. While Ennis ends up living in a trailer, Jack lives until his death in a house financed in large part by his father-in-law. And nor do they have unfettered access to public land, as their time on Brokeback Mountain demonstrates.

In fact, the film continually reminds us that the men are always on borrowed ground and borrowed time, literally. In one of the film's later scenes, Jack meets a soon-to-be coworker who propositions him by mentioning that their boss has "a little cabin down on Lake Kemp." The man presses, "Said I could use it . . . We ought to go down there some weekend. Drink a little whiskey. Fish some. . . . You know?" This scene mirrors a later one in which Ennis attempts to placate a disappointed Jack by promising, "I'll try if I can get Don Wroe's cabin again. We had a good time that year, didn't we?" When Jack continues to bemoan Ennis's broken promise to meet up shortly, the latter asserts, "Jack, I got to work. In them earlier days I'd just quit the job. You forget what it's like bein' broke all the time. . . . It was hard enough gettin' this time." While we do get the sense that Ennis sometimes resists intimacy with Jack, the film validates Ennis's assertion: his financial instability has made it difficult to maintain their relationship and has perhaps even led to difficulties in his relationship with his wife and daughters. In short, then, men's access to other men in the film is always circumscribed by their class positions; even a romantic "getaway" ultimately constitutes a reminder of their relative poverty and powerlessness. This is true of Jack and Ennis's time on Brokeback Mountain, as well: the explicitly commercial stipulation to stay with the sheep is what (at least briefly) keeps them apart. It is when they refuse those interests, and their own financial exploitation as a result of them, that they first come together.

Oddly enough, many critics, particularly queer critics, overlook or even misread Jack and Ennis's subordinate class statuses; my attention to class here is thus part of my overarching attempt to model an expansive practice of queer ecological reading. Nick Davis, to take one example, refers to the film as "bourgeois melodrama" (635). This is a particularly dubious claim, considering the details of class outlined above and considering that Ennis, as discussed below, explicitly rejects the confines of the bourgeois family. Dwight A. McBride, similarly, observes that "one ready way to provide critique of a social norm (classism/elitism, family rivalry, heterosexism/heteronormativity) is to have it be the primary obstacle to the success of the central love story in a film (Titanic, Romeo and Juliet, and Brokeback, respectively). The social forces of heteronormativity keep Jack and Ennis from realizing the happy progress of their love story" (96). McBride does not perceive classism/elitism to be a pertinent aspect of Jack and Ennis's story, much less an obstacle, despite the film's repeated references to the men's hardscrabble lives.

In fact, class directly informs the double bind that is Brokeback Mountain itself: Jack and Ennis cannot own any part of it privately, but as it is land reserved and managed by the federal government, it is not truly available to them as members of the public, either. And their time there is circumscribed by their lower-class status—working for private interests in which they will never share, with little comfort and no job security. Through this double bind, the film depicts what Gordon Brent Ingram, Anne-Marie Bouthillette, and Yolanda Retter term "deterritorialization": "the loss of identifiable queer sites . . . and thus substantial portions of a local landscape, through homophobia, capital, or environmental deterioration" ("Strategies for (Re)constructing

Queer Communities" 451). While Brokeback Mountain is never a fully "queer site," it is the closest Jack and Ennis have ever gotten to one. And the fact that the men never return to it—while they do return to the outdoors in various fishing and camping trips throughout the years—suggests that it has either been completely taken over by commercial interests, or is otherwise circumscribed by forces of surveillance. As Ingram, Bouthillette, and Retter note, further, "[f]or . . . sexual minorities, these losses of access, safety, comfort, and freedom of expression are compounded by their experiences as women, people of colour, or poor people. . . . . [T]hese groups endure hypermarginalization and invisibility because of poverty and lack of basic environmental resources—including raw space" ("Surveying Territories and Landscapes" 91). Jack and Ennis face a lack of "access, safety, comfort, and freedom of expression" not just because of their queerness, and the surveillance visited upon them, but because of their failure to achieve a certain economic status. We thus see that the alienation of the queer from nature is not something chosen, something *a priori*, or something inherent, but something enacted through the combined forces of capitalist exploitation and heterosexism.

"I'm Not You": Divergent Sexual-Ecological Principles in *Brokeback Mountain*

Through these stagings, the film enacts an intersectional queer ecological politics—one that links classism, homophobia, and environmental destruction/commodification, while also demonstrating, both positively and negatively, the ways in which the queer and the natural might be interrelated. But its characters do not embrace this politics in equal measure. Jack insists upon a resolution to the pair's in-between state that accepts, rather than rejects, the bind in which they find themselves. Specifically, he wants to own private land that he can use for commercial purposes. At several points in the film, Jack insists that he and Ennis could build this kind of life together: "What if you and me had a little ranch together somewhere, little cow-and-calf operation, it'd be some sweet life. Hell, Lurleen's old man, you bet he'd give me a down payment if I'd get lost." Later, after Jack's death, his parents recount to Ennis that he had had a "foolish" fantasy of getting a ranch with another man—who, it is implied, was his lover—suggesting that he maintained this interest independent of his relationship with Ennis. As Thomas Byers observes, "the ranch of which Jack dreams is a fantasy of domesticity modeled on ideals of heterosexual marriage and family" (5). Indeed, this "sweet life" would actually be bankrolled by Jack's previous participation (though ultimate failure) in heterosexual domesticity. Moreover, it would entail a relationship to the natural world based primarily on capital accumulation, rather than pleasure, identification, or community.

While the film suggests that same-sex domesticity is ultimately untenable, at least under the current social conditions of Wyoming, the fact that Jack insists upon it is nonetheless notable. I argue that his insistence represents a failure of imagination, a failure to recognize any other options besides private heterosexual domesticity or private homosexual domesticity. It is a foreclosure of more creative, and more queer, possibilities—relating to another person or persons in a way not sanctioned by the state and not modeled on heterosexual institutions, and relating to nature in a way other than the private and domestic. In fact, the era in which Jack and Ennis's story first starts is actually the era in which queers and other outsiders sought out such possibilities through communal living, polyamory or "free love," feminist households, and other countercultural lifestyles. As Timothy Miller reports, "homosexual communes (usually separate ones for men and women, although combined ones in a few cases) were a part of the 1960s-era communal landscape. . . . Lesbian communes made the larger, earlier mark, with most gay male settlements coming after 1975" (138). Notably, the majority of these early communities were located in the American West. But such alternative lifestyles are inconceivable within Jack's framework. He takes no issue with the fact that homosexual encounters are prohibited in town, nor with the prospect that such encounters will become increasingly unfeasible in the wilderness because of its development.

Like Carol White in Safe, then, Jack responds to his own suffering not by developing an intersectional, ethical consciousness around the environment and environmental injustice, nor by questioning the regime under which he lives, but by attempting to fit more comfortably within that regime. More specifically, his interest in the private represents a de facto acceptance of the commodification of nature and of the concomitant disciplining of queerness as something unfit for public appearance. Lacking in both class consciousness and queer consciousness, then, he represents what Lisa Duggan has termed the "new homonormativity"—"a privatized, depoliticized gay culture anchored in domesticity and consumption" (50). While developed over the course of the film, these points are foreshadowed very early on, such as when Jack playfully lassos Ennis on Brokeback Mountain. This act both aligns Ennis with non-human nature and marks Jack as separate therefrom; it anticipates later scenes in which Jack ropes calves on the rodeo circuit in pursuit of prize money, staged encounters that value animals only in terms of sport. In that early lassoing scene, the pair's horseplay quickly turns into fisticuffs, indicating that their divergent sexual-ecological principles will—at least as much, if not more so, than homophobia—be the downfall of their relationship.

In contrast, Ennis consistently holds out against the possibility of domestication. As Jack awkwardly puts it, "I'm not you. I can't get by on a coupla high-altitude fucks once or twice a year." Indeed, the latter's anti-domesticity is thoroughgoing; for one thing, though he appears to be a loving father, he immediately shuts down the request of his daughter Alma Jr. (Kate Mara) to live with him after he divorces Alma. For another, his distaste for romantic commitment of any kind is stressed several times over. When his girlfriend Cassie (Laura Cardellini) asks Alma Jr. if the girl thinks he will ever settle down, she replies, "Maybe he ain't the marryin' kind." And even Jack asks Ennis during one of their rendezvous on Brokeback Mountain, "All this time and you ain't found no one else to marry?" Jack's odd question—considering that, earlier, he mistook Ennis's divorce from Alma as a sign that Ennis wanted to settle down with him—suggests just what a deeply ingrained value domesticity is in this milieu, its rough-and-tumble frontierland reputation notwithstanding. Ennis rejects not just the emotional trappings of domesticity, but its materialist dimensions. When Alma Jr. comes to visit him in his trailer, she remarks, "Daddy, you need more furniture," to which he replies, "If you got nothing, you don't need nothing."

That "nothing" that Ennis finds so gratifying could also be called "nature." As Hiram Perez reports, Annie's Proulx's short story "Brokeback Mountain" "suggests a sensual gratification in the smells and sounds of ranch work," particularly in such passages as these: "[Ennis and Alma's] bedroom was full of . . . sounds . . . of squalling and sucking and Alma's sleepy groans, all reassuring of fecundity and life's continuance to one who worked with livestock" (as quoted in Perez 79). For Perez, this passage raises provocative questions, including, "Might not the sensuality of his work complicate how we assess Ennis's sexuality? Why assume that his yearning for a cowboy lifestyle is not continuate with sexual desire? . . . Is it impossible that Ennis's labor on the ranch provides sensual—even sexual—gratification?" (79). While the film does not raise these issues quite as explicitly as the story, we might say that it inculcates in the viewer a pleasure in "nothing," or nature: based on a thirty-two-page short story, the film spends its two-hour-and-fifteen-minute running time not primarily on action or dialogue, but on languid, contemplative shots of natural beauty. But perhaps more important for my argument here, Perez is reminding us that sexual desire often has less to do with a gendered object choice than with the physical and economic context in which one might experience pleasure. Ennis is sexually attracted to "the natural"—but in particularly non-heteronormative ways. His sexuality is not just *like* the natural world, but part and parcel thereof. In turn, the threat of that world's commodification is also a threat to his sexuality. We should recall, then, not just Jack and Ennis's "animalistic" first sexual encounter, but the "animalistic" character of his subsequent relations with his wife: Ennis becomes aroused in that "bedroom full of . . . sounds of squalling and sucking," attempting to penetrate Alma "doggie-style" just as he did with Jack.

It should be noted that, compared to the works treated in Chapter 1, *Brokeback Mountain*'s characters do not self-consciously or explicitly discuss their connection to nature. But I would argue that this state of affairs actually reflects the connectivity and empathy that we are to understand they already possess: for "one who worked with livestock," such relation would be second (or perhaps, first?) nature.[10] After all, unlike Jess in *Stone Butch Blues*, Jack and Ennis are humans for whom nature is no abstraction or distant memory, but a daily reality; when we meet them, they have not yet experienced the full division from the natural that a capitalist-homophobic regime will enforce. Moreover, the film regularly captures the men's intimate knowledge of and facility in dealing with non-human nature. We might think of their ability to kill and prepare an elk by themselves, or Ennis's caution to Jack that a certain horse "has a low startle point," or how both men care for the more vulnerable sheep in the flock—swaddling the babies in slings on their horses, as Ennis does, or digging burrs out of their legs, as Jack does. While the first act might not fit into a sentimentalized view of nature, in which killing would have no place, all of these acts fit into a vision of ethical sustainability, in which humans understand, appreciate, and care for non-human nature and make use of it in minimally invasive or non-institutionalized ways.[11] We should also remember the film's sparse dialogue; this feature evokes the relationship between these characters and the natural world, a relationship that does not need to be articulated through human language. And in fact, the taciturn nature of our protagonists indicates, at least in Ennis's case, their preference for a simple, anti-social, nature-oriented lifestyle.

Despite this empathetic attunement to nature, though, there is at least one failure of empathy in the film worth noticing. One scene in the film depicts Jack's apparent predilection for patronizing Mexican male prostitutes. By this time living in Texas and working for Lureen's father, Jack, bitter and distraught, passes a road sign that reads, "El Paso, 65 [miles]" and "Juarez—Mexico Border 68 [miles]." We then watch as he walks down a dark border-town alleyway, up to a young Mexican man who asks, "Señor?" Jack gives a slight nod and the two walk off into the darkness. This scene, I argue, further highlights the divergence between Ennis's and Jack's principles. Again, like Carol White, Jack seeks solace for his marginalization from someone even more marginalized than he, in the process exercising his relative privilege as a wealthy, white American male. That is, while he is sexually/socially oppressed himself, Jack is relatively unconcerned with the oppressive circumstances under which this Other lives: unable, presumably, to come and go as Jack does, and a world away from the nouveau-riche bracket that Jack has recently infiltrated, though a mere three miles separates them. The film invites the viewer to critique the nonchalant, exploitative behavior Jack displays in this scene; at the very least, it would be difficult for us to ignore the street prostitute's socioeconomic marginalization, considering the film's class consciousness up until this point. Meanwhile, Ennis, as the character more attuned to nature, remains poor and yet relatively free of such ethical missteps. This is not to suggest that *Brokeback* sees sex trade—or wealth, for that matter—as immoral, per se. Rather, it is to point out how the film links Jack's economic, ecological, and sexual acquisitiveness, and promotes as an alternative a locally attuned sexual-environmental ethics.

We should note that Ennis's refusal of sexual (and, therefore, ecological) commodification, as compared to Jack's embrace thereof, has been understood by critics such as Perez as anti-futurist. Drawing on Judith Halberstam, Perez claims that, "[i]n opposition to Jack's desire for domesticity modeled on marriage, Ennis's commitment in the relationship suggests an alternative (or queer) temporality. After all, the urgency and intensity of their desire is dictated by the fleetingness of their encounters" (75). Perez also sees the men's use of postcards as a medium of communication as exemplifying "how Ennis is gratified by ephemera" (76). But this reading does not account for the fact that Ennis, in fact, cares very much about longevity and life cycles. After all, Proulx's description of the family bedroom tells us that the sounds and smells were "reassuring of fecundity and *life's continuance* to one who worked with livestock" (as quoted in Perez 79, my emphasis). We might also think of how the film depicts Ennis's tense discovery of the corpse of a sheep (attacked by predators after he has failed to watch over them), or his tender care for both the sheep and, later, his children. Moreover, the film sets up the future as a major concern for Ennis in another sense: as I've noted above, encroaching modernization and privatization of land threaten his way of life. Finally, the claim that Ennis is "gratified by ephemera" does not seem entirely accurate considering how his work as a ranch hand is seasonal—cyclical and repetitive—though it may render him expendable as a worker. Indeed, that Ennis could want an ephemeral or peripatetic love life and not care about capital accumulation,

and yet be married to a repetitively patterned job working with "life's continuance" among animals and land is a kind of paradox, a queer ecological
one, that makes a great deal of sense. What I mean to show here, then,
is the problematic implications of queer anti-futurity for environmental
concerns. Queer anti-futurity not only prevents us from seeing the ways in
which queer texts articulate care for nature's fate—even if, or even as, they
embrace "ephemera"—but it threatens to discount the idea of such care.

For all of these reasons, I insist that we have to understand Ennis's position on domesticity as something other than internalized homophobia.
Indeed, when he scoffs at Jack, "two guys living together . . . no way. Now
we can get together every once in a while way the hell out in the middle of
nowhere," we realize that *anyone* living together in any traditional or familial formation is anathema to him. Of course, the film shows us through
a graphic flashback one possible outcome of "two guys living together":
as a child, Ennis's father forced him to look at the corpse of a local man
murdered because he ran a ranch with his presumed partner. But the fact
remains that Ennis resists the idea of any kind of organized and manageable
desire, a resistance that just so happens to entail a preference for public
natural space. Ennis is afraid not quite of his own queerness, or others'
reactions to it, but of being literally and figuratively fenced—or, as it were,
lassoed—in. More pragmatically, we could simply say that Ennis prompts
us to ask, if even private forms of queerness are still regarded as excessively
public, so much so that they occasion murder, what do we have to lose by
insisting on the public?

Not only does Jack not share or sympathize with Ennis's anti-domestic
ethos, he often seems not to recognize its existence. At one point during
an outdoor rendezvous, Jack insists, "You know it could be like this, just
like this, always." "Yeah, how you figure that?" Ennis responds. Jack again
launches into his case for the "calf-and-cow operation," not seeming to
comprehend that such an arrangement *wouldn't* be "just like this." Virtually everything would be different: they would be on a private ranch, not in
(partly) public woods; they would be cooking in a kitchen, not over an open
flame in the outdoors; and they would spend their time running a business,
not exploring the wilderness and making love.

I don't mean to suggest that Ennis always espouses a perfectly consistent queer politics, however. We might recall, for example, the early scene
in which he explodes in anger at two foul-mouthed bikers at a Fourth of
July fireworks show in a public park, growling, "I got two little girls here!"
This move represents the kind of de facto privatization of public space to
which I've alluded: the private family is, ironically, assumed to have a greater

right to public space than those who live outside of that institution, those who don't actually have homes and property to which they can retreat. The demands of the family automatically trump the demands of anyone outside of the normative bounds of desire. I would therefore suggest that Ennis has internalized such logic, but that he clearly struggles against it, especially as the film progresses.

This point becomes more acute when we recall the historical developments unique to the period captured in the film. As Carl Hallberg reports,

> From 1953 to 1969, Wyoming's Natural Resources Board and State Engineer's Office embarked upon an ambitious campaign to develop water projects across the state in order to promote or enhance agricultural, industrial or residential development. . . . Writing in 1958, the manager of the Fremont Irrigation Company complained that the application processes had little changed since the turn of the century: "The *wast[e]* of time and manpower and the extra expense, not to mention the long delay in allowing the *settler to enter on his land*, is all *unnecessary*." (my emphasis)

Hallberg explains that waves of enthusiasm for Reclamation—specifically, water projects—continued throughout the postwar period. As he recalls,

> Equally optimistic was Roy Beck, executive director of the Natural Resources Board, who believed that such work in Wyoming still had great potential. In 1970, he commented to Ellis Armstong, commissioner of the Bureau of Reclamation, that with the Riverton Reauthorization Bill and the Seedskadee Project, "we can turn around the Reclamation program in Wyoming."

Riverton, as we might remember, is the town to which Alma eventually convinces Ennis to move. According to the U.S. Bureau of Reclamation, Riverton was established when Native American residents ceded portions of the Wind River Indian Reservation to the United States; "Provisions were [then] made for the disposal of these lands under the homestead, townsite, coal, and mineral land laws."[12]

Broadly speaking, Reclamation in the American West was initially justified through the concepts of "homesteading" or "homemaking." As Theodore Roosevelt declared in his 1901 State of the Union address, "The reclamation of the unsettled arid public lands presents a different problem. Here it is not enough to regulate the flow of streams. The object of the government is to *dispose of the land* to settlers who will *build homes upon it*. To accomplish the object water must be brought within their reach." He concluded that "Our people as a whole will profit, for successful *home-making is but another*

name for the upbuilding of the nation" (Chisholm 853, my emphasis). Catriona
Sandilands has tracked how this kind of natural domestication has been
linked, ideologically or materially, with white heterosexual domesticity.
She offers the example of Oregon's Donation Land Act (DLA), which "encouraged a heterosexual pattern of colonization because of the way land
was allotted to settlers" ("Unnatural Passions?" 16): white males over the
age of twenty-one were given 160-acre parcels, and an additional 160 for
their wives. Sandilands points out, drawing on the work of Peter Boag,
that "[w]omen were not eligible for allotments as single people, and it
was clearly in the advantage of men to have the two parcels" (16)—thus
very young girls suddenly became marriage material. But the story does
not end there. Sandilands argues that "the DLA . . . imposed a monolithic
culture of single heterosexual family-sized lots on the land, with significant effects on the economic and environmental history of the region from
nuclear family farming patterns . . . and even increased forestation" ("Unnatural Passions?" 16). As Jack and Ennis live in a time when this notion
of natural landscape as implicitly heterosexual domestic space was being
enthusiastically *revived*, their struggle is thus not over landedness on the
one hand and sexuality on the other, but over the two as imbricated. And
Ennis's rejection of domesticity can't *not* be a rejection of the belief that
land and non-human nature exist only to be owned.

Queer Wildness vs. Gay Domestication: *Brokeback Mountain* in the Context of Neoliberalism

Through its meditations on the public and private, *Brokeback Mountain* contributes to contemporary political debates over issues such as same-sex marriage. To begin with, it interrogates the idea that domestic respectability
should be the goal of those with unorthodox desires. Several queer theorists, including José Esteban Muñoz and Michael Warner, have launched
such interrogations. As Muñoz writes, "homonormative" figures such as
lawyer Evan Wolfson, a prominent same-sex marriage activist and founder
of Freedom to Marry, "cannot critique the larger ideological regime that
represents marriage as something desirable, natural, and good. [Wolfson's]
assimilationist gay politics posits an 'all' that is in fact a few: queers with
enough access to capital to imagine a life integrated within North American
capitalistic culture" (*Cruising Utopia* 20). This politics, in other words, represents a failure of queer-utopian imagination. Muñoz and Warner have also

warned us that the assimilationist same-sex marriage agenda further abjects certain types of individuals from the body politic, particularly as public rights are tied to marriage. In addition to poor queers, these individuals include transgender people, those in polyamorous relationships, and those who choose not to marry. We might also add that the fight for same-sex marriage endorses the government's intervention into what has otherwise been deemed a private matter—not unlike the U.S. Forest Service's ceding of its public lands to private interests in Brokeback Mountain. Returning to the film, we see that Jack's plan would change the face of the nuclear family slightly but would not challenge that family's social goals, its privileged status, or its economic underpinnings. And it does not challenge the shift in the human relationship to nature—from empathetic identification to ownership and mastery—that such a plan would entail.

Jack's interest in assimilation also invokes the ever-shrinking public sphere that critics such as Lisa Duggan have recently decried. As she describes it, "[i]n the United States specifically, the neoliberal agenda [has entailed] shrinking public institutions, expanding private profit-making prerogatives, and undercutting democratic practices and noncommercial cultures" (xv). This agenda, as Duggan traces it, begins after the civil-rights era and continues into the present. (Other analysts locate its beginning right after World War II.) I propose that Brokeback Mountain's status as a public space turned private, and Jack's endorsement of this trajectory of privatization, map directly onto these historical shifts—which have found minorities striking the same bargain that Jack does, between the loss of free space and social-sexual freedoms and the achievement of relative acceptance (or, sometimes, just bare survival). The film's critical portrayal of this scenario leads me to part ways with critics such as Martin F. Manalansan, who calls the film a "neoliberal portrait . . . based on a privileged form of market-generated individualism that operates on ideas of universalism and similitude established at the expense of economic and racial inequalities" (99–100). While Manalansan may be right that the film's *appeal* rests upon a universalized gay subject, it takes rather notable pains to critically reify "privileged form[s] of market-generated individualism" and to highlight, rather than to overlook, economic inequalities.

Of course, the picture of gay assimilation may be more complex than its queer-theory opponents make it out to be. Marriage and other legal mechanisms may offer crucial protections to queers, especially the most vulnerable populations. For instance, Mignon R. Moore reminds us that "[b]ecause black same-sex couples are more economically disadvantaged on average than are white same-sex couples, at the same time that they are more likely to be raising children, they are disproportionately harmed" by laws against fostering or adopting children, laws against including children they co-parent on their health insurance plans, and more generally by their inability to legally marry. In this sense, we can theoretically distinguish between same-sex marriage as elitist status-mongering and same-sex marriage as a protection against further oppression. We might then imagine that individuals who choose to marry might still maintain radical or progressive agendas. But my point is that Jack and Ennis are increasingly denied such complex, creative possibilities. To be part of *nature-and-culture* or *public-and-private* are no longer options for these lower-class queer men under the dual regimes of homophobia and Reclamation. At the same time that their queerness is censured, they are asked—not just by the powers that be, but by many audience members who fantasize for them a happily-ever-after[13]—to capitulate to a private culture that will entail a disavowal of the spontaneous and free access to public nature. For Jack, this makes sense: private financial gain, private domesticity, and middle-class respectability go hand in hand, while his incipient white privilege will theoretically allow him to collect these spoils with impunity. But Ennis rejects this bundle of ideals and holds out for that more utopian future by insisting on a public life, but one that affords some measure of privacy. This might look something like a public park in which he can enjoy a fireworks display with his little girls, and/or with his male lover—without doing violence to others trying to occupy the same sphere, and without having violence done to him.

It is worth taking a longer view of gay liberation to understand just what a major departure Jack's homonormativity represents—and how the film opposes this position. Beginning in the 1950s, U.S. GLBTQI activists negotiated, remapped, and even rejected the private–public distinction. Duggan explains that "homophile activists intervened in postwar conflicts by steadily expanding the notion of sexual or personal privacy to include, not only sexual relations between consenting adults at home, but freedom from surveillance and entrapment in public, collective settings. . . . This complex maneuver. . . . defin[ed] a kind of right-to-privacy-in-public . . . This project worked along with efforts to expand the allowable scope of sexual expression in public culture, both commercial and nonprofit/artistic" (52). As I have suggested, this private–public distinction routinely punishes queers while privileging heteronormative individuals. The latter enjoy moving across both spheres, and their interests are used to justify the exclusivity of certain public spaces, while the former are relegated to the private, and further managed within that sphere. In turn, heterosexuality becomes naturalized as healthy sexual expression—open and visible, rather than shameful, secretive, or desperate. Thus homophile efforts made space for the private in public life, while also critiquing those very concepts.

By the 1980s, antigay forces had finally conceded to GBLTQI activists the right to privacy but insisted that never should it meet its supposed opposite, publicness. The late 1980s and the early 1990s therefore saw orchestrated attacks on, for example, the National Endowment for the Arts for its funding of "obscene" artists such as Robert Mapplethorpe and Andres Serrano. But what Duggan—and, I argue, *Brokeback Mountain*—finds even more alarming than these antigay campaigns is the fact that contemporary gay politics has largely acquiesced to this particular mapping of the public and private and has given up the fight for privacy in public. While the fight for same-sex marriage represents this shift most prominently, it is only one manifestation thereof; many gay organizations and activists have advocated more broadly for "a politics that offers a dramatically shrunken public sphere and . . . 'responsible' domestic privacy" (Duggan 53). Considering the fact that the "private," like "the natural," is redefined and remapped at the whim of homophobic authorities, and considering that heteronormative "private life" gets to be much more public, mobile, and flexible than queer "private life," the concession of this ground is grave indeed: the injunction to "keep it private" threatens to disappear queers altogether.

And it threatens to disappear nature. Environmental historian Philip Shabecoff tells us that the Eisenhower era, which ended two years before *Brokeback*'s plot begins, saw the largest giveaways of natural resources and lands to private companies and individuals since the nineteenth century—at least until the Reagan era, when *Brokeback*'s plot ends. He recounts that Douglas McKay, Eisenhower's secretary of the interior, "attempted to block public power projects and turn energy resources over to private companies. He also tried to abolish a number of federal Fish and Wildlife Service areas and to transfer Nevada's big Desert Game Reserve to the state's fish and game department." For these efforts, "he was dubbed 'Giveaway McKay'" (84). Samuel P. Hays observes that the contemporary U.S. environmental movement also focused on the public in a different sense: it "played an important role in civic enterprise, . . . enabling people to feel that they could 'make a difference.'" It was able to do so because "[e]nvironmental issues were broadly conceived public issues; they represented the interests of a broad-based segment of the public, and they involved environmental conditions that were widely shared" (196). Not surprisingly, then, Hays reports that "[t]he most vigorous participants in the environmental opposition were private industries and developers" (196). The same battle that GLBTQI activists were fighting over the private versus the public, then, was being fought by environmental activists in the same period. As *Brokeback Mountain* has it, these battles are one and the same.

Thus, while critics such as Herring have accused *Brokeback Mountain* of "historical amnesias" (Herring 94), I would have to vigorously disagree. As I have shown, it captures many of the major shifts of the postwar era, from the final development pushes in the American West, to the neoliberal turn in gay activism and American politics at large, to the fact that "[p]ublic space in the twentieth century, more than any other time in history, has been dominated by the state's attempts to suppress, constrain, and otherwise regulate sexual desire and consensual activity—particularly for women and sexual minorities" (Ingram, "'Open' Space as Strategic Queer Sites" 123). The film critically presages the scenario that we arguably inhabit today—in which queer desire turns into gay acceptability at the price of social conformity and commodification; in which the democratic public sphere and publicly accessible natural space become things of the past; in which health and safety are commodified; and in which these realities become naturalized.

When taking stock of the film's presentation of this scenario, we must note one particular way in which it differs from its literary source. Proulx's short story "Brokeback Mountain" offers an additional option for queer life that the film does not: Denver, an urban space that would offer some kind of gay community. Thomas Byers argues that the absence of Denver within the film "confirms the film's binarization of two alternatives for gay life: Jack's fantasy ranch and Mexico" (9), where Jack solicits prostitutes. Further, Byers claims that this elimination has two particular ideological effects: "First, the notion of a genuinely alternative structuring of sexuality and kinship relations, as opposed to simply an alternative object-choice, remains beyond the pale. Second, any hope for a viable gay community of more than two members is removed from the map" (9). In this view, *Brokeback Mountain* endorses the neoliberal case for same-sex marriage voiced by commentators such as Andrew Sullivan: if gays are not allowed access to private domestic life, they will be forced into seedy, loveless encounters.

But there's another option that has dropped out of sight in such discussions: that one of queers freely occupying public, natural spaces. Most critical accounts have ignored this option, perhaps presuming its impossibility. But I have demonstrated how the film holds out for it, offering us a glimpse at how queer individuals might identify with the natural world, and critiquing that world's capitalist and rhetorical exploitation for heterosexist purposes. The disappearance of public, natural spaces, and their reterritorialization as private zones, is precisely *Brokeback*'s subject. So while I agree with Byers that the omission of Denver is pivotal, I believe that we can read it quite differently, particularly if we take the interrelationship between environment and sexuality seriously. The omission might very well suggest that the option of escaping to an urban center—be it Denver, New York, San Francisco, or elsewhere—is beside the point: one should not have to sacrifice one's connection to the natural landscape, and one's identity as a rural individual, in order to survive as a queer. Indeed, as Kath Weston has noted, "the movement from rural to urban space has become symbolically overloaded in 'coming-out' stories" (as cited in Mortimer-Sandilands and Erickson 17).

This interpretation takes on added weight when we recall that neither of our protagonists has much money of his own, and that neither seems particularly suited to urban life—especially not Ennis, who reflects that "the most travelin' I've ever done's been around the coffeepot looking for the handle." Put one way, even if it we thought it appropriate to advise those queers who experience discrimination or censure in the public sphere to just hit up a gay bar or move to a "gayborhood," Jack and Ennis are people who cannot easily take up that solution. If the queer can now only get to nature, literally and figuratively, through the expenditure of capital, then a poor queer is in quite a bind indeed. The film's omission of Denver puts this bind into sharp relief, then: homophobia and capitalism link together to ensure that the men have virtually no public natural space open to them, and no way of experiencing the natural landscape apart from commodifying or otherwise mastering it. Even Jack's public reaction to Ennis's refusal of private domesticity—picking up a street prostitute in Mexico—is highly commercialized, and enabled by global capitalism as well as by white, male, American privilege. I argue that the film thus captures a pivotal historical moment, one in which same-sex desire begins to look particularly "unnatural" when it runs up against a capitalist, anti-environmentalist, and neoliberal framework. The film's critique is therefore aimed not at the limitations on the expression of gay identity, as so many critics have maintained, but rather at the process by which queer desire gets transformed into gay identity—a process that entails the privatization of public, natural space.

Perhaps more positively, I also see the film's omission of Denver's gay community as a rejection of the "gay ghetto" model. As a student in one of my Queer Ecology courses once quipped, "They'll take away Brokeback Mountain, but they'll give you a gay bar." This brilliant comment registers a reality in which urban consumerism is gay identity. It is worth revisiting Gordon Brent Ingram's work here:

> The increasing commercialization of communal sites [causes] many to be
> . . . increasingly unavailable to less privileged queer groups. The greater the

commodification of space and loss of secure access to formerly public sites (a central characteristic of globalized capital), the more the preclusion of collectivity. Today, instead of authentic access to space and community, sexual minorities have been granted a poor substitute of the globalizing-capital standard fare, the "spectacle" where capital is accumulated to such a degree that it actually becomes an image, rather than authentic access to resources. ("Marginality and the Landscapes of Erotic Alien(n)ations" 50)

Jack and Ennis, the poor-white itinerant ranch hands, lack this authentic access to space and community. But the film refuses to fill that gap with the "poor substitute" of the urban gay bar, dance club, or shopping district, those things that Denver would provide.

Of course, some queer scholars have understood the gay bar as a space that is both private and public, or even predominately public. In his work on World War II–era gay life, for instance, Allan Bérubé writes, "Lesbians and gay men took advantages of a more tolerant social climate during the war to stake out a new public turf in [gay and mixed] bars. Later, in the 1950s and 1960s, the successors to these wartime bars . . . became a major battleground in the fight for public meeting places free from harassment" (93). But my point here is that the options Jack and Ennis face in 1960s–1980s Wyoming are strictly circumscribed in the ways Bérubé describes—and that this circumscription mirrors the shrinking of the public sphere under the neoliberalism of that postwar period. Indeed, the circumscription depicted in *Brokeback* invokes the severely limited options for public existence faced by poor queers and queers of color in the present-day United States. Consider, for instance, Dean Spade's report on the contemporary state of New York's famed Stonewall neighborhood, the site in the 1960s of gay, lesbian, bisexual, and transgender resistance to police harassment and economic exploitation: "a coalition of gay and straight high-income renters and home owners have teamed up to rid their streets (their group is literally called RID, or Residents in Distress) of the queer and trans youth of color who have . . . formed a community in the public spaces of that neighborhood for years. The residents . . . have pressured politicians to increase police presence in the area, resulting in extensive harassment and false arrests (particularly against trans youth of color)" (48)—youth who tend to be homeless or marginally housed. Whether intentionally or not, then, Spade suggests that gay privatization frequently goes hand in hand with the further marginalization of poor people and people of color. Once again, we see the insidious pattern whereby an Othered group fails to empathize with other Others.

Brokeback Mountain does happen to contain several scenes set in bars, and one in particular illuminates its commentary around ghettoized, commercialized gay space. Shortly after Jack and Ennis's summer on Brokeback Mountain, Jack competes in a rodeo and visits the small local bar, where he attempts to buy a drink for the rodeo clown. The man becomes hostile, walking away after throwing his money toward the bartender in disgust. Jack's attempt to pick up a man in a de facto straight bar is notable on multiple counts. For one, it's representative of the kind of privacy-in-public for which early gay activists fought. For another, it indicates a belief, however misguided, in a space that is heterogeneous rather than ghettoized (though of course still commercialized). Jack's disappointment in this scene thus registers not just a recognition of his "misreading," or of public hostility toward queer desire, but of the fact this is not after all a heterogeneous, communal public space—one that would include queers and straights, rodeo cowboys and rodeo clowns, and maybe even those of different socioeconomic classes. Rather than fight to create such a space, Jack soon turns to a kind of desperate assimilationism. But his naiveté here, coupled with the film's refusal to depict the option of the gay ghetto, has an important utopian effect; it gestures toward a horizon of possibility that might still be met.

Brokeback's intertext Surf Party also features a scene set in a bar. Rudy's, a beachside dive named for its Japanese American owner (Lloyd Kino), caters to the local surfers, including minors, and no legitimate money appears to be exchanged. Thus it's neither a commercialized space, nor a zone of segregation, nor a consolation for rejection from the larger public sphere—as are the gay bars to which I've alluded. Moreover, Rudy's multi-racial, multigenerational, mixed-gender establishment harbors those who refuse quiet domesticity and the dominant definition of a "clean," "natural" space: a beach clear of amorous teenagers, beach bums, idle surfers, and other riffraff. The decline of this utopia begins when Sergeant Neal raids the bar. But it's aided by a larger development: the growing agreement among most of the film's characters that the beach, and the image of the surfer more generally, needs cleaning up.[14] This acquiescence, compared to Ennis's resistance, highlights the queer thrust of Brokeback Mountain.

Poststructuralist Pastoral:
Brokeback Mountain as Metatext

Brokeback Mountain's critique of the domestication and privatization of desire depends in large part upon its status as a film—and upon its self-reflexivity as regards that status. It calls attention, sometimes negatively, to the very act that makes it legible as a text: watching. To begin with, it drives home the issue of biosurveillance by directly implicating the viewer in that phenomenon.

I have already cited the binoculars scene, in which the shot–reverse-shot sequence makes clear that Aguirre's view was *our* view. In turn, we are forced to recognize our agency in observing, our public intrusion into what was intended as a private interaction. The drive-in scene works in a slightly different manner, however. Unlike an illicit tryst or secluded mountainside, a drive-in movie screen is something that we expect to be observed by the public. But the placement of a movie screen inside of a movie, especially inside of a movie focused on surveillance, cannot but reify the act of observation, the act that we ourselves are undertaking.

D. A. Miller locates *Brokeback*'s filmic self-reflexivity not in its scenes centered on surveillance, but on the broader level of performance. As he argues, "though *Brokeback Mountain* does not otherwise seem to aspire to the cinematic avant-garde, there is something about Ledger's ever-'on' performance that almost suggests one of those postmodern shifts of narrative level in which a character behaves as though *he knows he is in the movie we are watching*" (56, emphasis original). While I find Miller's assessment compelling, it seems crucial to acknowledge this character's status in the filmstory as a paranoid, surveilled individual. That is to say, while both might coexist within the same film, there is a difference between a character behaving as though he knows he is being watched by external, or non-diegetic, viewers, and one behaving as though he knows he is being watched by internal, or diegetic, viewers. The latter allows us to be moved, maybe even horrified, by our role in the former.

So the question then becomes, if the film implicates us as viewers in the surveillance of the queer and the natural, are we not then placed in an oppressive position to both? And is the film's visual apparatus itself not then homophobic, as well as ecophobic? Miller seems to believe that the answer is yes, at least when it comes to queerness. He remarks on our "heightened appreciation of spectatorial privilege [in watching the film]: to see without being seen. . . . [E]ven as others are debarred from inspecting the gay penetralium, *we get to keep looking*. . . . [A]nd better still, we never have to hear ourselves addressed by [Ennis's] question" (55–56)—that is, "What the fuck you lookin' at?" But how is it that we can recognize our spectatorial privilege and yet not hear a question about spectatorship as being addressed to us? Indeed, Miller seems to roundly contradict his own claim, in going on to argue that "Ennis [is] always being watched like a hawk—if not by Jack, or Joe Aguirre, or Alma, then, in a far more continuous surveillance than theirs combined, by us spectators. . . . Only the fictive surveillance intrinsic to our spectatorial position, after all, allows us to diagnose the 'paranoia' of Ennis's belief in the fictive surveillance that he imagines to know all about him. *We* are his paranoia" (56). I would propose that knowing ourselves to be Ennis's paranoia—and knowing that the fictive character's belief in the fictive surveillance is thoroughly accurate—could hardly produce on our part a sadistic relationship, unless the viewer refuses the empathy that the film otherwise cultivates. I propose that *Brokeback*, instead, produces a kind of self-consciousness about our viewership that forces us to examine that privilege. Like *Safe*, then, *Brokeback Mountain* does not just take up questions of sympathy, empathy, and identification within its diegesis; it explores them formally and therefore makes the viewer a participant in that exploration. It conditions us not just to observe the natural and the queer in ethical, non-exploitative ways, but to, first, *observe how we observe*.

We should also acknowledge that, while the film features multiple viewers who, like us, are privy to what Ennis initially hopes to keep private, it distinguishes between different *types* of viewers. Consider, for instance, the difference between Joe Aguirre on the one hand, and, on the other, the bikers Ennis encounters at the fireworks show and the cowboy who passes him vomiting in that early scene. The cowboy and the bikers are Jack and Ennis's social equals: marginal, lower-class, transitory figures. And the threat they pose to Jack and Ennis would be better described, at least from a queer perspective, as progressive possibilities. The cowboy stands to offer comradeship, sympathy, or even empathy—he has, after all, stopped when he sees a man in distress—and, perhaps in Ennis's paranoid imagination, more queer desire. And the bikers are clearly countercultural figures. Moreover, in their refusal to stop their ribald banter, they insist that public space not cater exclusively to the heterosexual, reproductive family. In contrast, Joe Aguirre is a relatively privileged, quasi-omniscient figure of discipline. *Brokeback*'s treatment of Jack and Ennis's time on Brokeback Mountain, coupled with this characterization of Aguirre, ensures that the revelation of his surveillance comes as a shock to the viewer, one that prompts us to disidentify with the perspective that we have just been unwittingly sharing. I argue that the film's staging of the viewer-as-surveiller does not, therefore, ultimately validate the ecophobic/homophobic practices of surveillance and public-versus-private mapping that I have been tracking throughout this chapter. It leads us to question those practices, while also offering the cowboy and the bikers as alternative sites of viewer identification. After all, there is a difference between the gaze of a fellow freak and that of a policing authority, between cruising Ennis and stalking him.

The film's self-reflexivity allows it to achieve several other queer goals. First, and on the most basic level, our metatextual involvement in the publicizing of Jack and Ennis's relationship prompts us to ask if privacy for such a couple is really the best-case scenario, or even a sustainable one. Indeed, if there's a difference between the cowboys and bikers on the one hand, and Aguirre on the other hand, we might recognize that there's a difference between a progressive publicizing of queer desire and a humiliating one, between looking *with* and looking *at*. Ideally, then, our watching can model, or even function as, public community-building,[15] whereas Aguirre's kind of watching can only ever be private-interest surveillance. Second, and more specifically, the film thus *enacts* a program of privacy-in-public like that advocated by gay activists beginning in the 1950s. It validates to a certain extent Jack and Ennis's interest in conducting a private relationship, but it challenges the homophobic insistence that queerness must *only* be private; it refuses to confine that relationship to the domestic sphere, or to render it invisible. In short, *Brokeback* encourages an empathetic queer habit of viewing—just as, as I have shown in the previous chapter, *Safe* facilitates a kind of seeing that registers, without reproducing, the limitations of the dominant perspective.

As queerness and the natural world are interconnected per the film (and per this book), *Brokeback*'s self-reflexive techniques also prompt us to examine our surveillance of the latter. The empathetic queer habits of viewing it inculcates, in other words, are also ecological habits of viewing. Miller's strange turn of phrase—that "Ennis is always *being watched* like a hawk" (56)—reminds us (inadvertently?) that Ennis and the natural world are aligned as objects. Further, the film's tendency to highlight the act of viewing reminds us of how the nature of the film does not merely exist, but is framed in particular ways for particular viewers. It thereby points to how certain parts of nature are aestheticized, making them "count" more than other parts—and, more broadly, how what we perceive as, simply, natural might be socially constructed or ideologically inflected. This level of consciousness chimes with the work of poststructuralist ecocritics from the past several years, who have dared to suggest that the natural world might not be taken as a self-evident reality. As William Cronon declares in his pivotal collection *Uncommon Ground: Rethinking the Human Place in Nature* (1995), wilderness "is quite profoundly a human creation. . . . Wilderness hides its unnaturalness behind a mask that is all the more beguiling because it seems so natural" (69). While, understandably, these positions have been met with some hostility,[16] it is important to note that poststructuralist ecocritics have been much more willing than their theory-resistant counterparts to consider seriously how the concerns of gender, sexuality, race, and class—those issues so central to the story of *Brokeback Mountain*—intersect with environmental concerns.

This awareness of biosurveillance is all the more important considering how *Brokeback* has become known as much for its aesthetically pleasing rendering of the natural landscape as for its depiction of human relationships. This notoriety is perhaps best epitomized in the remarks of conservative Christian film reviewer Steven Isaac: "[Ang] Lee is a skillful moviemaker and storyteller. And his film is crammed with emotionally compelling scenes and three-dimensional characters. . . . And, to be trivial for a moment, the scenery is sensational." Isaac's commentary sounds disingenuous in at least two senses. For one, it reads as an attempt at deflecting the reader's attention away from Isaac's own attention to the film's queerness. For another, the scenery is not "trivial," considering—as I have shown throughout this chapter—that its depiction is deeply intertwined with that of its "three-dimensional [queer] characters." It seems, in fact, that Isaac knows this—perhaps even better than many a queer critic. But his commentary nonetheless points to the possibility of losing (or hiding?) ourselves in the film's sweeping natural vistas. The film's reification of its own processes of framing and its explicit class consciousness work against this possibility. They complicate the aestheticization of nature in which the film undeniably participates, as well as the very conditions of capitalism under which the film itself was produced—even if they do not fully counter them. Like those poststructuralist ecocritics cited above, the film questions how we come to understand what nature is, while simultaneously calling for its defense. It refuses, to paraphrase David Mazel's praise of Rebecca Solnit's work, to "reduce the complexities of environmental politics to a simple image of a picture-postcard wilderness" (*American Literary Environmentalism* 161).

And in fact, the film uses actual postcards to capture the complex positions of the queer and the natural under biosurveillance and neoliberal privatization. Postcards constitute the most common mode of communication between Jack and Ennis; the men reconnect for the first time when Jack announces his impending visit to Riverton by postcard, and they arrange their subsequent meetings through the same means. This mode of communication, notably, functions both publicly and privately; postcards constitute private correspondence that is technically available to the public eye, and they travel through public means. To that extent, the use of postcards resists the expectation that the queer remain private. (After all, both men presumably have access to less open means of communication, such as letters and telephones.) At the same time, we must remember that postcards have, from their very inception, frequently functioned as displays of private wealth, even as they depict public places such as parks and natural wonders. That is, a postcard announces one's mobility and worldliness, while also registering the fact that a particular space has been commodified.[17]

The difference between Jack's use of the postcard and Ennis's is important, then: Jack always sends picture postcards, whereas Ennis always sends plain ones. The first time Jack writes, we are given a view of the message on the back, framed by a description that reads, "El Capitan and Signal Peak—View from Highway . . . between Carlsbad, N.M. and El Paso, Texas. Signal Peak, from which the Apaches sent up smoke signals, is the highest peak in Texas." Ennis then flips the postcard over to see the color image of the peak. When he heads to the post office to respond, he selects a plain postcard with a pre-stamped Abraham Lincoln postage mark (a figure, of course, with rather queer resonance).[18] These two types of cards correspond to Jack and Ennis's personal and domestic philosophies; more than indicating his relative finan-cial prosperity compared to Ennis, Jack's postcards represent and in fact enact the commodification of nature. Jack's later choice of a Brokeback Mountain postcard, one of the last images in the film, further suggests his interest in commodifying his and Ennis's experience of both nature and desire.

The use of postcards also allows the film to critique what Mazel calls "[t]he abjection necessary for the materialization of . . . nature" (*American Liter-ary Environmentalism* xxv). As I have noted, Brokeback Mountain has already come under the control of state and federal officials, as well as private live-stockmen, by the time Jack and Ennis reach it. Whatever indigenous popula-tion it may have harbored has long since been decimated, and its population of wild animals is, likewise, in the process of being managed. The postcards invoke these processes of abjection. To wit: Signal Peak's status as a site worthy of recognition in postcard form depends upon the disappearance of those Apaches who once inhabited it. The postcard, in turn, confirms them as a thing of the past. While Jack and Ennis are white men with compara-tively greater privilege, they are likewise abjected: sent away from Brokeback Mountain, and barred from returning, because of their failure to facilitate a capitalist enterprise. In turn, their subsequent encounters in the outdoors are marked by paranoia. We should also note that all of those who work on Brokeback Mountain are of lower status in terms of economics, race, and/ or immigration status.[19] Interestingly, Jim Kitses points out that "Despite an importance in the West's economic history that rivals that of cattle, sheep have been assigned a marginal role in the movies. Traditionally, they have been the source of conflict, their place on the frontier contested as a threat to cattle ranches. In this way they have been seen as interlopers, the property of a lower class of immigrants and minorities" (26). While I do not mean to conflate Jack and Ennis's position with those of people of color in the Ameri-can West's history, my point is that the film calculates the cost of privatizing natural public space in more ways than one.

Finally, as I have suggested above, the postcards in *Brokeback Mountain* remind us of the aestheticized framing of nature that happens in the "real world," as well as within the film itself. That is, the postcards indicate that the human experience of nature, particularly in the postmodern era, is highly mediated—just like the views of nature offered by the film itself. I therefore disagree with Manalansan's claim that "[Jack and Ennis's] romance is literally and figuratively elevated by the whiteness of the space and memorialized in an immaculate postcard" (99); *Brokeback*'s use of the postcard has much more critical potential than he assumes, particularly when we consider how the film as a whole questions the move from queer desire to commodified gay identity. Just as Ennis is framed by the lens of Aguirre's binoculars, so has the natural landscape been framed by the lens of a photographer for the postcard, and by the lens of the cinematographer for the film. All three kinds of framing constitute attempts to render the land and/or the queer "useful," but only the last, by virtue of its intertextuality and self-reflexivity, allows us to think critically about such attempts. And just as the mass-produced postcard points to, and constitutes, the commodification of nature, so is queer desire subject to problematic commodification. The movie's last scene reifies the difference between domesticated, commodified gay identity and undomesticated, non-commodified queer desire, juxtaposing Jack's glossy color postcard of Brokeback Mountain with Ennis's view of the "real world" outside his window.

Brokeback Mountain's presentation of nature as subject to ideological construction has important queer ecological implications. For one thing, if what we perceive as nature and the natural is not a given, then queerness's status as unnatural, and as *out of place in nature*, is cast into doubt as an inviolable truth. We might then say that *Brokeback Mountain* specifically indicts naturalization— the process by which institutions such as heterosexuality, whiteness, capitalism, and marriage are established as natural. It mourns the loss of queer identification with nature that comes about through the production of domestic heterosexuality as the ideal, as well as through the production of mainstream gay identity as a bid at that ideality. But it also recuperates queerness, defining it not as the opposite of nature, but as the excess of Nature.

The film's engagement with the concept of naturalization has academic/ intellectual implications, as well. As I have shown in my introduction, queer theory has long had a negative view of the natural. While sometimes understandable, this view has both precluded queer forms of environmentalism and occluded the queer environmentalism that does exist. But perhaps more importantly, it has failed to acknowledge those machinations that establish what counts as natural in the first place. We might consider, for example, José Esteban Muñoz's work on camouflage as a queer artistic medium that refuses "a certain natural order"; in writing specifically of Jim Hodges's work, he notes that "[a] natural representational order as restrictive directive is . . . redeployed as . . . artifice that disrupts the tyranny of nature as a coercive mechanism" (*Cruising Utopia* 140). In opposing nature and artifice, Muñoz takes that natural order as a given, as simply extant, rather than as produced through ideology or rhetoric. He thereby endorses the discriminatory alignment of the queer with the artificial and, by extension, the heterosexual with the natural. Moreover, he suggests, perhaps inadvertently, that nature *itself* is "tyrannical." A focus on naturalization, instead, makes for a queer approach to the natural world that is at once pragmatic, hopeful, and complex. *Brokeback Mountain* takes up this focus, tracing out, and then rewriting, an ideological genealogy that has come to rest on the idea of queerness as unnatural.

Conclusion

I have tried here to explicate an unacknowledged ecological message within one of the most, if not *the* most, well-known GLBTQI films in history: that queers should not forfeit their right to a positive relationship to the natural simply because monogamous, futurist, reproductive, domestic heterosexuality has been naturalized. *Brokeback* delivers this message in terms that are unique to the post-1960s era—including postmodern self-reflexivity and an understanding of social construction—while also militating against many of the developments of that era—including Reclamation and neoliberalism. This message is perhaps best understood when placed again against that of *Surf Party*. As that older film progresses, we learn that Skeet Wells, Terry's brother from Phoenix, is the head of a local surfing gang and that he is perceived by many as a no-good punk. Meanwhile, Len, the young surfer who warned Terry about parking her trailer on the beach, begins unofficially enforcing Sergeant Neal's efforts to clean up the beach of trash like Skeet after the sergeant threatens to ban surfing altogether (see figure 11). In leveling that threat, the sergeant observes to Len, "there isn't one legitimate surfer that's done anything about . . . the beer parties, [the] annoying [of] families, obscene language, dressing [changing clothes] on the beach, taking over the whole ocean." So, just as there is a "legitimate" way to be a non-heterosexual cowboy, or ranch hand, in *Brokeback Mountain*—to domesticate, privatize, and/or commodify your desires—there is a "legitimate" way to be a "Beach Cowboy" in *Surf Party*—to keep natural space safe for the private, domestic family. The irony of the term "legitimate surfer" is the same irony that queer theorists such as Michael Warner and Mariana Valverde have found in the concept of the "respectable homosexual."[20] But as those theorists have shown, such entities not only do exist, they are increasingly becoming the only viable mode of existence.

Thus what at first appears in *Surf Party* to be a tale of spontaneous teen rebellion turns out to be a tale of voluntary teen self-discipline. Here, we might recall both Ennis's paranoid existence under the panopticon and Jack's desire for a "calf-and-cow operation." That is to say, the kids of *Surf Party* are not interested in throwing off the authoritative regime that blocks their free access to nature and sexuality, but, rather, in finding their place in that authoritative regime. This becomes most clear in the film's second half, when the teenage characters move from questioning authority as embodied by the police, to policing each other. For example, when Terry's friend Sylvia, one of the three Phoenix girls, comes home from Skeet's house at 5 A.M., Terry asks if she was alone with Skeet. When Sylvia snaps, "Are you my mother?" Terry replies, "*Somebody* should be."

While Terry thus proves dedicated to tempering the rebelliousness of the very group with whom she ran away to the California coast, Len Marshal similarly steps up the do-gooding, blaming Skeet for the injury of a young man who was trying to get into the surf gang by "running the pier," or surfing between the pilings.

"Did you try and stop him? That would be taking responsibility," Len demands of Skeet.

"What responsibility?" Skeet sneers.

"They're threatening to close the beach," Len responds.

"There's other beaches," Skeet scoffs.

"The king doesn't fight. He moves, huh?" Len returns.

Figure 11. Sergeant Neal lectures Len Marshal at his surf shop in *Surf Party*. Twentieth Century Fox Film Corporation, 1964.

That line makes us think of Jack, considering his willingness to escape into a life of private domesticity with both Ennis and his wife Lureen. But it also resonates with the scene in *Brokeback Mountain* where Jack sings along to "King of the Road," the Roger Miller song that was a hit in 1964, the same year of *Surf Party*'s release. The lyrics of "King of the Road" center on the singer's decision to opt out of the strictures of polite society—as the rebellious teens of *Surf Party* initially hope to, and as Ennis actually does: "Third boxcar, midnight train / Destination . . . Bangor, Maine. / Old worn out suits and shoes, / I don't pay no union dues, / I smoke old stogies I have found / Short, but not too big around / I'm a man of means by no means / King of the road."

Len Marshal makes his stance vis-à-vis the public–private distinction, and vis-à-vis Skeet Wells in particular, explicit a few scenes later, declaring, "I believe in surfing. I think it's worth protecting." In other words, he understands public natural space as something that requires constant monitoring and restrictions to access, so that it may be free of undesirable elements—beer parties, obscene language, families being bothered. We might note at this point that Len, who runs the local surf shop, has the surname Marshal. Like Joe Aguirre, this figure of authority has a vested financial interest in the cleansing of the natural space in question. In fact, the film imagines virtually the same scenario that Ennis initially rails against in *Brokeback*, which I have identified as an example of his internalization of privatization efforts: the bikers he confronts at the fireworks show, just like the surfers to which Sergeant Neal refers, are drinking beer, using obscene language, and annoying families. But whereas Ennis's violently pro-domestic stance soon shifts, Len pursues the role of marshal with zeal until the very end. The film has him representing the first of the multiple options that *Brokeback* cites: to be straight in nature, as opposed to being queer in the city or queer in nature. In censuring Skeet Wells, Len Marshal wipes out the last possibility—re-installing the first in a form that *appears* to be righteous rebellion.

If it weren't already clear that *Surf Party*, just like *Brokeback Mountain*, is an account of queer cleansing and conformity—the difference of course being that the first idealizes that account and the second condemns it—we should consider the twist at the end of the first movie: Skeet Wells turns out to be a gigolo, not unlike the prostitutes Jack visits in Mexico. A party at what has appeared to be his bachelor pad is interrupted by the arrival of a much older wealthy woman who stalks into the bedroom, interrupting a canoodling Skeet, and declares, "This is MY home. The party is over, you'll have to go back to work. . . . You don't have many more years left in your profession. Or should I say, specialty?" (figures 12 and 13). Just as in *Brokeback*, a figure of economic authority has surveilled, and then pun-

Figures 12–13.
In Maury Dexter's
Surf Party, Skeet Wells
is humiliated when
his wealthy lover
arrives unexpectedly
to discover a
swinging party at
her home. Twentieth
Century Fox Film
Corporation, 1964.

ished, the coupling of two illicit lovers. And Skeet is thus revealed to be, just like Jack and Ennis, virtually penniless and homeless, with no land to claim as his own and no right to natural public space—as that which he has occupied, the beach, has been reestablished as heteronormative: family-friendly, culturally mainstream rather than countercultural, under constant surveillance, and open only to people of the leisure class, not squatters, homeless people, or other derelicts. We should recall here that the presence of the girls' "home," the trailer, was the initial problem in the film. Living on the beach under such conditions is bad, per Surf Party, because it opposes the middle-class domesticity toward which one should be striving. But lying on the beach can be good, because it marks that natural space as an exclusive site of middle-class leisure. (Recall, again, that Ennis lives in his trailer for years, through the very last scene of *Brokeback Mountain*; on the other hand, the girls' trailer occupation of the beach lasts one night.) The only thing that could be better would be to own a beach house, or to own the beach *itself*—making its privatization officially complete.

The film's concluding events confirm *Surf Party*'s adherence to these philosophies. Sergeant Neal gives Skeet a lift to the bus depot, where he is to buy a ticket back to Phoenix. Meanwhile, Terry and her friends head back to Phoenix with their trailer in tow. What seems to be an abrupt ending—the budding romance of Terry and Len is never consummated, for example—perfectly suits the film's logic when it comes to sexuality and natural space. Potential delinquents have been set on the straight and narrow, and the beach has been sufficiently cleared of riff-raff. The principals of the film, except for the new marshal in town, Len, have all disappeared from the space that was so hotly contested. The beach of *Surf Party* thus starts to look like the public parks devoid of humans after a crackdown on gay cruising, or the empty bus benches that have been designed to discourage homeless people from sleeping on them:[21] its functionality lies not (just) in its exclusive use by those in power, but in how it broadcasts the undesirability of the queer: the unmarried, the sex worker, the polyamorous, the poor.

In opposing the ideology of *Surf Party*, the film that its opposite-sex couple pays to watch while snuggling in public, *Brokeback Mountain* asks us to imagine a visibility that is not the result of surveillance, but that is also not a commodity. While I have argued that Lee's film redefines the tragedy of homophobia in terms of privatization and environmental exploitation, we can also see that it works to rewrite the plot of *Surf Party* from a queer, even optimistic, perspective—despite the fact that it has no musical numbers or party scenes and that it constitutes a heavy 135 minutes as opposed to a breezy 67. Whereas *Surf Party* establishes public natural space as intrinsically heteronormative, *Brokeback Mountain* calls for queer desire that is both public and natural—that is, unruly, unmanaged, spontaneous, and free. Perhaps it is in that drive-in scene, then, that the film actually becomes most self-reflexive. Ennis, as a character in the film *Brokeback Mountain*, watches the film that *Brokeback Mountain* is rewriting. In *Surf Party* and in his own life, he will watch the countercultural elements of society acquiesce to the demand for a "pure" (that is, commodified, heterosexualized, white, middle-class) nature. But unlike "King" of the beach Skeet Wells, or "King of the Road" Jack Twist, Ennis will decline to move.

5 Attack of the Queer Atomic Mutants

The Ironic Environmentalism of Shelley Jackson's *Half Life*

> It didn't matter if the Arms Race ground to a halt, if a bomb was never used on a foreign country again, for the U.S. government had begun a war against the people and land here long ago and was going to lay siege to them until the half-life of the longest-lived radioactive elements was multiplied many times over.
>
> —Rebecca Solnit, *Savage Dreams: The Landscape Wars of the American West*

> An ironic ecology . . ., rather than either dominating or venerating nature, would . . . value and proliferate "impure" and vernacular mixings of nature and culture, new shared meanings and practices, new ways of dwelling with non-humans . . . Its defining legacy would be neither the nuclear power station, nor the nature reserve, but a living, evolving plurality of shared forms of life.
>
> —Bronislaw Szerszynski, "The Post-Ecologist Condition"

Since the 1940s, Western cultural producers have imagined myriad new organisms that U.S. nuclear technology might produce, from giant ants (1954's *Them!*), to shrinking humans (1957's *The Incredible Shrinking Man*), to creatures that steal human brains and spinal cords (1958's *The Fiend without a Face*).[1] Shelley Jackson's 2006 novel *Half Life* imagines a politicized minority population of conjoined twins. One of these twins, Nevada-born twenty-eight-year-old San Franciscan Nora Olney, serves as the novel's ostensible narrator. We are privy to her innermost thoughts and neuroses as her madcap quest for the removal of her comatose twin, Blanche, unspools. In the affirming sociopolitical world of *Half Life*—constantly ridiculed by the witty, sardonic Nora—medical intervention for conjoinment is abhorred, not to mention against the law. Nora's removal of Blanche would thus be understood as a murder of the most politically incorrect kind.

Half Life might be described as typically postmodern in several ways. For one thing, its form is intertextual and multivocal: it consists of a main text, Nora's self-conscious account of her quest, interspersed with items that she collects for her "Siamese Twin Reference Manual," including fliers for "twofer" film festivals, declarations made by twofer political subgroups, and lyrics to popular songs featuring conjoined characters. The novel also features incessant wordplay; frequent allusions to popular culture, literature, and critical theory; and various academic and political in-jokes. For instance, one page of the Reference Manual features a list of groanworthy titles from a twofer bookstore, including *Altar Ego: My Twin Took Holy Orders*, *Fat in Spite of Myself: When One Twin Overeats*, and *I Love Me! [and You]*. Similarly, Nora's cataloging of her roommate's bookshelf turns up *Autogeminophilia*, an allusion to Ray Blanchard's now widely challenged "autogynephilia" theory, which holds that male-to-female transgender people are sexually attracted to the idea of themselves as women; and *The Geminist Manifesto*, a pun on "Gemini," or the Twins, as well as on Marx's *The Communist Manifesto* and the term "feminist" (91). In yet another inspired move, the novel cites literary critics' claims that Shakespeare was two-headed (245–46)—a reference to real-life critics' attempts to claim Shakespeare as queer, as female, as a corporate author, et cetera.[2] Jackson's targets, then, range from the progressive and intellectual (the cultural institution of the feminist bookstore, Marxism, feminism, New Historicism) to the popular and profane (self-help and reality-TV discourse). Given the frequency of these parodic allusions, we might say that *Half Life*'s dominant affective mode is irony. But the novel is also ironic on the highest of narrative levels, insofar as the main character is a minority striving against a social structure not because it is oppressive to her, but, rather, because it is accepting. Perhaps more importantly, her efforts to escape such acceptance by becoming a "singleton" are eventually undercut: not only does Nora never rid herself of her sister Blanche, but Nora's narrative voice begins to blur with that of the ostensibly unconscious Blanche. *Half Life* thus ridicules its own structure, that of the hero's quest for freedom.

Perhaps most obvious in terms of postmodern irony is *Half Life*'s queerness. The world of the conjoined twin populace is humorously modeled on queer communities and their politics, while Nora is also described as queer (she's a lesbian with a history of sleeping with men). Conjoinment itself, as I show in the second section of this chapter, also has significant queer resonance: throughout U.S. history, it has been paralleled with non-normative gender and sexuality, and has posed the same kind of categorical crises as have queer desires. In this sense, conjoinment is not unlike transgenderism: as an embodiment, it thwarts normative expectations for sexual activity, romantic relationships, and reproduction. *Half Life* thus brings dis/ability into the picture along with sexuality, gender, gender identity, race, and class. Finally, *Half Life*'s queerness inheres in the novel's narration. When what seems to be Nora's voice blurs into an ambiguous perspective, the reader is thereby forced to question how normative, stable identities are achieved. Eric Savoy's observation on queer irony is particularly helpful here; as he notes, "[i]f the queer text is necessarily double-voiced, then its most prehensile rhetorical mode is irony" (134). In terms of narration, and in terms of its conjunction of text and intertext, *Half Life* speaks in a voice that is certainly double, if not multiple.

Because of its relentless irony, the novel is often difficult to take seriously—and, for some, to enjoy.[3] Indeed, it's the most "unserious" work I treat in this book, not to mention the most fantastical. One might then presume that it has no real political thrust, much less an environmentalist one. And in fact, *Half Life* has not been recognized in critical scholarship as having any significant ecological investments. Bronislaw Szerszynski's work on environmentalist rhetoric offers a possible explanation for this reception: he observes that "[e]nvironmental politics has . . . been dominated by a moral earnestness that has gone hand in hand with its over-estimation of the epistemic power of science, and by a neglect of the way that meanings and values about nature are not just socially situated and partial but also shot through with ironies and aporias" (351–52). In other words, irony and sincerity have been largely understood as mutually exclusive, at least from an environmentalist perspective. Simply put, *Half Life* just doesn't look or sound like environmental literature. But I maintain that it effectively takes on a very serious set of issues: environmental degradation and its attendant social ills, specifically those associated with the real-life history of nuclear testing in the American Southwest. And I argue that irony is crucial to, even constitutive of, the novel's ecological project. This chapter thus questions the idea that, to perform effective ecological work, one has to be "taken seriously." It seeks to expand our understanding of what environmental literature can be, considering that its hallmarks have long been earnestness, sincerity, and even self-righteousness and sanctimony.

This chapter, as does this book on the whole, participates in a larger, long-running debate around the ability of postmodern and poststructuralist modes to do "real" political work.[4] One of the major questions framing this debate is, if postmodernists and poststructuralists question reality,

how can they care about the "real world"? Alex Callinicos, for instance, has
defined "postmodern irony" as "the knowing and detached appropriation
of experiences by an elite that regards itself as too sophisticated for *simple
pleasures and unqualified commitments*" (205, my emphasis)—among which,
the enjoyment of nature and environmentalist action could presumably be
counted. Others have asked, if postmodernists and poststructuralists reject
identity, how can they address discrimination based on identity? Arlene
Stein, for instance, has complained that queer theorists fail to account
for "*real*, persistent structural differences in style, ideology, and access to
resources among men and women" (50, my emphasis). Considering how
contemporary queer novels and films, not to mention queer theory and
sensibility, tend to embrace modes such as camp, irony, and postmodern-
ism/poststructuralist skepticism, it's no wonder that fictions like those in
my archive are rarely read as having notable activist investments, least of
all environmental ones.

But recently, scholars such as Mariana Valverde have effectively undercut
such assumptions about apoliticism and ironic/postmodern modes. Valverde's essay "Justice as Irony: A Queer Ethical Experiment" acknowledges
the claim, attributed to Slavoj Žižek, that "many communities around the
world have stopped believing not just in this or that ideology but even in
the very possibility of a firm Truth." However, she argues, "that doesn't
mean that we cynics, we postmoderns, . . . we queer theorists, etc., are in a
position to actually make do without the *form* of ideology. We are all bound
to act as if subjects existed, as if freedom of the will existed . . . This necessary contradiction can be decried in tragic terms. But it also can be seen as
humorous, more specifically, as a permanent irony" ("Justice as Irony" 89).
To put it in the terms of this book's project, acting on firm beliefs (such
as that environmental degradation is wrong, or that it is happening in the
first place) while maintaining deep skepticism (say, about the fact that the
environment is a self-evident "real thing" rather than a constructed reality) is
deeply ironic, but also potentially crucial. Such a stance opposes the work of
queer theorists such as Lee Edelman, who locates queer irony in the refusal
of all political positions; as he maintains, "politics, however radical the
means by which specific constituencies attempt to produce a more desirable
social order, remains, at its core, conservative insofar as it works to *affirm* a
structure, to *authenticate* a social order, which it then intends to transmit to
the future in the form of its inner Child" (*No Future* 3, emphasis original).
As I outline in my introduction, this take on futurism makes not just queer
politics, but queer *ecological* politics, impossible—especially considering
how environmentalism is future-oriented at its core.

While irony inheres in the gap between those two modes of affect—sincerity and skepticism—Valverde also recognizes it as a defining feature of political action itself. She claims that "when political movements lose their irony, their sense of humor, their capacity to see that . . . [they] ought not to take their own truths too seriously . . . [they] become uncomfortably similar to the powers they seek to challenge." Thus "[i]rony . . . may be an important resource . . . to constantly remind us of the profound gap between law and justice" (86). I would add that a sense of irony may also allow us to recognize the hypocrisy inherent in many types of injustice; we might recall, for instance, Greta Gaard's observation that homophobia depends upon the belief that queers are "unnatural," while those who hold such beliefs frequently show little concern for the natural world. Perhaps, then, the most chilling aspect of something like anti-environmentalist George W. Bush's claim that "[m]arriage cannot be severed from its cultural, religious and *natural roots* without weakening the good influence of society"[5] (my emphasis) is its disinterest in its own irony. *Half Life* shows us, instead, how irony and contradiction might be enthusiastically deployed for ethical purposes.

In this chapter, I explore how *Half Life*'s ironic, postmodern, and queer features model ethical approaches to the problems of environmental health and justice invoked by its Atomic Age setting. I show how its choice of conjoinment as the nuclear-engineered mutation of concern is a queer ecological one, how its ironic stance toward environmental destruction constitutes a progressive kind of pastoralism, and how the novel's complex mode of narration allows it to enact the breakdown of human sovereignty—the mode that has historically informed domination of the non-human. I thus offer *Half Life* as a model for how effective ecological responses might emerge not *in spite of*, but *through*, an entrenched irony.

What Nuclear Technology Has Joined Together: The Making of the Queer Mutant

Half Life's explanations for the conjoined population are as wacky as the scientific montages found in *Them!* and *The Incredible Shrinking Man*. But they also intervene poignantly in the environmental histories associated with nuclear technology. One news source archived in Nora's "Siamese Twin Reference Manual" observes that "It is generally believed that the dramatic growth in the conjoined twin population worldwide was caused by radioactive fallout. The assertion is supported statistically by the distribution, both temporal (mid 20th century) and geographical (advanced industrial nations), of the first wave of births" (47). But as this theory is "not supported by lab results[,] . . . some groups . . . aver that [twinning] has nothing to do with [radiation]," believing instead that "it was a deeper, more metaphysical split that took place when the first nuclear bomb was exploded at the Trinity site on July 16, 1945" (47). In other words, the novel presents conjoinment as either the material result of nuclear testing, or as the metaphysical result of such testing's physical and psychic tolls—or both. Considering the otherwise fantastical text's gestures toward real-life history—for example, the date cited in the quotation above is that of the actual Trinity site test—the reader would likely understand these tolls as encompassing everything from the deaths of 120,000 or more Japanese civilians at the end of World War II; to the irradiation of Western Shoshone and other Native American communities in Nevada, New Mexico, and Utah; to myriad cancers contracted by Nevada Test Site workers during the Cold War; to untold numbers of related illnesses in the near and distant future.[6] Such things cannot be adequately represented by classical narrative form, as I have suggested in Chapter 3, nor through a strictly realist framework. Thus I would argue that queer and/or postmodern form, and the queer, postmodern form of *Half Life* in particular, is not only not apolitical, but in fact ideally suited to taking on concrete political issues such as the environmental injustices induced by nuclear testing.

But *Half Life* presents a twist on doomsaying accounts of nuclear technology. A document in the Reference Manual reports that "[i]n 1951, recognizing the need for a national activity of penance, a despondent American government began bombing itself. . . . The spot they chose for the National Penitence Ground or Proving Ground or, later, Test Site . . . was Nevada" (154). Nora's grandmother reports how the humans, animals, and landscape of Nevada were devastated: "The Sadness was supposed to be a secret, but when the wind was blowing northeast, as it generally was, it told stories. (. . . 'America is sad. Iodine-131, cesium-137, strontium-90.') . . . Some farmers inquired of the Atomic Energy Commission why, please, their lambs were born with their hearts on the outside of their bodies? 'Malnutrition,' said the Atomic Energy Commission. Hair fell out. 'Nerves.' Also teeth. 'Don't forget to floss.' Skin lesions. 'Sunburn.' Breast cancer, bone cancer, thyroid, liver, lung cancer. 'It's worrying about fallout that makes you sick, not fallout itself'" (156).

American Sadness, in the view of many of the novel's characters, is a tragic missed opportunity for true penance. But it allows Jackson to rewrite the history of nuclear testing in the United States by highlighting its domestic effects, and to rewrite the Atomic Age mutant narrative to explicitly implicate the U.S. government—not to mention the privatization of environmental-justice concerns. After all, the government's position that "It's worrying about fallout that makes you sick, not fallout itself" sounds an awful lot like the mantras of privatization found in Todd Haynes's *Safe*, including, "The only person that can make you get sick is you."

Indeed, Jackson's novel invokes the fact that the U.S. government has never officially apologized for the loss of life in Hiroshima and Nagasaki, and that it was not until 2010 that the United States sent a representative to the annual memorial ceremony at Hiroshima. And it also reminds us of how compensation for U.S. citizens and workers affected by nuclear fallout has been tragically slow in coming.[7] The novel thereby responds to narratives such as *Them!* and *The Incredible Shrinking Man*, which, although of course ridiculous, quite seriously pin responsibility for mutation not on the U.S. government but on individual mad scientists—who in turn stand in for communists, Russians, homosexuals, and other threats to the American way of life.[8] In such texts, the question is not "Is nuclear technology safe?" or "Is its deployment ethical?" but, rather, "Is it in the right hands?" Imagining a scenario in which nuclear fallout becomes a question of domestic responsibility for the United States, *Half Life* obviates the xenophobia and American exceptionalism, as well as the attendant reckless competitiveness, that have driven developments in nuclear technology and the representation thereof.

Of course, by all of *Half Life*'s accounts, the queer configuration that is conjoinment is inseparable from the environmental and social devastation wrought by nuclear technology—but, in another one of the novel's ironic twists, citizens understand conjoinment not as a horror on the order of giant ants or shrinking men, but as a blessing, an instructive phenomenon. One group insists that the aforementioned metaphysical split is "no accident, but the essential next stage in the spiritual evolution of a species finally advancing beyond self-interest" (47), while the group Mutatis Mutandis and the League of Mutant Voters' Joint Position Statement puts it succinctly,: "Radioactivity leads to mutation, mutation leads to The New Human (Twofer), the New Human will lead us to a peaceful tomorrow" (111). Even more boldly, the "Siamists" "believe we should revere the waste, and the Penitence Ground and the trinite and the fallout . . . as the sacred *relics* of the birth of the new world" (105, my emphasis). In other words, *Half Life*'s citizens learn to simultaneously criticize the government's deployment of nuclear technology and embrace its fallout, for how it provides a different model for the future—one attuned to interdependence and interrelationships among the human, the non-human, and those who fall in between. In thus depicting the embrace of mutation, and in making our experience of reading dependent upon a mutant, and queer, narrator, the novel rejects the fundamental premise of most classic Atomic Age texts, in which mutation, the abnormal body, and, by extension, queerness, are categorically horrifying. This depiction also complicates the oppressive view that queerness is a postmodern disease, with transgenderism the result of technological experimentation (as I discuss in Chapter 2) and homosexuality the result of decadent urbanity (as I discuss in Chapter 4). Instead, Jackson imagines a love of the "post-natural" that does not entail a rejection of the natural—nor even a distinct break from it.

Jackson's inclusion of the twofer in this imaginative model allows her to offer an alarmist environmentalist vision that does not rely on normative values around gender, sex, sexuality, and embodiment. Noël Sturgeon has written extensively on such alarmism, studying the "association continually created between homosexuality, evil, and environmental destruction" in pop cultural texts, which she finds to be "coupled with an anxiety about the successful reproduction of white, middle-class, nuclear family form that is presented as 'normal' and 'natural' without any critique of its complicity in the overconsumption of corporate products in an environmentally destructive system" (263). But these anti-queer anxieties are not relegated to pop cultural texts such as the Atomic Age mutant narrative; they appear throughout scientific and political discourse to this day. For instance, Theo Colborn, Dianne Dumanoski, and John Peter Meyer's *Our Stolen Future: Are We Threatening Our Fertility, Intelligence, and Survival? A Scientific Detective Story* (1997) mobilizes fears about decreasing male virility and the decline of the nuclear family, and abhorrence of feminine boys and masculine girls, in order to sound the alarm about environmental toxins. The authors report that "[w]ildlife studies vividly demonstrate that [synthetic] chemicals have the power to derail sexual development, creating intersex individuals that are neither male nor female" (xvi), and they also point to so-called gay gulls as bearing disturbing implications for human development. In one passage—which an ironic environmentalist stance would allow us to see as inadvertently humorous—the authors report that "the *husband-and-wife team* [of George and Molly Hunt, UC Irvine researchers] did establish that . . . female gulls were setting up *housekeeping* together and producing . . . nests with extra eggs" (5, my emphasis). While the Hunts theorized that this configuration might have an evolutionary advantage, Colborn et al. see it as another piece of evidence for the decline of the human as we know it. One of their conclusions, then, is that "it is particularly important that women minimize the consumption of animal fat *from birth until the end of* their childbearing years. They bear the next generation and the responsibility to protect their children from contamination" (214, emphasis original).

While I would not argue the point that the work of Colborn, Dumanoski, and Meyer points to an increasingly, frighteningly toxified world, its gender and sexual politics are highly questionable. They subtly (and falsely) link social changes to environmental changes—suggesting the likes of same-sex marriage as the result of a degraded natural world, and advancing a kind of pastoral in which nature could be restored along with the nuclear family. Thereby, as Giovanna Di Chiro argues, they establish a kind of "eco(hetero)normativity" that draws on homophobic, transphobic fears to stir public action (202). Moreover, we should note that the claim that women "bear the next generation and the responsibility to protect their children from contamination" chauvinistically charges individual women, and not families, neighborhoods, consumers, or corporations, with maintaining the health of the environment.

We can see here the importance of texts that are both ecological *and* queer, *and* ironically minded: in *Half Life*, the environmental "wake-up call" is one that depends not upon homophobia, transphobia, or heterosexism, but upon the queer. *Half Life* rolls its eyes at the scare tactics of Colborn et al., boldly linking queerness to environmental degradation, but in an entirely different way than those scholars have. As I have outlined, it is not the queer configurations that nuclear contamination produces that the novel raises as a point of concern—but, rather, the other costs to human and non-human health and well-being. In fact, those in *Half Life*'s fictional world locate the response to ecological degradation in its very queer byproduct's ontology: a recognition of the inherent connectivity of all life. Simply put, ecological degradation emerges from a failure to recognize or respect human and non-human connectivity, while in turn the twofer models such connectivity. Rather than the opposite of environmental health, or a product of postmodern society run amok, queers are, instead, at the forefront of the call for ecologically minded action. The novel thus rewrites not just the history of the Atomic Age, but the history of contemporary American environmental thought, such that it culminates in a queer relationship to the non-human world.

Here, Jackson demonstrates that it is possible to think both queerly—in questioning norms of embodiment and sexuality—and futuristically. The "Siamists," the League of Mutant Voters, and "Mutatis Mutandis," however ridiculous they may sound, find no contradiction between their radical social agenda and their forward-looking ecological agenda ("the

New Human will lead us to a peaceful tomorrow" [111].) Or, perhaps we should say, these activist figures rejoice in that contradiction, *enabled* by their willingness to sound ridiculous. This depiction has several additional implications in terms of queer theory, ecocriticism, queer politics, and environmental politics. For one, it offers an alternative to the theoretical concept of "queer time," the contrarian mode that focuses on the fleeting and the ephemeral at the expense of the future. In my introduction, I show how "queer time" precludes queer investment in sustainability, that mode so crucial to environmentalism. And indeed, futurity and sustainability are crucial mindsets when it comes to nuclear technology—the results of which are often unpredictable, and the effects of which can ramify not just in the present but for thousands of years hence; both the first epigraph for this chapter and *Half Life*'s own title invoke this disconcerting fact. *Half Life*'s futurity also circumvents traditional pastoral thought, which idealizes a long-gone, pristine nature. This circumvention is important, because such visions cannot accommodate anything like the vibrant queer society that the twofers in the novel inaugurate. In other words, Jackson suggests that we can't wish to return to an earlier moment in time, a time before, say, nuclear technology laid waste to the earth, because that would be a time before queer bodies and desires could circulate in relative safety. Thus any queer critique of nuclear technology, or of other forces with potential for serious ecological-social impact, has to be both anti-nostalgic and futurist, concerned with the present and forward-looking.

In this sense, it is important to consider *Half Life*'s status as speculative fiction. It is futuristic insofar as it draws on science-fiction tropes, and insofar as it concerns itself with long-term ecological impact. But as an alternate-reality narrative, it is also attuned to the present (or at least *a* present). We might then conclude that its very generic ontology has environmental implications: it asks that we see our present-day actions as meaningfully linked to possible futures—that we speculate, or imagine, that we are connected to beings in a different dimension than ours.

The Queerness of Conjoinment

Thus far, I have focused on the idea that conjoinment is a clear, and queer, sign that humans in the novel (and, we might say, in the "real world") need an understainding of how treatment of the earth impacts human life and vice versa. But how, exactly, is the conjoined queer? To begin with, the twofer communities of *Half Life* are overtly modeled on queer communities. Much of the novel's action takes place in San Francisco's Castro District—in reality, the city's historically gay neighborhood, while, in the novel, the epicenter of twofer activism. Jackson parodies the identity politics associated with these kinds of queer communities, such as the move toward inclusive, non-gendered language: in addition to "twofer," the conjoined population has introduced "tyou" as a form of address, and "everytwo" as a substitution for "everyone." This coinage resonates humorously with real-life feminist and transgender activists' attempts to popularize "hir" and "ze" for "his" and "her" and "she" and "him," respectively.[9] Jackson also delves into approaches to GLBTQI history that have been widely debated among activists and academics. One source within the novel notes that "Revisionist scholars . . . claim that a sizeable population of twofers has existed throughout history ('theirstory')" (47). Similarly, real-life activists have reclaimed figures from history as lesbian, gay, bisexual, or transgender in order to legitimate contemporary GLBTQI life—which many theorists and historians have maligned as problematically ahistorical, if not, in many cases, wishful thinking.[10]

But the allegory extends much further. Jackson's particular choice of "mutant" invokes a long history of parallels between queerness and conjoinment. To begin with, many medical historians and scholars have noted that conjoinment is particularly "like" being queer, whereas singular corporeality is particularly "like" being straight. David Clark and Catherine Myser observe that "the compulsion to assume a properly singular corporeality—like singular [normative] sexuality—has a tremendous, even killing force in our culture" (350). They argue that "[s]ingular corporeality can be usefully compared to the category of 'sex,' since it operates as 'a principle of intelligibility for human beings . . . no human being can be taken to be human, can be recognized *as* human unless that human being is fully and coherently' in possession of its 'own' body" (351). Here, Clark and Myser echo Judith Butler's claims about gender as human legibility. Likewise, the novel's protagonist frequently reflects upon her status as less than human, referencing, for instance, political campaigns designed to "cu[t] the twofer vote in half" (137).

While being conjoined is like being queer, the converse seems to be true, as well. In hir memoir *Exile and Pride: Disability, Queerness, and Liberation*, disabled transgender activist Eli Clare observes that "[q]ueer people deal with gawking all the time: when we hold hands in public, defy gender boundaries and norms, insist on recognition for our relationships and families. . . . [B]oth [queer and disabled people] have been considered freaks of nature" (96). Clare also notes that federal and state regulations make it difficult for disabled people to marry, have children, and keep those children—reminding us that struggles for marriage equality and adoption rights are not unique to GBLTQI individuals. Ze shows us, as this book also hopes to, that sexuality cannot be understood apart from categories such as gender, ability, class, and race.

More specifically, being conjoined excites fears of excessive, public sexuality, just as being queer does. Allison Pingree reports that, when famed conjoined twin Violet Hilton, sister of Daisy, sought to marry her beau in the 1930s United States, marriage licenses were refused "'on moral grounds;' 'on ground that the bride is a Siamese twin;' on 'the question of morality and decency;' as 'a matter of public policy'" ("The 'Exceptions'" 181). As Pingree explains, "the twins' particular form of aberration perfectly embodies what many by then had come to fear: . . . that heterosexual, companionate marriage might not be the only form of intimate 'bonding' between two people; and that the division between public and private might not be so clear after all" ("The 'Exceptions'" 183). Alice Dreger, likewise, notes that "conjoinment is socially troubling . . . [because] it makes public a physical intimacy that usually marks only private relations" (19). As I have described in detail in the previous chapter, queer sexuality is perceived as excessive, and excessively public, in and of itself—a perception that, ironically, links it to non-human nature. And in fact, we might note that conjoinment itself constitutes a queer pairing, insofar as it always entails the union of two people of the same sex, who possess "extra," or "excessive," body parts. Nora corroborates these perceptions, recounting how her conjoinment has garnered her much unwanted attention; her dates "freely propose strange [sexual] formations involving Blanche" (42), and she wonders if anyone is really interested in her or just in the prospect of a built-in ménage-à-trois.

We should also acknowledge that conjoinment has often been compared to marriage, but in ways that reveal anxiety over the status of heterosexual unions. Pingree maintains that a major problem with the Hilton twins was how they "replicat[ed], literaliz[ed], and thus supplant[ed] the marriage contract" ("The 'Exceptions'" 183). She also notes that critics of the New Woman "symbolize[d] domestic and marital transgression through the corporeal anomaly of conjoined twins." For instance, "in 1928, Henry Carey published an essay in *Harper's* claiming that 'woman's emancipation' was a 'threat to family life.'" He titled this piece "This Two-Headed Monster—The [New] Family" ("The 'Exceptions'" 176). Interestingly, Nora's "Siamese Twin Reference Manual" includes, among other documents, a waiver from the underground organization she approaches for separation surgery, and we see that she has checked the box labeled "irreconcilable differences" as her justification—a phrase, of course, best known for its appearance in divorce law. Elsewhere, Nora at once acknowledges the equivalence of conjoinment and sexual coupling, and opposes its usual normative deployment, noting, "couples are always monstrous. Everyone senses this and grows uneasy in their company. Nobody likes to watch the blending of things that should be separate" (63). That is, while she despises her own twoferism, it seems she despises the privileging of monogamous, dyadic romantic relationships even more.

But conjoinment is not just an allegory for queerness, or vice versa. The two "conditions" appear alongside each other within the novel: as Nora declares, "I was the lesbian, not Blanche" (43). And San Francisco's Castro District is home in the novel not just to twofers, but to queers, and to those who occupy both categories. And of course, just as conjoinment and queerness intersect in the novel, so do they in real life. For one, scholars have noted that heterosexism and general anxieties about queerness directly affect the treatment of conjoinment by medical professionals and the media. Dreger cites a 2002 *USA Today* article that reports, "*the moment* the team of more than forty doctors and nurses at UCLA . . . completely separated the heads of . . . one-year-old . . . twin girls Maria de Jesus and Maria Teresa, neurosurgeon Jorge Lazareff paused and spoke to the assembled room: ' . . . We now have two weddings to go to'" (62, emphasis original). Similarly, Clark and Myser quote a 1995 PBS documentary that observes, "[Dao, one conjoined twin] will require extensive reconstructive surgery to her bladder and colon, but today's procedure will leave her with a complete set of reproductive organs. If she survives, like Duan, she will be able to have children when she grows up." According to "this utilitarian calculus," Clark and Myser argue, "social productivity and re-productivity are interchangeable values" (347). Much has also been written about the "original" Siamese twins, Chang and Eng, whose fecundity shocked moral sensibilities, per Pingree and Dreger, and, according to Cynthia Wu, "alluded to non-normative, non-Christian sexual practices" (33). (The brothers were married to a pair of white sisters and had twenty-two children between them.)

So what does it mean for the novel to have conjoinment *coexist with*, and not just *stand in for*, queerness? What does it mean to acknowledge that queerness *intersects* conjoinment, rather than just paralleling it? Some critics have taken this shuttling between fantasy and reality, allegory and literalism to be a defining feature of the text's postmodernism; Steven Shaviro notes that the novel is "'postmodern' in the . . . sense that it . . . speaks unresolvable multiplicities with one voice. We move, in a single paragraph, from, say, a description of . . . the . . . sparse vegetation of the desert . . . to pure linguistic play, to outright, florid hallucination: and none of these is marked out from the others, they all share the same degree of actuality and presence within the world or body of the text."[11] I want to propose, further, that this

style is indicative of the novel's version of queer ecology. For one thing, the
presence of familiar political realities subtends the clever allegory, and vice
versa, allowing the novel to hover at all times between sincerity and skepticism. Indeed, for its potential for puns and parody, Half Life demonstrates
through the trope of the conjoined twin a deep concern for the fate of the
non-normative body—which, as I have suggested, is often used as evidence
for, or even framed as a cause of, environmental degradation. The novel's
fictional world, in which the disabled person is pressured not to conform,
and in which medicine has gone underground, illustratively inverts our
present world—in which the drive toward medical intervention and normalization is incredibly powerful. But in literalizing queerness even as she
allegorizes it, Jackson also pushes beyond the work of those postmodern,
poststructuralist ecocritics who suggest that we might think of the environment like how we think of sex—as constructed and yet material.[12] No
experience can be reduced to mere allegory or point of comparison in Half
Life, but nor is any experience totally stripped of symbolic meaning. This
logical economy is of a piece with queer ecology's innovative proposal:
that the queer is not just like the natural, or vice versa, but that the two are
interrelated conceptually and materially. The twofer of Half Life embodies
this insight.

Perhaps more obviously, the novel's interest in interrelationship also
allows it to draw attention to the complex overlapping of categories such
as race, class, gender, sexuality, ability, embodiment, and immigration
status—what feminist and critical race studies scholar Kimberlé Crenshaw
has termed "intersectionality." Perhaps the most political/critical aspect of
Half Life's diegesis in this sense is its awareness of how often the (white)
queer—be it those with non-normative genders or desires, or those with two
heads—has the potential to acquiesce to the status quo. For instance, the
novel references the processes by which conjoinment might be normalized
at the expense of other minorities; at one point, Nora discloses that "[w]ith
two heads you don't walk by the projects. The inhabitants were notoriously
peeved that yet another minority had edged them out for help and housing,
due to better lobbyists, better connections, and fatter pocketbooks. The rise
of the twofer . . . had thrust the singleton poor even further down the lad-
der" (53). The novel thus distinguishes between two levels of conjoinment
(radical and dedicated to social justice, and mainstream and dedicated to
assimilation), the way queer theory distinguishes between being "gay" and
being "queer." And it also suggests that, while Nora may be a minority in
terms of embodiment, she is the majority in terms of race and class. I have
just suggested in Chapter 4 that the latter distinction plays out in ecological

terms, with the "queer" becoming "gay" and giving up claims to natural space in the process. *Half Life* dramatizes the implications of this distinction, while reminding us that non-normativity is not enough, from a queer ecological perspective; one must recognize the multiplicity of experiences of injustice, and one cannot depend upon the oppression of another group for one's own liberation. Considering that, in our own current world, same-sex marriage has become the celebrity cause *du jour*, while black Americans have meanwhile slipped further into poverty with little public outcry, the humorous image of the twofer proves to be a potent allegorical figure indeed.[13]

"The Desert Is Not Easy to Love": Empathy and the "Ugly" Landscape

At the same time that the novel stages the intersection of multiple identities, it also mocks the possibility of a stable identity (and, self-reflexively, mocks that mocking). Such anti-identitarian mocking is a trademark of poststructuralist frameworks such as queer theory. And it has allowed or at least accompanied the development of categories such as transgenderism, wherein individuals identify with a gender other than the one assigned to them at birth, and "straight queers"—individuals who are heterosexual in practice but aligned politically or socially with GLBTQI or otherwise non-normative lifestyles.[14] In addition to the novel's ultimate refusal to distinguish between Blanche and Nora (discussed further in this chapter's last section), it gives us a character who humorously troubles her given identity: Nora's roommate, an experimental filmmaker and pornographer named Audrey who was born a "singleton" but feels cognitively and philosophically as if she has a conjoined twin. Audrey's self-applied label of "twofer-identified" reminds us of the complex, sincere, and yet ripe-for-parody designations that have proliferated over the past several decades, including not just "transgender" and "straight queer," but "woman-identified woman," "male lesbian," and "womyn-born womyn."

At one point, Audrey insists to Nora that "a blurry identity isn't as rare in nature as you seem to think" (73). She hereby reconciles the queer with the natural and wryly participates in the kind of reclamation that we've seen from scholars such as evolutionary biologist Joan Roughgarden, whose 2004 book *Evolution's Rainbow* reports on a wide array of "homosexual" and "transgender" behavior among animals. But Audrey's wryness, and the irreverent tone of the passage overall, allows her to still observe the caveat of another evolutionary biologist, Marlene Zuk, that "using information about animal behavior to justify social or political ideology is wrong"

(177), or at least problematic.[15] The exchange between Audrey and Nora proceeds quite hilariously: "'Don't you remember the lantern fish?' 'I do not remember the lantern fish' [Nora replies]. . . . 'The man lantern fish is small and basically helpless. He starves to death if he doesn't run into a woman lantern fish. When he does, he . . . sinks his teeth into her side . . . His jaw begins to dissolve. Her skin starts to grow over him, covering his eyes, his gills—' 'Gross!' '—until finally her bloodstream breaks into his and her blood starts circulating in his veins.' We were both silent. 'He is no better than an appendage,' she added unnecessarily" (74).

This passage serves to remind us that, while we speak of human gender and sexuality as constructs, we often think of nature, the non-human, as simply there, and as immune from construction. At the same time, while we might recognize that the human and the non-human are equally subject to oppressive construction, and equally interconnected, we have to admit that the non-human exceeds, and acts independently of, the grasp of human consciousness. If nothing else, the novel highlights the ridiculousness of referring to a "man lantern fish."

I want to propose that this specific facet of *Half Life*'s queerness—its troubling of stable identity—is crucial to an ecological mindset. To begin with, I have suggested throughout *Strange Natures* that empathy for the non-human is a key element of environmentalism, and of queer environmentalism more specifically. An unstable or "loose" identity allows for such empathy, enabling one to imaginatively inhabit other positions—the non-human, the sub-human, and, as in the proposed legal rubric cited in *Half Life*, those considered to be less than a full human. It effectively reduces the distances that, as Roderick Nash has shown, must be overcome for one to extend ethical care across different categories. As he summarizes, "[g]eographical distance eventually ceased to be a barrier in human-to-human ethics, and in time people began to shake free from nationalism, racism, and sexism" (5)—as reflected in such milestone instances as the abolition of U.S. slavery. In more recent terms, Nash notes, "[t]he [1960s] began with an emphasis on human rights, but by its end, as perception of an environmental crisis increased, the stakes began to widen to include nature" (166). To throw into question what counts as human in the first place—as *Half Life* does, through its narration, and by presenting us with characters whose ontology is neither human nor "natural" in the traditional sense—means that the barriers one must overcome to extend empathy might not be so rigid in the first place. This is a different scenario, of course, from essentialist iterations of ecofeminism that maintain that women are in a more privileged position to care for nature: it is the very unmooredness of someone like Audrey, I propose, that allows one to shuttle between disparate positions.

Queer anti-identiarianism might also open up care for those entities beyond the normative realm of identification—expanding not definitions of *humanity*, but, as do the works I treat in Chapter 2, definitions of *what deserves care*. One source catalogued in the "Siamese Twin Reference Manual" observes that "[t]he divided pronoun has released agency from grammar's lock-hold and set free the principle of change. Many of our new sentences will be hopeless cripples . . . but others will give rise to new forms of beauty, that those of you locked in an earlier age cannot imagine. What will these differently abled sentences say?" (112). We could take this sentiment as mawkish, but we could also recognize in it traces of that very queer mode, camp sensibility: "I know it's ugly/bad; I love it in spite of it being ugly/bad. I love it *because* it is ugly/bad."

In Chapter 2, I have detailed how a queer extension of empathy is important when it comes to "sub-humans" such as transgender people, working class people, plants, and animals. But *Half Life* suggests that this extension of empathy is particularly important when it comes to *landscapes* that have not been considered valuable, either because they are perceived as lacking aesthetic value, because they do not meet idealized definitions of "nature" or "wilderness" (they are faceless and not furry, perhaps), or because they have been degraded—oftentimes, as a result of the other two perceptions. We see this ameliorative empathy in action when *Half Life*'s characters both defend the desert land that was considered ugly enough to bomb and find beauty in the otherwise grotesque. For instance, at the same time that Nora's "Granny" laments the "American Sadness" that irradiated her land, causing her husband's death from cancer and her own breast cancer, she sighs, "Such sunsets we had . . . You never saw such colors" (155). Here, Jackson recalls Don DeLillo's 1984 postmodern classic *White Noise*, wherein the narrator worries, "Have I raised [my son], unwittingly, in the vicinity of a chemical dump site, in the path of air currents that carry industrial wastes capable of producing scalp degeneration, glorious sunsets? (People say the sunsets around here were not nearly so stunning thirty years ago)" (22). Interestingly enough, ecocritic Dana Phillips observes that critics have been largely uninterested in DeLillo's treatment of nature, which he attributes in part to "the fact that one has to adjust one's sense of nature radically in order to understand how, in *White Noise*, natural conditions are depicted as coextensive with, rather than opposed to, the malaise of postmodern culture" (236). This is true of *Half Life* as well, and, in fact, of all of my archive. Phillips develops the notion of postmodern pastoralism, explaining that "the postmodern pastoral, unlike its predecessors, cannot restore the harmony and balance of culture with nature, because the cultural distinctions the pastoral used to make—like that between the city and the country—have become too fluid to have any force . . . Neither culture nor nature are what they used to be. But perhaps DeLillo's point is that they never were, that the distinction between culture and nature cannot be taken as an absolute" (245). Phillips shares my conviction, then, that a postmodern, poststructuralist stance, especially toward the non-human world, need not be understood as apolitical. In fact, insofar as Granny's commentary on the sunset appears in the context of her fight against further irradiation, she indicates that one can both love an adulterated landscape and criticize its adulteration, and recognize beauty in ecological disaster without condoning the disaster itself—just as one could recognize a landscape as "ugly" and still decline to do violence to it.

We might turn to activist-memoirist Jan Zita Grover to find a powerful example of the queer implications of ecological empathy for the non-ideal—and, conversely, the ecological implications of queer empathy for the non-ideal. Grover's 1997 memoir *North Enough: AIDS and Other Clear-Cuts* details her transplantation from San Francisco to the woods of Minnesota after experiencing burnout as a volunteer for AIDS patients. Grover was part of a generation of lesbians who cared for the mostly gay and male victims of the epidemic, care that itself exemplifies cross-identification and the extension of empathy. Hoping to find respite from the city and the epidemic, Grover instead encounters an epidemic of clear-cutting. *North Enough* details her eventual acceptance of the land and simultaneous self-education in environmental politics and local ecology; just as she has found beauty in the emaciated, lesion-ridden bodies of her friends, she learns "to love what has been defaced, to cherish it for reasons other than easy beauty" (20). Jackson's text, which likewise celebrates the "grotesque" mutant body, contains a similar pronouncement: "the desert is not easy to love" (50).

This ethic of care for the "ugly" that Grover outlines and Jackson dramatizes has implications beyond the queer. We should note that those landscapes considered "ugly" and/or "useless," and which are subjected to industrial and/or governmental abuse, are usually those populated by people of color, be they crowded urban areas or "barren" desert landscapes historically populated by Native Americans. This is no coincidence, as environmental justice advocate Robert Bullard explains: "not only are people of color differentially affected by industrial pollution, but also they can expect different treatment from the government. Environmental decision making operates at the juncture of science, economics, politics, special interests, and ethics. The current environmental model places communities of color at special risk" (*The Quest for Environmental Justice* 31). In other words, attitudes toward a certain landscape and attitudes toward the people who inhabit that landscape are deeply intertwined, as are socioeconomic and aesthetic ideals. All these determine what counts as "the environment" to begin with, not to mention which environments deserve saving. In making these points through a queer allegory, *Half Life* both allows us to think of the "mundane" ways in which environmental injustice usually plays out, and asks us to add sexuality and embodiment to the environmental justice framework—which has traditionally focused on race, class, gender, and immigration status.

An "Emptyish State": *Half Life* and the Real-Life History of Nuclear Nevada

The love for "grotesque," Othered bodies and ugly, non-ideal landscapes is particularly important in the desert milieu Jackson depicts. Astrid Ensslin notes that, in the American literary and cultural imagination, the desert has stood "as an ecosystem characterised by aridity—extreme temperatures, drought and sparse vegetation"—an ecosystem that, in works such as T.S. Eliot's *Waste Land*, "epitomises loss of fertility, dissonance between the sexes, [and] disillusionment with heterosexual relationships" (205). Interestingly, Ensslin's article, which was published before the release of *Half Life*, notes that Jackson's breakthrough hypertext work *Patchwork Girl* features a female character associated with the desert—in this case, Death Valley. Ensslin argues that "Shelley Jackson joins a canon of female American writers focusing on frontier women's lives." Drawing on Carol Fairbanks, she points out that "female frontier accounts in the nineteenth century primarily described the Prairies in positive terms, as 'fruitful,' 'new' and 'beautiful,' evoking a hopeful image of the 'vast' and 'solitary' plains otherwise derogated by male writers" (212). While Ensslin's collapse of the desert and the prairie here is questionable, the point remains that the former space has indeed been largely perceived as barren and lifeless.

Half Life describes how that perception has enabled certain destruction. Nora observes that "[t]he spot [the U.S. government] chose for the National Penitence Ground or Proving Ground or, later, Test Site, was the emptyest [sic] part of an emptyish state, Nevada. 'Unfortunately,' Granny said, 'there is no such thing as empty.' . . . Moreover, in a [government] memo, the locals were described as a 'low-use segment of the population.' 'Low-use,' said Granny. 'What language'" (154). Real-life inhabitants of the Nevada desert have advanced similar critiques; one so-called downwinder told writer Rebecca Solnit that "One of the reasons they did the testing in the area that they did is because this is a, and I quote, 'virtually uninhabited area.' . . . Well, frequently the indigenous people, the only reason they have to put up with what they have to put up with . . . is . . . [t]hey just don't have the numbers to have the political clout to keep that kind of thing from happening to them. [W]e have a moral right, but we don't have any political rights, apparently" (154–55). The shift in pronoun from "they" (the indigenous people) to "we" is particularly meaningful in terms of the non-identitarian ethos I have outlined above; this white interviewee both recognizes that the indigenous people in question constitute a different group, and insists upon solidarity when it comes to "political rights."

Half Life takes pains to make the point Solnit does, that "[o]f course the indigenous people of the desert saw in it not a land of austerity and absence, but an abundance for those who were careful, attentive, and reverent" (65). Much of Half Life consists of Nora's recollections of her and Blanche's childhood in Too Bad, Nevada, which allude to how their attentiveness furnished them with intimate knowledge and revealed the desert ecosystem to be very much alive. For instance, Nora recalls that "[s]omeone who didn't know the desert like [Blanche and I] did might not have even noticed that some of the rocks . . . were dusted with yellow-ocher" (381). Elsewhere, Nora expresses her wariness of discourse that either dismisses or romanticizes the desert. She insists that "[t]he cowboy poets lie. Tumbleweeds rolling emptily in the winds of dusk, desiccated ruins . . . : these things aren't sad. I have survived a thousand sunsets without a tear" (379). A bit more darkly, when Nora finds herself stranded in the desert near the end of the novel and planning her next move, she observes that "[t]he desert punishes spontaneity" (394). Not coincidentally, "carefulness," "attentiveness," "reverence," and "non-spontaneity," or "patience," are the same terms that, in Chapter 2, I showed to be related to a queer ethics of care attuned to transgender existence—care based on love and sympathy, not the desire for gain or productivity. A queer ethics of care, which may overlap with an indigenous ethics of care, would likewise allow one to revalue land that has been maligned as queer—without disavowing queerness or repositioning the land as implicitly heterosexual or cisgender.

Of course, the desert is queer not just insofar as it is "ugly," but insofar as it fails to meet heterosexist standards of (re)productivity and usefulness. I have described, in Chapter 4, how these standards underwrite the simultaneous exploitation of Brokeback Mountain and its queer inhabitants. The same holds true, if not more so, for the difficult, arid landscapes in Half Life: common descriptors for the desert, including "barren," "vacuous," and "anti-domestic," can be, and have been, used against queers. Further, scholars such as Arthur Evans have commented on the historical perception of Native Americans—the original inhabitants of the American

West's deserts, and some of the most vocal opponents of nuclear testing in the twentieth century[16]—as queer. Evans reports that "the widespread homosexuality of the North American Indians," not to mention their non-Western heterosexual practices, including the positioning of females on top of males, "was given as an excuse by the invading Christian whites for their extermination" (as quoted in Gaard, "Toward" 126).

Here, again, we see a major irony: the forces that malign queer sexuality as "wasteful" and "unnatural" are often the same that wreak destruction against nature and humans, and that care very little about the wasteful, over-consumptive character of Western/Euroamerican life. And once again, we see that structures such as racism, homophobia, and ecophobia work in tandem. *Half Life* indicts this negative queering of the desert landscape, suggesting that it is precisely the inability to love this non-ideal, to love the queer, that has led to ecological destruction; hence, the importance of the queer twofer. Here, we are in a very different framework from that sketched out by scholars such as Annette Kolodny, in which the ideal of a fertile landscape shapes American identity. As Kolodny explains, drawing on Henry Nash Smith, "'the idealized figure of the farmer' . . . became a kind of emblematic self-image for the new nation as a whole." This image encapsulates a "tension . . . between the initial urge to return to . . . a maternal landscape and the consequent impulse to master and act upon that same femininity" (27). The desert landscape, insofar as it is perceived as infertile, hostile, unproductive, and decidedly *non*-maternal, requires a new understanding of the domination of the non-human world: that it is often through homophobia, not just sexism or racism, that such domination operates.

We should also note that the desert landscape can be considered queer in quite another, non-oppressive sense: as a world in which myriad non-reproductive but nonetheless generative interactions take place between different species and ecological elements. In her article "Biophilia, Creative Involution, and the Ecological Future of Queer Desire," Dianne Chisholm explicates the work of nature writer Ellen Meloy, whose "earthy curiosity for the erotic vitality" of desert life in particular inspires her to "trac[k] interspecies couplings across the desert's vital landscape on a map of co-adaptation, which standard ecosite grids and biological taxonomies fail to chart" (359–60). It is worth surveying Meloy's florid (if you will) prose: "You can tell [desert paintbrush] by its fiery scarlet and early bloom, as if it wants these curvaceous sweeps of sandstone to itself before the wildflower season's full Baroque. . . . Paintbrush . . . invades the vascular tissue of another plant and absorbs its nutrients. Sometimes [it] nudges up seductively close to the host, a flashy scarlet starlet in pickpocket position" (as quoted in Chisholm 368).

Such passages remind us, first, that reproductive life as we normatively imagine it (insemination, growth, birth and rebirth, etc.) is not the only kind of vitality to be found in any given ecosystem, and, second, that interactions between the human and the non-human might be reclaimed as erotic, and as queer, in the most positive of senses.

Stacy Alaimo has documented a similar kind of reclamation in the work of feminist writers of the late nineteenth and early twentieth centuries. She argues that in texts such as the 1927 novel *Cactus Thorn*, "in which the desert appears as a seductive mistress, [Mary Hunter] Austin takes the historically entrenched image of a feminine nature and turns it against itself, contesting discourses that position women and nature as resources for exploitation." Austin's vision of the desert as "sexual but not maternal" (Alaimo, *Undomesticated Ground* 64) chimes with Meloy's view of the desert as creative but not necessarily procreative (Chisholm 369). Importantly, both Meloy and Austin acknowledge that their insights are indebted to indigenous peoples and, in turn, have anti-racist and not just feminist or queer implications—thus demonstrating their truly ecological character. What all of these texts show us, then, is that the desert's negative conception in the dominant framework as "queer" and "non-reproductive" cannot simply be denied (since the desert *is* queer and non-reproductive in the ways cited above), and it cannot just be inverted (to construe the desert as, in fact, not-queer or reproductive and thereby validate heteroreproductive demands). It is crucial, then, that *Half Life* makes queerness central to progressive ecological activism: to do otherwise would be to accept the dominant construction of the desert as queer *in a negative sense*. The implications for queer theory and queer ecology are profound: *Half Life*, like the other texts in my archive, reimagines "nature," "queer," and "futurity," rather than accepting their dominant definitions.

Failing all such insights about the desert's vitality, of course, the U.S. government constructed "dummy" towns—among other platforms—for the purpose of nuclear testing in the New Mexico and Nevada desert. *Half Life* frequently alludes to these towns, as well as other manner of replica, from a dollhouse that figures prominently in Blanche and Nora's childhood, to the ghost-town tourist trap that their grandmother creates with their mother's butch female lover. Here, again, a sense of irony proves necessary to a queer ecological framework attuned to environmental justice: it allows us to recognize not just the fallacy of the desert as an empty, wasted space, but the absurdity of a scenario in which a government builds only to destroy, and in which the construction of *fake* homes allowed scientists and government officials to ignore the *real* homes that already existed, including non-human habitats. (We might say, further, that the "empty" desert test space serves as a strange ideological mirror image of the crowded urban areas of Japan where the "real thing" would take place.) Simply put, *Half Life*'s ironic postmodernity is better attuned to the strangeness of such a scenario of environmental degradation than a more earnest and straight-forward approach would be. As Bronislaw Szerszynski argues, "irony can help us both *diagnose* and *respond* to the crisis in public meaning which helps sustain unsustainable behaviour" (337, my emphasis).

We should also remember that "ironic" doesn't necessarily mean "hu-morous"; sometimes, it means the recognition of a *lack* of humor, or the recognition of ignorance. Solnit again proves instructive here, recounting the trials of one Native American family, the Dunns, to protest government seizure of the land: "The first letter sent off six months before had been forwarded by the Secretary [of the Interior] or one of his underlings to the Bureau of Indian Affairs, where a diligent bureaucrat had answered Car-rie's fairly rhetorical questions straightforwardly and humorlessly. [Carrie Dunn:] *Do you understand the relationship that traditional Western Shoshone have with the land?* [Bureau of Indian Affairs response:] *My staff informs me that many Western Shoshones have a strong attachment to aboriginal lands and consider them sacred*" (179).

The bureaucrat's attempt at regurgitating the Western Shoshone land ethic falls flat, revealing a gap between textbook knowledge and experiential knowledge, and reminding us of how the privileging of the former has led to the devastating suppression of the latter. Here, the person *defending* the earth, and not the one pursuing its exploitation or destruction, is the one with a sense of humor, serious subject matter notwithstanding.

An ironic mindset is also well suited to probing the particularly strange postmodernity of nuclear testing itself. Solnit tells us that

> Test is something of a misnomer when it comes to nuclear bombs. A test is controlled and contained, a preliminary to the thing itself, and though these nuclear bombs weren't being dropped on cities and strategic centers, they were full-scale explosions in the real world, with all the attendant effects. I think that rather than tests, the explosions at the Nevada Test Site were rehearsals, for a rehearsal may lack an audience but contains all the actions and actors. The physicists and bureaucrats managing the U.S. side of the Arms Race had been rehearsing the end of the world out there, over and over again. (5)

In other words, the history of nuclear technology in the Southwest is marked by contestation over what counts as "real." As Solnit suggests, a performance might be just as serious as the "real thing"—though its status as a perfor-mance allows that seriousness to be elided. In a rather strange way, then, the U.S. government employs a postmodern, poststructuralist skepticism of reality and emphasis on performance. But this is an unethical deployment of those stances: a calculated dissimulation, a downplaying—an instance in which, as Douglas Colin Muecke describes it, an "ironist pretends not to be aware" of the existence of "an upper level or point of view that invalidates his own" (as quoted in Szerszynski 341). In this case, the upper level is, in fact, the view from the ground, from the grassroots. Recall, for instance, the passage in *Half Life* that references "downwinders'" questions for, and responses from, the government: "[We are experiencing] [s]kin lesions. 'Sunburn.' [We have] [b]reast cancer, bone cancer, thyroid, liver, lung cancer. 'It's worrying about fallout that makes you sick, not fallout itself'" (156). To respond effectively to such manipulative discourse, the earnestness, truth-seeking, and ethical mandate typical of environmental activism is desperately needed—but so is a sense of irony, a sense of the absurd, and a strong skeptical eye.

Half Life dramatizes these questions of postmodernity and performance at multiple points, and it does so self-consciously, of course. For instance, Nora recalls the "Time Camera" photo shop in the fabricated ghost town of her and Blanche's childhood, remarking, "You could tell it was the past from the pictures. Under the lens, pleather was leather, pop beads were pearls, and the shitty shine of the peeling chrome on the prop sword was the solemn gleam of polished steel. (Oddly, the one real sword, a dress sword we had got from the Grady junk shop, never looked as good in photos)" (144). This passage articulates the prototypical postmodern condition, wherein the difference between the authentic and the inauthentic has collapsed—and, in fact, where the inauthentic actually trumps the authentic. Here, again, Jackson invokes DeLillo, specifically the "Most Photographed Barn in America" sequence from *White Noise*. In this sequence, the narrator, Jack Gladney, travels with his colleague to a rural tourist attraction whose frequent representation is its own draw; his colleague declares, "We're not here to capture an image, we're here to maintain one. . . . [The tourists] are taking pictures of taking pictures" (13). On the one hand, we could read both Jackson and DeLillo's scenes as exemplifying how the human disconnection from the real and the authentic has allowed for environmental destruction. That is to say, forms of mediation such as photography or the Internet, to which *Half Life* refers incessantly, potentially allow one to distance oneself from the natural world. But the respective tone of each passage is one of irony rather than tragedy; both novels are skeptical of claims to anything like authenticity, and, by extension, to an inviolable category such as "Nature."

Such irony and skepticism remind us that what counts as authentic, and what counts as natural, is contingent, subject to shifts in economics, public morality, foreign relations, and aesthetic values. But conversely, and perhaps more positively, we might think of Noël Sturgeon's claim that, "[u]nless we are willing to recognize the deeply political and ideologically variable status of 'nature' in our culture . . . we cannot adequately discuss and decide these important questions about our interaction and use of the environment." Thus "a relentlessly critical examination of claims to the natural is the best way to learn to respect natural beings and processes (including our own natural status as animal-humans . . .)" (*Environmentalism in Popular Culture* 23). In other words, recognizing the constructedness of the natural world is not a cause for despair, nor for apathy—nor, on the other hand, for destructiveness. It is the *ends to which a given construction works* that we must critically scrutinize. Indeed, the questioning of categories such as "naturalness," fruitfulness, beauty, and authenticity can lead us to question their opposites, "unnaturalness," barrenness, ugliness, and inauthenticity—and, in turn, to question the practices that emerge from those categories. For its part, *Half Life* suggests that the perceived barrenness or ugliness of a given space does not justify its destruction—and not just because those terms are utterly subjective, but also because such spaces might have values that we cannot recognize, including their own intrinsic value.

While I have shown, thus far, how queer, postmodern, and poststructuralist values can allow us to revalue maligned landscapes, I want to show explicitly how (queer/postmodern/poststructuralist) irony can foster the kind of empathy with which this book has been concerned. To begin with, one of irony's central functions as a rhetoric is to highlight and/or create distance—to, say, point to a gap between what is being claimed and what is in fact the case, or to hold something up for scrutiny by critically commenting on it. To take one relevant example: David Guggenheim's *An Inconvenient Truth* juxtaposes denials of global warming with images of melting polar icecaps. Through this ironization, the film indicts global warming denial. But *Half Life* pokes fun not just at anti-environmentalism, but at humanism, individualism, ontological stability, and the very categories of "non-human" and "human." Thus its self-effacing irony works toward the anti-identitarianism I have discussed previously. It enables an empathetic queer ecology whereby one might identify across, rather than within, given categories, and whereby one might imaginatively occupy the place of another. More specifically, though, I want to claim that a thoroughgoing, dissident irony encourages care for the unloved and the abject. After all, there is nothing more ironic than finding beauty in a desert landscape that the powers that be consider ugly—as the novel's activist population does—or finding yourself attracted to those who fail to meet normative standards for a human body, as Nora's roommate and countless others in *Half Life*'s alternate reality do. Irony and a sense of humor, in fact, embolden these figures to forge ahead with their unorthodox affections. Thus irony's distancing need not be its endgame mechanism. It can create a conceptual gap into which a human who feels closer to nature than to other humans, or a singleton who identifies with twofers, can easily step. Importantly, as I show in greater depth below, *Half Life*'s brand of irony does not (necessarily) entail a rejection of the entity under critical appraisal. It is not a cruel or dismissive irony, then, but one that is simultaneously compassionate, introspective, and good-humored.

"I" is "Not Good Enough": Modeling Queer Ecological Ethics through Narrative Form

While self-reflexive from its start, *Half Life* takes a major shift toward metafiction in the third of its four sections. The first two sections consist of a retrospective narration that covers recent events, such as Nora's decision to do away with Blanche and her journey to England to seek medical intervention, as well as earlier events, such as Nora's memories of the sisters' childhood in Nevada. These two sets of events are interspersed with materials from the "Siamese Twin Reference Manual." In the third section, though, the retrospective narration has "caught up" to the ostensible present moment from which our narrator has been operating; in a nod to Vladimir Nabokov's pioneering postmodern novel *Pale Fire*, she directly addresses the reader in the present tense, explaining, "I am writing this, now, from the desk of the Twilite Inn."[17] After this direct address, Nora announces that she has been writing a diary during the time of her retrospective narration, and proceeds to excerpt it. The diary introduces serious doubt as to the ontological status of the previous sections; the speaker admits that she "can't shake the feeling that someone's reading over my shoulder" and then muses, "Who's writing this book, anyway? I am. Not good enough" (373). The action that precipitates all these musings is Nora's awakening in an underground London clinic just before separation surgery, to find that she, and not Blanche, has been marked for removal. As Sascha Pöhlmann summarizes, at this point in the novel we start asking such questions as, "Is it Nora telling the story, or is it Blanche? If so, did Blanche take over at some point, or has she always been telling that story? Is Nora impersonating Blanche, is Blanche impersonating Nora, are both impersonating each other, or is it a third (fourth, fifth) voice?"[18]

The novel thus throws the reader into a space of radical uncertainty, and even paranoia, a positioning that has both queer and ecological implications. To begin with, we should remember that the challenge posed by the conjoined body is a challenge to heterosexual privacy and self-restraint; recall Allison Pingree's observation that the Hilton twins embodied the fear "that the division between public and private might not be so clear after all" ("The 'Exceptions'" 183). *Half Life* has thus queered our readership by placing us, unwittingly, in a public position: the figure who was supposedly dormant during our reading is not only conscious, but has perhaps been speaking to us from the very beginning. The effect is an uncanny one of having been watched without permission. On the one hand, we as readers may feel quite disturbed. On the other, we might rejoice in the fact that this effect is what social and medical mores seek to limit: the public, excessive nature of the queer or abnormal body.

Nora's self-dissolution has queer implications in a rather different sense: it recalls queer theorist Leo Bersani's well-known argument about self-shattering. Such an allusion, of course, is not surprising for a text that thanks Avital Ronell and Judith Butler in its acknowledgments, that gives characters the last name Foucault (290), and that includes such dialogue as, "Vyv hates Siamese essentialism, but it seems to me that being a twofer must have influenced his work on set theory" (95). In his 1987 essay "Is the Rectum a Grave?," Bersani muses on the "terrifying appeal of a loss of the ego" (217) and the dismissal of the "sacrosanct value of selfhood" (222) to be found in anal sex, concluding that "if sexuality is socially dysfunctional in that it brings people together only to plunge them into a self-shattering and solipsistic *jouissance* that drives them apart, it could also be thought of as [gay men's] primary hygienic practice of nonviolence" (222). In a recent interview, Bersani reports that he is "now interested in masochism not as pleasure in pain so much as the pleasure of at once losing the self and discovering it elsewhere, inaccurately replicated . . . it still means a certain pleasurable renunciation of one's own ego boundaries, the pleasure of a kind of self-obliteration" ("A Conversation" 174–75). There are clear disjunctures between this argument and the storyworld of *Half Life*. For one thing, Nora is obviously not a gay man, though she is queer. For another, the novel does not delve into the psychoanalytic particulars of ego formation as Bersani does, despite Jackson's occasional allusion to Freud (79) and the suggestion that Nora has been shaped by her sexualization as a "twofer." But I dwell on Bersani here because I want to highlight how Jackson is likewise interested in a queer critique of the "sacrosanct value

of selfhood," in the idea of "discovering [the self] elsewhere, inaccurately
replicated," and in "practice[s] of nonviolence." But whereas Bersani's
"nonviolence" is generally abstract, *Half Life* clearly defines it as environmentalist, and as coalitional. That is, Nora's self-dissolution opens out
onto politicized connections with semi- and non-human Others—and
even with the reader herself.

That is to say, the ambiguous, disintegrating narrative structure forces the
reader to participate in the (re)construction of the storyworld—or, rather,
reveals the hand she has had in that world's construction all along. As Stéphane Vanderhaeghe notes, "Through an interplay of binary oppositions,
Jackson fashions the (twin) metaphor of writing and reading, inciting her
reader to intervene in the text and dig deeper into it to (un)cover meaning
under the successive layers of whiteness that reveal the blankness of a page
that is slowly being erased as one reads/runs over it."[19] If the book has turned
out to be about the process of its own construction, or deconstruction—as it
seems to be, with the novel's explicit references to itself as a text, such as "the
reader will notice that my narrative has begun to loop the loop" (341)—and
if the ostensible author has turned out to be (at least sometimes) the reader,
then we are, like Nora, implicated in the very postmodern, and specifically
Barthesian, process of reading-writing. The novel makes its readerliness
explicit in declining to solve its own mystery at its conclusion; the last line
is, "Nora?"

The questions *Half Life* asks about the construction of the storyworld are
also questions about the "real world," including the non-human natural
world. As Pöhlmann observes, "When Nora wonders in her diary whether
the world is 'in my mind, or in the world' . . . it is a question of the conditions
of both knowledge about and the being of that world . . . Her perception of
the world is in fact linked to the actual creation of that world early on." If we
participate in the creation of that world, and if, to paraphrase Dana Phillips,
the distinction between natural conditions and postmodern culture cannot
hold, then the novel asks us to take responsibility for how we construct "the
world," broadly speaking. After all, we might remember, the fundamental
premise of the novel is that the advent of the twofer has occasioned a vision
of shared ethical responsibility for the earth and all its inhabitants. Likewise,
Jackson seems to suggest, those who construct exploitative views of natural
spaces—such as of the desert as barren and ugly—must take responsibility
for their implications of those views.

Some critics have in fact suggested that the question at the heart of *Half
Life*'s unique narrative ontology is an ethical one. It is worth quoting Christopher Kilgore here at length:

Jackson designs the novel's complex form to ask how ethics can survive a conception of self that rejects the subject's foundational singularity. Jackson emphasizes the plurality that underlies all formulations of the narrative "I" and suggests that Nora's "extraordinary embodiment" causes such fascination because its form calls attention to problems with the notion of "self" that traditions of first-person speech tend to elide. Nora's account offers a way to rebuild the "person" concept so that it can *both* acknowledge the self's multiplicity *and* accept the social demand for singularity and responsibility. It is this simultaneous narrative endorsement of singularity and multiplicity, an "I" and a "we" at the heart of subjectivity, that makes this unnatural narrative so remarkable.

As I have been arguing, though, it's not just any kind of ethics with which *Half Life* concerns itself, but environmental ethics. Here we should revisit the odd story of "American Sadness": the government, in bombing "itself," was really bombing innocent others. Nora recounts how her grandmother explained the situation to her: "Granny drew two tadpoles, Yin and Yang. . . . 'Say the black tadpole is America. Then the white one is un-America. When bombing un-America, America must also bomb the un-America in herself'" (154). In shattering the self and creating a "we" that is literally and figuratively indivisible, the novel militates against the disingenuous, dissimulated "we" implicit in "American Sadness." It also indicts the ways in which those who are responsible for environmental disasters rarely have to experience their consequences firsthand. Finally, and more broadly, it asks us to collapse the distinctions of "us" and "them," "self" and "Other" that drive environmental destruction in the first place. As the fallout from nuclear technology has taught us, there is no reliable barrier between those two sets of groups, no ontological distinction between the human and non-human that will prevent, say, people from getting sick from airborne radiation or contaminated cow's milk, as did many living near the Nevada Test Site and, even more disastrously, near Chernobyl.

Thus, while readers and critics alike have complained about the novel's "devolution" into ironic wordplay and philosophical questioning,[20] we might say that there was no other option for a novel with a queer ecological agenda. *Half Life*'s "unnatural narration," as Kilgore dubs it (8), is actually well suited to questions of nature and ecology: our ostensible human narrator is never wholly singular, in ways that model the ecological, feminist, queer, and anti-racist values of interdependency, intersectionality, self-shattering, and plurality. And the novel ultimately refuses to uphold the sovereignty of the individual human and her quest for self-realization. Instead of positing clear distinctions between the self and the Other, the human and the non-human, the conscious and the unconscious, it takes us to a place of radical undifferentiation, a place where everything is understood to be intimately connected to everything else. Just as I have shown in the last two chapters that queer filmic techniques are also techniques of environmentalism and environmental justice, so do we see in *Half Life* that queer literary form is ecological form. Thus, to the question of whether ethics can survive the dissolution of the self and of stable identity, *Half Life* responds that ethics might in fact *grow most effectively out of such dissolution.*

Conclusion

The greatest irony of all, then, is that *Half Life* turns out to have participated in what it ridiculed from the start. For the vast majority of the book, the plot has been driving toward our (apparently) first-person, autodiegetic narrator's un-P.C. removal of her twin—a setup that largely prevents us as readers from desiring any other outcome. This setup has also made P.C. twofers, twofer-identified singletons, Siamists, Siamystics, and other odd phenomena of this post-atomic age (as well as real-life academics and activists) even riper targets for parody. So perhaps the strangest thing about this very strange book is that it collapses its own structuring logic. It pulls the rug out from under us not just by throwing its narrator into question, but by questioning the very allegiances it has encouraged its readers to develop. As Tania Barnes observes, "Readers who have been spurred along equally by the book's mystery—what does Blanche want?—and by its imaginative evocation of another world will feel frustrated by the confusing denouement and open-ended conclusion." While many if not most of us have spent the novel cheering on a quest for human sovereignty, for the correction of abnormal bodies, and for a disavowal of "blurred identity"—even if we've otherwise endorsed *Half Life*'s interest in ecology—the book suddenly abandons those goals. Nora "herself" concludes, "I have spent my whole life trying to make one story out of two: my word against Blanche's. But we are only as antithetical as this ink and this page" (433), which is to say, inseparable and interdependent, even if different. In the same way, we have spent our time reading the narrative as Nora's alone—only to find ourselves unable to make any definitive attempt at narratorial identification. We may feel betrayed by all these developments, but we may also laugh at what fools we've been. Not only did we not anticipate what eventually happens, but we expected a normative conclusion to a very queer story.

The novel thus avoids the pitfall Szerszynski identifies, in which "the ironic attitude itself is the one thing that is unironised. The postmodern ironist," he concludes, "is thus not free but captured by their own alienation from the public world, by an ironic attitude that becomes a new immediacy, a new and equally constraining horizon of thought" (349). Jackson, in contrast, employs a comprehensive irony, one that does not depend on elitism—the novel laughs not just at us, but at itself—and that does not simply respond to the absurdities of corporate and governmental exploitation with counter-absurdities on the same ideological order. As Szerszynski observes, when environmentalists and other leftist activists *do* employ irony,

> it is [usually] a "corrective" irony. Firstly, it operates by setting up the tension between two levels of meaning, only in order to more resolutely effect a resolution onto one of them. Movements reveal situational ironies in order to shame their targets into repentance . . . Schweppes, Shell or British Nuclear Fuels, for example, present themselves as responsible corporate citizens, but are revealed to be otherwise. Secondly, it positions the ironist as an outside observer of the irony, on the moral high ground looking down, rather than implicated in it. Such a positing of the ethical actor seems inadequate for an age in which the logic of politics is that of Baudrillardian simulation. (347–48)

In other words, to merely point to the absurdity of something like the government blasting a dummy town in the middle of the Nevada desert, and then to present "the truth"—that the land is being irradiated in ways that will destroy flesh-and-blood humans, as well as non-humans—would be to appeal to some universal truth that everyone can supposedly recognize. More specifically, to merely do so would be to forget the absurdity of one's own position: in this case, pleading with a government that has wiped out millions of indigenous people in the past, and that is planning to wipe out hundreds of thousands of people of color in the present, to spare the indigenous flora, fauna, and peoples scattered across the Nevada desert. It's important to note, then, that *Half Life*'s main disclosure—that Nora will not end up removing Blanche—is not one that reestablishes a definitive moral order, or that recuperates a familiar reality out of the chaos. Quite the opposite, in fact. The disclosure that Nora will not end up removing Blanche is dependent upon the fact that we as readers *no longer know the difference between Nora and Blanche*—itself a direct demonstration of ecology, or interconnection—and upon the fact that Nora doesn't know the difference, either. Or, should we say, Blanche?

Importantly, then, Jackson's novel concludes by taking us back to the desert: not just the sisters' place of origin, but the place where they first experienced the interdependence of human, non-human, post-human, and quasi-human life forms. After the aborted separation surgery, we find this snippet from "Nora": "'I'm through,' I said out loud. . . . I've had my run. All right, Blanche, I'm all yours" (375). After one childhood-recollection chapter and a page from the "Siamese Twin Reference Manual" on Boolean logic, our protagonist/s wake/s up in Nevada. But the reconciliation undertaken there is not just personal or familial; Nora and Blanche have returned on the occasion of a historic event. A flier offered to "Nora" by a hotel clerk announces,

> OXYMORON! PRO Nuke? NO Nuke? Join us! Historic Self-Contradictory Action at the NTS. Pro-nuke and No-nuke activists join together in demanding that Nevada's National Penitence Ground be turned over to the people effective immediately. The Nuclear Abolitionists, Parents for a Radiation-Free Tomorrow, and The Western Shoshone, long opponents of nuclear testing and waste storage, have forged a historic agreement with pro-nuke forces including the RadioActivists, Mutatis Mutandis, and the . . . League of Mutant Voters. . . . "We see in the Oxymoron the opportunity to find common ground on an issue that has bitterly divided our community. Declassifying the NPG will put Grady on the map as a destination for tourists and pilgrims alike, creating abundant jobs for locals, while putting an end to the Sadness that is poisoning the state of Nevada." (392)

This grassroots effort seeks to end once and for all the victimization of the human and non-human through government domination and nuclear technology, while still embracing the "mutant," created of nuclear technology. Notably, this flier is not separated out into a "Siamese Twin Reference Manual" entry like the multiple other documents the novel contains. Rather, it is included within the body of the main text. In fact, after this point, the novel does not include any other excerpts from the manual. Thus, just as Nora and Blanche have become unified, so does the text become more of a whole—at least as far as a postmodern, self-reflexive, polyvocal text can be. Indeed, the text's ontology is comparable to the political reality anticipated by the flier: a united front that does not require homogeneity.

Ultimately, then, *Half Life* announces itself as the very stuff it has parodied: multivocality, hippy-dippy mysticism, tree-hugging, political correctness. We realize that its humor and flippancy toward GLTBQI and ecological politics were actually, or also, gestures of embrace. This fact becomes most clear when we receive an update on Audrey's happy condition near the novel's end, after Nora and Blanche have reintegrated back in the desert; while the unhappy twofer Nora once scoffed at her twofer-identified roommate's desire to be conjoined, the narrator/s now report/s that, at that moment, Audrey "consults a baby name book. She has just had word that her tissue has accepted the plastic form, and she should start thinking about choosing a name for her new head" (434). All along, then, *Half Life* has been "serious," but with an ironic affect. We might therefore say that the novel constitutes an example of praxis, or the practical application of theory: it's not just *about* queer and ecological principles, but an enactment of them. It puts into motion Szerszynski's vision of a "thoroughgoing ironic environmentalism"—which, he believes, "would involve a reflexive awareness of the limited and provisional nature of human understanding, while at the same time not lapsing into cynicism or quietism" (350). In taking up pressing queer ecological questions through this "thoroughgoing iron[y]" and self-conscious absurdism, then, Jackson's novel tells us that we must be able to laugh, and to laugh at *ourselves*, as we undertake progressive political agendas. In short, it's not that *Half Life* has no truths to offer; it's just that it has refused to take those truths too seriously.

Conclusion
The Futures of Queer Ecology

In rereading contemporary queer novels and films as environmentalist polemics, I have argued that queer literature *is* environmental literature for how it grapples with the natural. As I have shown, the queer ecological fictions in my archive cannot take "the natural" at face value, because of how it has frequently been used against the queer, but nor can they reject "the natural" because of how it encompasses the threatened non-human world. Thus they must carefully explicate, negotiate, and reconfigure it. I have shown how this task is informed by intellectual heuristics unique to the contemporary period—from the anti-identitarianism of queer theory, to the irony of postmodernism, to the social constructionism of poststructuralist feminism and critical race studies—as well as by the activist commitments of that period—from second- and third-wave environmentalism to environmental justice. My own task of reading has likewise been informed by these heuristics and commitments, even as I reroute, or take issue with, aspects of them. For instance, I have shown how the queer theoretical concept of self-shattering, once limited to a sexual framework, can be put to use in environmental ethics—but I have rejected queer theory's anti-futurity, demonstrating that future-thinking is crucial to queer ecological thought. I thereby offer a methodology for the queer ecological study of film and literature, and a model for queer ecological action, that is attuned to tensions and productive contradictions: *Strange Natures* both *demonstrates that*, and *explains how*, skepticism of natural categories can coexist with sincere investment in the natural world.

Strange Natures steps into an interdisciplinary sphere of scholarship focused on human sexuality and the non-human world—a sphere that has only just begun to coalesce into the field many are calling "queer ecology." Thus I must stress that my work does not speak definitively for that field. Indeed, many of my fundamental assumptions here may stand at odds with those of other scholars engaged with it. Consider, for instance, Simon Estok's recent observation that "it is very strange that there has yet to emerge a queer ecocriticism"; as I have shown in my introduction and subsequent chapters, queer ecology and ecocriticism have been conceptually constrained by homophobic discourses that position queers as "against nature," as well as by queer discourses that embrace that designation as a form of dissidence. This history, I argue, makes queer ecology/queer ecocriticism, but not its belated entrance, "strange." Estok claims further that

> [q]ueer ecocriticism situates us theoretically to understand that the commodification of nature and of sexual minorities are similar, each depending on a large consumer base that seeks a vicarious experience, rather than the thing itself. In twenty-first century terms, this means zones of voyeurism offered by "queer" comic TV sites, or documentaries offering landscapes of ecotourism, all with little interest in subjectivities, identities, organizational potentials, and so on . . . [Q]ueer theory voiced silenced communities; queer ecocriticism voices "Nature" along with those communities. (214)

I appreciate Estok's suggestion that the commodification of queerness and the commodification of nature are similar; in Chapters 2 and 4 I show how the queer and the natural are in fact commodified at once. However, I take exception to his other comments. For one thing, his invocation of "the thing itself" is questionable; if queer theory has taught us anything, it's to be skeptical of claims to authentic identities and, by extension, authentic sites—especially considering how queerness been maligned as the artificial, urban, and nonreproductive foil of authentic, vital heterosexuality. I believe we should also be careful in thinking about who is granted access to that "thing itself"—as opposed to those who have no other choice than to stay at home and watch "documentaries." As I have shown in Chapters 3 and 4, environmental injustice often entails the alienation of poor people, queers, and people of color from healthy, natural spaces. Thus, firsthand, rather than "vicarious," experience of the natural world is a privilege, not necessarily an ethical stance. It is for such reasons that I have insisted throughout this book on a queer ecology that is attuned to social-justice concerns such as racism and classism. Finally, I'm troubled by the idea that a queer ecocriticism would "voic[e] Nature" (214). Aside from the fact that queer theory has never tried to speak for a given sexuality, just as poststructuralist feminism and critical race theory have declined to speak for all women or all people of color, it is highly unlikely that a

small group of intellectuals and activists could "voic[e] Nature"—rather than
voicing *concerns for* "Nature."

But my problems with Estok's comments indicate that there are, and will
likely continue to be, multiple visions of queer ecology and queer ecocriticism in the future. Future work might attend to some of the same concerns
I have treated here—including the definition and redefinition of the natural,
the social construction of the non-human world alongside that of human
gender/sexuality, the modes of affect and ethics that connect the human
to the non-human, and the politics of futurity—and in very different ways
than I have. And it will likely identify additional concerns and additional
relevant features of queer ecological texts. Future scholars might choose
different methodologies, and they almost certainly will focus on diverse
archives, genre-wise, time-wise, or otherwise. Indeed, contemporary films
and novels are obviously not the only kind of texts to which a queer ecological or queer-ecocritical lens has, or can be, applied. To offer some brief
examples: a queer ecocritical study of the explosion in "green" marketing
might investigate its reliance on heterosexist ideologies, or scholars might
investigate how countercultural undertakings such as *The Queer Farmer Film
Project*, Tennessee's IDA (the "Idyll Dandy Arts" rural commune), and the
vegan movement navigate nature in queer, biocentric ways.[1]

Queer ecology and ecocriticism might begin to draw on additional scholarly and political frameworks, and vice versa. For instance, while all of my
chapters focus in some way on race, class, gender, immigration status,
embodiment, and health status, in addition to sexuality and gender identity,
only Chapter 5 takes up dis/ability explicitly. Disabilities are sometimes
"natural" (cerebral palsy, dwarfism) and sometimes "unnatural" (anorexia,
dismemberment or disfigurement); thus dis/ability constitutes a rich site
for an investigation of how sexual and bodily ideals work together to frame
the natural world, and the field of disability studies could meaningfully
inform such work. To sketch out just one train of thought: this past summer, I visited Kentucky's Mammoth Cave National Park, where our tour
guide described how the caves were (wrongly) believed to constitute the
ideal rehabilitative environment for persons suffering from tuberculosis.
This belief is particularly interesting, considering that Mammoth Cave is
today inaccessible to persons who use wheelchairs, and considering that
the park's creation was sparked by the media sensation of Floyd Collins,
an explorer who became trapped and eventually died in a nearby cave in
1925. These events corroborate Mei Mei Evans's claim that "the theme of
(heterosexual white) men doing battle against Nature in order to achieve
'real man'hood" has been widespread; as she elaborates, "this ideological

construction creates a representational paradigm whereby heterosexual white manhood (i.e., 'real men') is construed as the most 'natural' social identity in the United States . . . According to this epistemological paradigm, those who have been socially constructed as Other (i.e., not white and/or not straight and/or not male) are viewed as intruders or otherwise out of place when they venture to or attempt to inhabit Nature" (183). Not surprisingly, then, Collins's story has been adapted into a stage musical and optioned for a feature film; it constitutes an archetypal tale of a heterosexual white man "doing battle against Nature" and literally risking life and limb in the process. We might compare the Collins archive to Danny Boyle's 2010 film *127 Hours*, which depicts real-life hiker Aaron Ralston becoming trapped in a Utah canyon before amputating his own arm and escaping. Both *Floyd Collins* the musical and *127 Hours*, while primarily presenting their heroes as incapacitated, offer several fantasy sequences in which they are mobile and physically intact. *127 Hours* also concludes with images of the real-life Ralston, his wife, and their infant son—a son he anticipated in one sentimental fantasy sequence. A queer ecocritical study might apply questions from queer theorists, disability-studies scholars, and scholars such as Evans to these texts, to determine what role reproductive futurism and able-bodiedness play in depictions of embattled heterosexual white manhood. And it might compare such depictions to the reality in which disabled persons are routinely ejected from the body politic due to their incompatibility with ideals of nature, material and ideological.

My focus here on the future is quite pointed, more so than it might be in a discussion of a different emerging paradigm. Throughout this book, I have demonstrated how queer theoretical work has tended to characterize futurity and future-thinking as heteronormative and pro-capitalist. It has thus preempted any serious consideration of environmentalism or ecology—insofar as those frameworks are futurist, or centered on sustainability and the long-term effects of consumer and corporate practices—and thereby constrained attempts to think queer ecology forward, or at all. I have, in response, shown how futurity and future-thinking can function as queer ecological values, particularly when it comes to combating corporate greed and social/environmental injustice. In fact, I maintain that a queer ecological focus on futurity can highlight the fact that lack of concern for the future more accurately characterizes regimes such as heteronormativity and global capitalism: while they may operate out of concern for the reproduction of the white, middle-class heterosexual family or for the accumulation of wealth, they also ignore their immediate and future costs to the poor, to people of color, to the environment, and even to themselves. (The Occupy Wall

Street movement that forges on as I write would not exist were that view not widespread among the so-called 99 percent.) The kind of queer ecological futurity I have traced out here is, instead, ethically attuned to the present and future health and safety of the biosphere as it encompasses the human, the non-human, and everything in between.

As this is a book that catalogues and proposes new ways of thinking and caring about the non-human natural world, it is necessarily anticipatory— and, we might say, futuristic. But I nonetheless have a grandly optimistic view of what these new ways could mean: that even, or perhaps especially, in our cynical "post"-everything age, individuals might learn to care about those persons and entities to whom they have no direct ties. In fact, I have suggested that the shirking of stable identities, epistemologies, and ontologies (moves for which critical theory, and queer theory in particular, are well known, and which have arguably sparked a "post-identity" culture) might lend itself most effectively to empathetic, politicized advocacy for the non-human natural world. My readings in Chapter 2, for example, have shown how the transgender individual, often treated as subhuman, can see hirself in the non-human context of flora, fauna, and landscape—and compassionately relate to other marginalized beings, such as factory workers and colonized peoples. In fact, all of the texts I treat here, save Surf Party, sketch out a specifically queer ecological ethic of care: a care not rooted in stable or essentialized identity categories, a care that is not just a means of solving human-specific problems, a care that does not operate out of expectation for recompense. In the so-called real world, such a scenario would be the most delicious, and queerest, irony of all, as Chapter 5 intimates: that it might be, say, the childless or unmarried person, or the queer who "lives in the now," or the person whose body is constructed through "unnatural technology"—in short, the person who has everything to lose and nothing to gain—who cares most for the future well-being of non-human and human others.

Because it crosses identity boundaries and looks skeptically at established ontological categories, the queer empathy I describe in Strange Natures is available to all (even you, dear reader). Just as the mantle of "queer" has been effectively taken up by heterosexuals because of its anti-identitarian stance, so might the queer ecological model of empathy avail itself to individuals from a wide range of backgrounds. Such a widely applicable model might prove crucial to our current times, when, from the majority of scientific perspectives, the ongoing survival of the planet is no longer guaranteed—and thus no longer the problem of a few unlucky, isolated groups—and when denial of global warming so often seems to go hand in hand with homophobic agendas.[2] And indeed, I have suggested throughout this book that the kind of empathy that environmentalism at large calls for so urgently right now is by definition queer, even when not directly linked to (homo) sexuality or sexual issues: one must care for nameless, faceless future beings, including non-humans, to which one has no domestic, familial, or financial ties. I thus offer *Strange Natures* with not a little bit of urgency, and with much openness.

Notes

Preface

1. See Bruhm and Hurley's *Curiouser and Curiouser*, which discusses the pre-sexual/ heterosexual character of mainstream depictions of children.

2. As I note in an article for the upcoming collection *International Perspectives in Feminist Ecocriticism* (ed. Simon Estok, Greta Gaard, and Serpil Oppermann), Edelman often takes to task figures such as Cornel West, without contextualizing their arguments in terms of their anti-racist and anti-classist efforts.

3. Catriona Sandilands asked such questions in her classic essay "Lavender's Green? Some Thoughts on Queer(y)ing Environmental Politics."

Chapter 1. Introduction

1. See Noël Sturgeon's *Environmentalism and Popular Culture*, which extensively discusses the processes of naturalization when it comes to gender, sexuality, environment, and other categories.

2. See, for instance, Halberstam's most recent book, *The Queer Art of Failure*, which features on its cover a photograph of a dead embryonic bird.

3. Similarly, as Michael Snediker observes, "Even as Butler and Bersani [chief among those arbiters of "queer pessimism"] have positioned their work in the context of AIDS, hate-crimes, and other lived domains of crisis, their work, with telling insistence, often depends on abstraction, on metaphor" (12).

4. This problem is explained—or, perhaps, enabled—by the fact that, as Robert L. Caserio notes in relationship to Tim Dean's work, "Edelman, or the antisocial thesis generally, does not distinguish structural claims about the unconscious from empirical claims about culture" (820).

5. Here, I particularly appreciate Dianne Chisholm's observation that "[i]f *No Future* benefits queer desire by giving it an easy target and a sado-aesthetic armature of

deployment, it disdains any attempt to rethink queer desire with respect to ecology's larger-than-pro-life crises" (377).

6. We also noted that these images promote what Sandilands has called "motherhood enviromentalism" (The Good-Natured Feminist xiii): a consumerist ideology that puts the environmental health and safety of children in the hands of middle-class mothers—and finds them at fault when things go wrong.

7. See John M. Broder's article "BP Shortcuts Led to Gulf Oil Spill," New York Times, September 14, 2011, at http://www.nytimes.com/2011/09/15/science/earth/15spill.html.

8. British newspaper The Guardian reported this comment on June 1, 1992.

9. Here, Berlant is writing of one of the poor black characters in Charles R. Johnson's short story "Exchange Value."

10. For better or worse, I am the author of the piece that uses the term "ecocriticism."

11. For example, Edward Abbey and Dave Foreman have spoken out against immigration. See Chapter 3, where I also discuss Christopher Manes's cynical celebration of the AIDS crisis.

12. Various examples of essentialist and/or broadly universalist versions of ecofeminism abound. To take just one, Karen M. Fox argues in an essay titled "Leisure: Celebration and Resistance in the Ecofeminist Quilt," "leisure is an important segment of women's lives for connecting with nature and reaffirming themselves and their relationships with nature" (155). To be fair, much ecofeminist work concentrates on the ways in which women and non-human nature have been similarly positioned—and thus how this positioning (and not necessarily some innate essence) may allow women to relate to non-human nature. See, for example, Carol J. Adams's The Pornography of Meat.

13. Morton claims that "[m]uch American ecocriticism is a vector for various masculinity memes, including rugged individualism, a phallic authoritarian sublime, and an allergy to femininity in all its forms" (274).

14. See Paul Dourish's "Points of Persuasion: Strategic Essentialism and Environmental Sustainability" and J. Proctor's "The Social Construction of Nature: Relativist Accusations, Pragmatist and Critical Realist Responses."

15. That is, Mazel's American Literary Environmentalism is intent upon proving not that there is no such thing as, say, Yosemite the physical place, but rather that beliefs about what Yosemite is, represents, and can be, along with ideals of race, class, and nationalism, shape our encounters with that entity.

16. Buell observes that "for first-wave ecocriticism, 'environment' effectively meant 'natural environment.' In practice if not in principle, the realms of the 'natural' and the 'human' looked more disjunct than they have come to seem for more recent environmental critics" (The Future 21)—whom Buell considers part of a "second wave." It should be noted that environmental historians such as Ramachandra Guha and Philip Shabecoff have identified three waves of environmentalism; arguably, second-wave ecocriticism emerges around the third wave of environmentalism.

17. Self-described "supporter of deep ecology" Orton is voicing, though not necessarily endorsing, this "environmental cliché." See his essay "Deep Ecology and the Left—Contradictions," cited below.

18. Among others, political scientist Stephen M. Meyer has amassed much evidence against the idea that environmental deregulation offers economic benefits.

19. Sandilands's 1994 essay "Lavender's Green" is widely acknowledged to be the pioneering work in the field. In 2011 the Modern Language Association held its first panel on the topic of queer ecology.

20. See "Bush Calls for Ban on Same-Sex Marriages," CNN.com, February 25, 2004, at http://www.cnn.com/2004/ALLPOLITICS/02/24/eleco4.prez.bush.marriage/.

21. In her review for *The Seattle Post-Intelligencer* on October 29, 1999, critic Paula Nechak remarked that *Boys Don't Cry* director Kimberly Peirce had accurately captured the "isolation of the Midwest, with its dusty desolation and nowhere-to-go frustration that propels people to violence and despair." For statistics on anti-GLBTQI hate crimes, see http://www.fbi.gov/ucr/ucr.htm#hate.

22. Cited on page 25 of Roy Martinez's *On Race and Racism in America: Confessions in Philosophy* (2010).

23. See Nicole Casta, "Pat Robertson's Contradictory Theology: God Won't Stop a Tsunami, but Might Respond to Gay Days with an Earthquake," May 2, 2005, at http://mediamatters.org/research/200505020002.

24. See http://www.devpsy.org/humor/god_hates_fags.html.

25. See Robert F. Kennedy Jr.'s *Crimes against Nature* (2004) and Suzanne Goldenberg's analysis "The Worst of Times: Bush's Environmental Legacy Examined," from *The Guardian* (http://www.guardian.co.uk/politics/2009/jan/16/greenpolitics-georgebush). Interestingly, Kennedy's title is a play on a euphemism for homosexuality.

26. See, for instance, Valentine's *From Nowhere to Everywhere: Lesbian Geographies* (New York: Routledge, 2000) and her collection edited with Bell, *Mapping Desire* (New York: Routledge, 1995).

27. See his chapter "Unnatural Predators: Queer Theory Meets Environmental Studies in Bram Stoker's *Dracula*," in Giffney and Hird's *Queering the Non/Human*.

28. The Center for PostNatural History (http://www.postnatural.org/) is a prominent example of this concept at work.

29. Many scholars agree that there have been three waves of environmentalism in the United States: the first being the Teddy Roosevelt brand of conservationism that began in the 1860s, the second being the Rachel Carson era of concerns about toxicity and consumerism that began in the late 1950s, and the third being our present moment. See also Ramachandra Guha's *Environmentalism: A Global History* (2000).

30. Shabecoff notes that, according to sociologist Denton E. Morrison, the rise of environmentalism at the end of the 1960s "came as something of a relief to a movement-pummeled white, middle-class America . . . [It] seemed to have potential for diverting the energies . . . of young people away from more bothersome movements" (109).

31. See the *PMLA* roundtable cited in this introduction for a discussion of queer theory's white- and male-centric reputation.

32. Betsy Hartman reports that "American environmentalism has had a long and strong relationship with eugenics" (as quoted in Hogan, "Undoing Nature" 34), while Andil Gosine claims that "[f]rom their preservationist-conservationist origins . . . leading North American environmental movements have invested in the production and circulation of discourses on 'overpopulation' that pit blame for global ecological disaster on . . . the world's poor" (149). See also Margot Francis's "The 'Lesbian National Parks and Services': Reading Sex, Race and the Nation in Artistic Performance."

33. African American writer/activist Al Young dramatizes this view in his short story "Silent Parrot Blues": "The average person can't understand what those Green Peace people and ecology people are driving at. I used to didn't understand it, either. Far as I was concerned, that was white yuppie stuff" (122).

34. See, for instance, Lauren Berlant's work on compassion, sentimentality, and optimism. In her article "From Care to Citizenship: Calling Ecofeminism Back to Politics," Sherilyn MacGregor reports that "One of the themes in contemporary ecofeminist literature is that women's care-related perspectives on human-nature relations should be adopted as a generalized normative stance, a form of ecological civic virtue" (57). MacGregor acknowledges that "there are important aspects to ecofeminist valuations of women's caring—particularly in light of the way non-feminist ecopolitical discourse ignores the work of care," but asks, "How can societal expectations that women be caring or the exploitation of women's unpaid caring labor under capitalism be challenged at the same time that the specificity of women's caring stance towards the environment is held up as an answer to the ecological crisis?" (57).

35. For instance, Buell believes that "'environmental' approximates better than 'eco' the hybridity of the subject at issue—[with] all 'environments' in practice involving fusions of 'natural' and 'constructed' elements" (The Future viii).

36. See Arne Naess and George Sessions's "Eight-Point Deep Ecology Platform," published in Bill Devall's Clearcut: The Tragedy of Industrial Forestry (1993), and David Orton's "Deep Ecology and the Left—Contradictions" (http://deepgreenweb.blogspot.com/2011/01/deep-ecology-and-left-contradictions.html). Orton claims that "Ecosocialists [whom we might align with social ecologists, against deep ecologists] deny the role of individual responsibility in destructive ecological and social actions. They don't recognize the necessity to practice voluntary simplicity so as to minimize one's personal impact on the Earth." He concludes by declaring that "[c]oming into a new relationship with the natural world is primary, and social justice for humans must keep this in mind. The Left can have a meaningful contributory role in a future ecologically focused and socially just post-industrial society, if it accepts and is transformed by the contribution of deep ecology and comes to see itself, in theory and in practice, as an ecocentric Left" (my emphasis).

37. See Amanda Hagood's 2010 dissertation, "The Domestication of U.S. Environmentalism, 1945–1962," which discusses the heteronormative anxieties of Jack Arnold's The Incredible Shrinking Man (1957).

Chapter 2. Post-Transsexual Pastoral

1. When it is clear that a transgender character or author identifies primarily as either female or male, I will use the pronouns "she" and "her" and "he" and "him," respectively. When a preferred identity is not clear, or shifting, I will use "ze" and "hir," pronouns popularized by Feinberg.

2. See previous note.

3. Rachel Stein finds in the poetry of Minnie Bruce Pratt and Adrienne Rich similar interest in literally/figuratively naturalizing the "unnatural" individual; she claims that the two "emphasiz[e] lesbian dis-location from social/natural spaces, and then also

resituat[e] lesbian desire within natural contexts" (288). I stress the fact that Feinberg, Mootoo, and Cliff undertake such operations with an explicit concern for non-human nature, not (just) for queer humans; moreover, I submit there is arguably more at stake in naturalizing the trans person than, say, naturalizing lesbians, gay men, or bisexuals: the trans person is considered "unnatural" and constructed not just in terms of desire or identity, but in terms of the material body itself.

4. Today, we might find many examples of failures to develop interlocking resistance, such as queer responses to California's Proposition 8 that blamed black and Latina/o voters, rather than investigating the historical oppressions and targeted campaigns that informed those groups' decisions—and rather than recognizing that the black, Latina/o, and GBLTQI communities are not mutually exclusive. Conversely, one might accuse some black and Latina/o voters of failing to recognize the ways in which their experiences of oppression mirror those of GLBTQI communities.

5. According to a recent estimate from the Human Rights Campaign, transgender people have a 1 in 12 chance of being murdered, compared to 1 in 18,000 for the average person (http://www.hrc.org/issues/1508.htm). The murders of transgender people are also more likely to be marked by "overkill"—excessive violence to the body beyond the point of death. See, for example, "Hate Crimes and Violence against the Transgender" by Tarynn M. Witten and A. Evan Eyler in *Peace Review* 11.3 (1999): 461–68.

6. The term "cisgender," referring to persons who feel aligned with their given gender identity, was reportedly proposed by Carl Buijs. For debates on the term, see http://transgriot.blogspot.com/2009/07/cisgender-isnt-insult.html.

7. As regards the first and third points, see Joan Roughgarden's *Evolution's Rainbow* and Marlene Zuk's *Sexual Selections*. As regards the second, see Donna Haraway's "A Cyborg Manifesto" and Anne Balsamo's *Technologies of the Gendered Body*.

8. See Susan Stryker for a long view of this picture.

9. In her 2008 *New York Times Magazine* article "When Girls Will Be Boys," Alissa Quart reports that "few transmen [elect to have 'bottom surgery'], in part because the operation is thought to be too rudimentary and in part because many transmen view it as unnecessary" (37).

10. By "modernist epistemology," Stryker means the belief that "real" phenomena exist, which are captured or displayed by representations. But transgenderism puts the "real" of sex into question through incoherent representation; a female gender for a male body, for example, undercuts the assumption that there is simply such a thing as a male body.

11. Halberstam's work on transgenderism also focuses on what she calls the "technotopic aesthetic, or one that tests technological potentialities against the limits of a human body anchored in time and space" (103).

12. See Susan Stryker's 2005 documentary *Screaming Queens: The Riots at Compton's Cafeteria* (co-directed by Victor Silverman).

13. See Jamison Green's concept of the "transgender childhood": "one in which the child unconsciously expresses [notable cross-]gender characteristics or behaviors" (13).

14. I believe that the role of nationalism in queer ecological thinking is an area worth exploring further. For now, I will note that Cliff's depiction of Harry/Harriet's militancy parallels Dionne Brand's 1996 novel *In Another Place, Not Here*; as John Corr observes, the

"queer relationship" of that novel's protagonists "embodies revolution against milita-rized globalization" (114).

15. Here I mean materialism in three of the multiple meanings of the term: as the emphasis on material objects and material accumulation; as the belief that the greatest value lies in material progress; and as the idea that physical matter is the only measure of reality.

16. He describes how, "[o]n the one hand . . . [a]s more adults have been drawn into the free labor system, and as capital has expanded its sphere until it produces as com-modities most goods and services we need for our survival, the forces that propelled men and women into families and kept them there have weakened. On the other hand, the ideology of capitalist society has enshrined the family as the source of love, affection, and emotional security, the place where our need for stable, intimate human relationships is satisfied" (109).

17. In sexuality studies, the overwhelming focus has been on how queer sexualities and identities have changed over time. Some exceptions exist, of course, such as Jonathan Ned Katz's *The Invention of Heterosexuality* and Stephanie Coontz's *Marriage, a History*. As we have recently seen in arguments against same-sex marriage, the (alleged) historical continuity of heterosexuality remains a popular public notion.

18. Dineh people are historically from New Mexico, Arizona, western Texas, south-eastern Colorado, Utah, and northern Mexico.

19. See his *Simulacra and Simulation*.

20. As Greta Gaard writes of teaching the novel in an ecofeminist literary studies course, "students grappled with the implications of Jess's choice to alter [hir] body . . . possibly because the body has been considered a locus of identity, a pure site of nature that should not be tampered with" ("Hiking without a Map" 241).

21. For instance, when Tyler says on page 25, "I was, I remind you, a child, and children were innocent, if not ignorant, in those days," it's not clear if ze is "thinking" of us as Asha, as other potential recipients of hir story, or, metatextually, as readers in the "real world." But my point is that it doesn't matter: even if we are supposed to understand that ze is speaking to Asha, we are still absorbing Tyler's story.

Chapter 3. "It's Just Not Turning Up"

1. Shoshana Felman, *Writing and Madness* (Ithaca, N.Y.: Cornell University Press, 1985), 210; emphasis original.

2. *Camera Obscura*'s special issue from 2004, *Todd Haynes: A Magnificent Obsession*, fea-tures several essays concerned with Haynes's generic appropriations. In 2010, Haynes adapted James M. Cain's 1941 source novel *Mildred Pierce* into an HBO miniseries star-ring Kate Winslet.

3. See, for example, John David Rhodes's "Allegory, *mise-en-scène*, AIDS: Interpreting *Safe*."

4. Danielle Bouchard and Jigna Desai have noted that "there has been no sustained investigation of the ways in which the film [*Safe* links] Carol's illness with the privileges that come to certain subjects, specifically [in terms of] US empire" (359). This chapter

attempts one such investigation but insists that we look at how U.S. empire operates at the mundane level of the "domestic."

5. As Lisa Lynch explains, "environmental illness, or multiple chemical sensitivity (MCS), can be broadly defined as a breakdown of the immune system caused by chemical overexposure." It has yet to be recognized "as a medical reality by the majority of health professionals, . . . [and] the CDC has not assigned diagnostic criteria for MCS" (207).

6. One notable exception is Stacy Alaimo, who briefly treats the film in her essay "Discomforting Creatures: Monstrous Natures in Recent Films."

7. I count Susan Potter's, Laura Christian's, and Danielle Bouchard and Jigna Desai's among these. Gaye Naismith directly cites the blind spots of Second Wave feminism, noting that the upper classes in *Safe* define themselves via the exclusion of "Othered" bodies. Yet her conclusion is that "in the absence of a feminist consciousness that could possibly grant them some sense of agency or power, Carol and her friends remain enclosed within the patriarchal structure of the family" (367). Since it is undeniable that the female characters in *Safe* exercise agency and power by overseeing various bodies of color and lower class, we might ask why the "solution" would not, instead, be the presence of a feminist consciousness that would *critique* these configurations of agency and power—and their relationship to the ideal patriarchal family.

8. The film's beginning shots are taken from inside a car, moving toward an initially unclear destination, backed by Ed Tomney's eerie synthetic score. Critics such as Reid and Christian have noted how *Safe* often plays like a horror film (but without the expected payoffs of gruesome discoveries or "Gotcha!" moments).

9. Christian Metz's *The Imaginary Signifier* notes the apparent "numerical 'superiority'" (43) of film, due to its synthesis of multiple axes of perception. Like Metz, Haynes stresses that visual access does not equal total omniscience. Visual access, in fact, often serves to obscure the fact that the viewer does *not* have complete knowledge.

10. I have taught this film several times, and each time we discuss this scene, students comment that they thought the DVD had become stuck, or that they find this scene terrifying—and some have both reactions in succession.

11. See Lawrence Buell's "Toxic Discourse."

12. *Hard Core*, Williams's 1990 study of pornographic codes, describes how the so-called money shot, or scene of male ejaculation, is employed as both narrative closure and visual proof that sexual pleasure has been experienced.

13. The concept of "mutual masturbation," for example, appeared around the time of the AIDS crisis.

14. This setting positions the film world in an older, more ignorant epistemological relation with AIDS, insofar as the syndrome was defined only five years prior to the film's milieu. And it contributes to a general sense of the film's milieu as "retro." This allows Haynes to characterize certain values as "outdated" but, more specifically, also contributes to what I will argue is Haynes's indictment of the Reagan era's neoconservative values (often called "1950s" in character). These values, as I briefly discuss, informed the slow and unsympathetic U.S. government response to AIDS in the 1980s.

15. Interestingly enough, critics such as Bouchard and Desai have referred to Peter Dunning as "gay" (366), although his sexual orientation is never specified in the film. It seems,

then, that the association between AIDS and queer sexuality has been so institutionalized that even the most careful, radical readings allow "AIDS" to point back to "gay."

16. Of course, as she has been set up as non-maternal and non-reproductive, and her doctor never mentions a pregnancy test, it seems clear that assumptions have also been made about the impossibility of her being pregnant—which is, admittedly a non-normative impossibility, unlike the assumption that she cannot have AIDS.

17. As José Esteban Muñoz puts it, "Carol could be the perfect model of idealized suburban femininity celebrated by the normative gay imprint" ("Dead White" 136).

18. Fulvia was a wealthy Roman woman born in 77 B.C.E. who married Mark Antony. I believe Fulvia's name invokes the ironic practice of naming slaves after prominent figures such as Roman noblemen and U.S. presidents. For example, the protagonist of Edgar Allan Poe's "The Man That Was Used Up" owns a slave named Pompey—a close associate, as it happens, of Mark Antony. Such allusions were intentionally humiliating, but there might be a more critical edge to Fulvia's name: while Carol may believe that her maid is respected and even invested in her home, we know that Fulvia has nowhere near the status of her namesake, or of Carol herself.

19. The *Oxford English Dictionary* defines "domestic" as "1. A member of a household; one who dwells in the same house with another; an inmate; a member of the family (including children and relatives). 2. a. A household servant or attendant. [2.] b. A domestic animal."

20. Davis's "Health and Safety in the Home" discusses the Whites' name at length. The Whitakers of *Far from Heaven* have a similarly symbolic name: Whitaker derives from "white acre."

21. For example, when Carol's doctor suggests she visit a psychiatrist, he hands the card to her husband, rather than to her. Christian and Davis have noted the patriarchal and heterosexist implications of this scene.

22. See Metz's *The Imaginary Signifier*, 48–49.

23. In fact, Carol's overall inarticulateness—which many critics have dwelled on in gendered terms—here gives way to a confident harnessing of language in the repeated mantra, "Fulvia? Fulvia?"

24. See again Doane, Naismith, Davis, and Rhodes.

25. See Gregory Squires and Chester Hartman's *There Is No Such Thing as a Natural Disaster: Race, Class, and Katrina* (Routledge, 2006).

26. See Bullard, *Confronting Environmental Racism*, 10.

27. See the 2008 U.S. Committee on Education and Labor report "Hidden Tragedy: Underreporting of Workplace Injuries and Illnesses" at http://edlabor.house.gov/publications/20080619WorkplaceInjuriesReport.pdf and Jon Anslow's "Are Migrant Workers More Vulnerable to Occupational Injury than Local Workers?" at https://dspace.lib.cranfield.ac.uk/bitstream/1826/2553/1/Thesis%20-%20Final%20edition.pdf.

28. See Lynne C. Einbinder and Kevin A. Schulman, "The Effect of Race on the Referral Process for Invasive Cardiac Procedures," in *Medical Care Research and Review* 57, supplement 1 (2000): 162–80 and "Ethnic and Racial Disparities in Emergency Department Care for Mild Traumatic Brain Injury" by Jeffrey J. Bazarian et al., in *Academic Emergency Medicine* 10, no. 11 (2003): 1209–17.

29. For a discussion of how the Western home traditionally seeks to differentiate between "inside" and "outside," see Philip Crang's article "Displacement, Consumption, and Identity," in *Environment and Planning A* 28, no. 1 (1995): 47–67. For a comparison with Eastern homes, see http://www.oldhouseweb.com/architecture-and-design/japanese-style-exudes-tranquility.shtml.

30. In *The Second Shift: Working Families and the Revolution At Home* (New York: Viking Press, 1989), Arlie Hochschild and Anne Machung note that women in dual-career partnerships come home to a "second shift" of child care and housework responsibilities. Ironically, Hochschild's work has inspired such self-help tomes as Kathy Sherman's *A Housekeeper Is Cheaper than a Divorce: Why You Can Afford to Hire Help and How to Get It* (Mountain View, Calif.: Life Tools Press, 2000)—a work clearly unconcerned with the prospects of a "second shift" for service workers.

31. See Buckingham-Hatfield.

Chapter 4. "Ranch Stiffs" and "Beach Cowboys" in the Shrinking Public Sphere

1. For example, Ara Osterweil claims that "Ang Lee succeeded in breaking the mainstream Hollywood taboo on homosexuality at the expense of creating a truly radical film" (26).

2. See B. Ruby Rich, "Hello Cowboy," http://www.guardian.co.uk/film/2005/sep/23/3.

3. See the U.S. Bureau of Reclamation's "Very Brief History" at http://www.usbr.gov/history/borhist.html.

4. See "Stemming the Rose: A Brokeback Mystery," at http://findarticles.com/p/articles/mi_hb3491/is_4_13/ai_n29323359/. My point here is that Proulx apparently chose to invent a phrase rather than to utilize one that might be more clearly recognizable as a homophobic epithet.

5. See the Southern Poverty Law Center's recap of the report at http://www.splcenter.org/get-informed/intelligence-report/browse-all-issues/2007/fall/the-oh-really-factor.

6. We should also observe the fact that, while same-sex marriage privatizes same-sex desire, many of its opponents believe it would infringe upon the public good.

7. See also Wendy Lynne Lee and Laura Dow's "Queering Ecological Feminism: Erotophobia, Commodification, Art, and Lesbian Identity."

8. See Foucault's *The History of Sexuality, vol* 1.

9. As Rosemary Hennessey reminds us, "for those of us caught up in the circuits of late capitalist consumption, the visibility of sexual identity is often a matter of commodification, a process that invariably depends on the lives and labor of invisible others" (31).

10. Perez observes that "the cowboy ethic of 'use rights' suggests a radically different relationship to land, resources, and community in contrast to privatization. This ethic, however, clearly situates the cowboy outside the law. This same ethic is intrinsic to Ennis's queerness" (78).

11. For all of these reasons, Ennis's Spanish surname "del Mar," meaning "of the sea," seems particularly pointed.

12. See the U.S. Department of the Interior's Bureau of Reclamation on Wyoming's Riverton Unit, http://www.usbr.gov/projects/Project.jsp?proj_Name=Riverton+Unit.

13. *Brokeback* has enjoyed quite the afterlife in the world of "fan-fic," or fan-authored fiction.

14. We should also consider how Rudy's presence alludes to the "natural order" of its milieu. Sergeant Neal's attempt to shut down his operation invokes the loss of property and personal freedom of hundreds of thousands of U.S. citizens of Japanese descent some fifteen years earlier.

15. Several scholars have produced reception studies on the film, including Harry M. Benshoff and Pilar Aurelia Bermudez.

16. See, for example, Gary Lease and Michael E. Soule's *Reinventing Nature? Responses to Postmodern Deconstruction* (1995).

17. As messages were initially prohibited, postcards at first functioned solely through the conveyance of images.

18. See Jonathan Ned Katz's *Love Stories: Sex between Men before Homosexuality* (2001), for an account of Lincoln's relationship with Joshua Speed.

19. Here, the film is a bit murky. One character is identified as a "Basque"; he takes the weekly grocery order from Jack and Ennis. Another character is credited as "Chilean sheepherder." Joe Aguirre's last name may denote Chicano or mestizo heritage—but, considering its resonance with that of the famed Spanish conquistador, we might read his character quite differently.

20. See Valverde's article "A New Entity in the History of Sexuality: The Respectable Same-Sex Couple."

21. See, for instance http://architectures.danlockton.co.uk/2008/12/18/anti-homeless -stools/.

Chapter 5. Attack of the Queer Atomic Mutants

1. For an exhaustive list, see the blogs Atomic Age Cinema (http://atomicagecinema .com/) and Radiation Cinema! (http://www.radiationcinema.com/).

2. An entire organization, the Shakespeare Authorship Trust, is dedicated to the question of who wrote under the name William Shakespeare. Several works of historical and literary fiction, such as Jennifer Lee Carrell's *Interred with Their Bones*, have proposed various answers. See also scholarly works such as Michael Keevak's *Sexual Shakespeare*, which investigates the question of Shakespeare and homosexuality.

3. On the GoodReads Web site, for example, readers describe the text as being marred by "self-congratulatory cleverness" ("Wealhtheow") and as "pretentiously writ-ten" ("Maggie").

4. See, for instance, Linda Hutcheon's *The Politics of Postmodernism*.

5. See "Bush Calls for Ban on Same-Sex Marriages," http://www.cnn.com/2004/ ALLPOLITICS/02/24/elec04.prez.bush.marriage/.

6. The numbers of those who died of radiation sickness are unknown. See the American Cancer Institute's reports on the Nevada Test Site at http://www.cancer.gov/i131/ fallout/contents.html.

7. See Steve Kanigher, "Former Test Site Workers Closer to Cancer Compensation from Government," http://www.lasvegassun.com/news/2010/feb/11/former-test-site -workers-closer-cancer-compensatio/.

8. The link between communism and homosexuality has been explored by numerous scholars, including Robert J. Corber and Harry M. Benshoff.

9. See http://www.one-colorado.org/news/become-a-transgender-ally/.

10. For instance, controversy has erupted over recent biographies of Abraham Lincoln and Gandhi, which claim that the figures in question were "gay."

11. See Steven Shaviro, "Geek Love Is All You Need," http://www.electronicbookreview .com/thread/fictionspresent/conjoined.

12. See Mazel's *American Literary Environmentalism*.

13. See Meizhu Lui, "The Wealth Gap Gets Wider," *The Washington Post*, March 23, 2009, at http://www.washingtonpost.com/wp-dyn/content/article/2009/03/22/AR2009032201506 .html (accessed August 7, 2012).

14. See, for instance, Calvin Thomas, ed., *Straight with a Twist: Queer Theory and the Subject of Heterosexuality* (Urbana: University of Illinois Press, 1999).

15. While I agree with Zuk's point that using evidence from animals to comment on humans can be problematic, I take issue with her suggestion that the human world is entirely separate from the non-human.

16. The Shundahai Health Network, for instance, is a Western Shoshone–founded group that works for nuclear disarmament.

17. In *Pale Fire*, the unreliable narrator—who has been on a madcap quest of his own, one that has thrown the very foundations of authorship into question—longs for "a comfortable table—not like the shaky little affair on which my typewriter is precariously enthroned now, in this wretched motor lodge" (28). Nora's middle name, Grey, invokes the alter ego of *Pale Fire*'s narrator, the assassin Gradus—who in turn is a direct analogue to Mr. Gray, the narrator's nemesis in *White Noise*.

18. See Sascha Pöhlmann, "How the Other Half Dies," http://www-copas.uni-regensburg .de/articles/issue_09/09_01_text_poehlmann.php.

19. See Stéphane Vanderhaeghe, "What's Black and White and Read All Over?," http:// lisa.revues.org/353.

20. *Publishers Weekly* declares that "Jackson's prose is nothing short of dazzling, but it's still not enough to give real tension to her oddball plot" (http://www.publishersweekly .com/978-0-06-088235-8), while Tania Barnes writes in *Library Journal*, "Readers who have been spurred along equally by the book's mystery—what does Blanche want?—. . . will feel frustrated by the confusing denouement and open-ended conclusion" (http:// www.libraryjournal.com/article/CA6352379.html).

Conclusion

1. Lauren R. Hall has started this kind of work with her research on the queerness of vegetarianism.

2. Drawing on Pew research, Andrew J. Hoffman reports that "75 percent of Democrats believe there is solid evidence of global warming, compared to 35 percent of Republicans and 53 percent of Independents" (2). Opinions on gay marriage break down similarly along political lines.

Bibliography

127 Hours. Dir. Danny Boyle. Perf. James Franco. Fox Searchlight Pictures. 2010. Film.

Aaron, Michele, ed. New Queer Cinema: A Critical Reader. Edinburgh, UK: Edinburgh University Press, 2004.

Adams, Carol J. The Pornography of Meat. New York: Continuum, 2004.

Adamson, Joni, Mei Mei Evans, and Rachel Stein, eds. The Environmental Justice Reader: Politics, Poetics, and Pedagogy. Tucson: University of Arizona Press, 2002.

Alaimo, Stacy. "Discomforting Creatures: Monstrous Natures in Recent Films." Beyond Nature Writing: Expanding the Boundaries of Ecocriticism. Ed. Karla Armbruster and Kathleen R. Wallace. Charlottesville: University of Virginia Press, 2001.

———. Undomesticated Ground: Recasting Nature as Feminist Space. Ithaca, N.Y.: Cornell University Press, 2000.

Anderson, Jill E. "'Warm Blood and Live Semen and Rich Marrow and Wholesome Flesh!': A Queer Ecological Reading of Christopher Isherwood's A Single Man." Journal of Ecocriticism 3.1 (2011): 51–66.

Armbruster, Karla. "'Buffalo Gals, Won't You Come Out Tonight': Boundary-Crossing in Ecofeminist Literary Criticism." Ecofeminist Literary Criticism: Theory, Interpretation, Pedagogy. Ed. Greta Gaard and Patrick D. Murphy. Champaign: University of Illinois Press, 1998. 97–122.

Bachelard, Gaston. The Poetics of Space: The Classic Look at How We Experience Intimate Places. Trans. M. Jolas. Boston: Beacon Press, 1994.

Bagemihl, Bruce. Biological Exuberance: Animal Homosexuality and Natural Diversity. New York: St. Martin's Press, 1999.

Barnes, Tania. Review of Half Life, by Shelley Jackson. Library Journal. July 15, 2006. Accessed March 2, 2011, at http://www.libraryjournal.com/article/CA6352379.html.

Barry, Peter. Beginning Theory: An Introduction to Literary and Cultural Theory. Manchester, UK: Manchester University Press, 2002.

Baudrillard, Jean. Simulacra and Simulation. Trans. Sheila Glaser. Ann Arbor: University of Michigan Press, 1981.

———. "We Are All Transsexuals Now." Screened Out. Brooklyn, N.Y.: Verso, 2002.

Beautiful Thing. Dir. Hettie Macdonald. Perf. Glen Berry, Linda Henry, Meera Syal. Sony Pictures Classics. 1996. Film.

Benshoff, Harry. "Brokering Brokeback Mountain: A Local Reception Study." *Jump Cut* 50 (2008): n. p. Accessed November 15, 2010, at http://www.ejumpcut.org/archive/jc50.2008/BrokbkMtn/index.html.

Berila, Beth. "Toxic Bodies? ACT UP's Disruption of the Heteronormative Landscape of the Nation." *New Perspectives on Environmental Justice: Gender, Sexuality, and Activism*. Ed. Rachel Stein. New Brunswick, N.J.: Rutgers University Press, 2004. 127–36.

Berlant, Lauren. "Cruel Optimism." *differences* 17.3 (2006): 20–36.

Bersani, Leo. "A Conversation with Leo Bersani with Tim Dean, Hal Foster, and Kaja Silverman." *Is the Rectum a Grave? And Other Essays*. Chicago: University of Chicago Press, 2010.

———. "Is the Rectum a Grave?" *October* 43 (1987): 197–222.

Bérubé, Allan. *My Desire for History: Essays in Gay, Community, and Labor History*. Ed. John D'Emilio and Estelle B. Freedman. Chapel Hill: University of North Carolina Press, 2011.

Bindel, Julie. "The Ugly Side of Beauty." *The Guardian*. July 2, 2005. Accessed May 15, 2006, at http://www.guardian.co.uk/world/2005/jul/02/gender.politicsphilosophyandsociety.

Biro, Andrew. *Denaturalizing Ecological Politics: Alienation from Nature from Rousseau to the Frankfurt School and Beyond*. Toronto: University of Toronto Press, 2005.

Bolcer, Julie. "Gay and Green on Earth Day." *The Advocate*. April 22, 2010. Accessed November 26, 2011, at http://www.advocate.com/News/Daily_News/2010/04/22/Gay_and_Green_on_Earth_Dy.

Bookchin, Murray. "Social Ecology versus Deep Ecology: A Challenge for the Ecology Movement." *Philosophical Dialogues: Arne Naess and the Progress of Ecophilosophy*. Ed. Nina Witoszek and Andrew Brennan. Lanham, Md.: Rowman and Littlefield, 1999. 281–301.

Bookchin, Murray, Dave Foreman, Steve Chase, and David Levine. *Defending the Earth: A Dialogue between Murray Bookchin and Dave Foreman*. Cambridge, Mass.: South End Press, 1991.

Bouchard, Danielle, and Jigna Desai. "'There's Nothing More Debilitating than Travel': Locating US Empire in Todd Haynes's *Safe*." *Quarterly Review of Film and Video* 22.4 (2005): 359–70.

Branch, Michael P., Rochelle Johnson, Daniel Patterson, and Scott Slovic, eds. *Reading the Earth: New Directions in the Study of Literature and the Environment*. Moscow: University of Idaho Press, 1998.

Broder, John M. "BP Shortcuts Led to Gulf Oil Spill, Report Says." *The New York Times*. September 15, 2011. Accessed November 10, 2011, at http://www.nytimes.com/2011/09/15/science/earth/15spill.html.

Brokeback Mountain. Dir. Ang Lee. Perf. Jack Gyllenhaal, Heath Ledger, Randy Quaid. 2005. Universal Home Entertainment, 2006. DVD.

Brooks, Peter. *Reading for the Plot: Design and Intention in Narrative*. Cambridge, Mass.: Harvard University Press, 1992.

Bruhm, Steven, and Natasha Hurley, eds. *Curiouser and Curiouser: On the Queerness of Children*. Minneapolis: University of Minnesota Press, 2004.

Buckingham-Hatfield, Susan. *Gender and Environment*. London: Routledge, 2000.

Buell, Lawrence. *The Future of Environmental Criticism: Environmental Crisis and Literary Imagi-nation*. Hoboken, N.J.: Wiley-Blackwell, 2005.

———. "Toxic Discourse." *Critical Inquiry* 24.3 (1998): 639–65.

Bullard, Robert D. *Dumping in Dixie: Race, Class, and Environmental Quality*. Boulder, Colo.: Westview Press, 1990.

———, ed. "Introduction." *Confronting Environmental Racism: Voices from the Grassroots*. Boston: South End Press, 1993. 7–14.

———, ed. *The Quest for Environmental Justice: Human Rights and the Politics of Pollution*. San Francisco: Sierra Club Books, 2005.

Byers, Thomas. "Liberal Ideology in *Brokeback Mountain*: Gay Marriage, Mexico, and Homo Sacer." Institut for Historie og Områdestudier. Aarhus University, Denmark. April 17, 2008. Lecture.

Butler, Judith. *Bodies that Matter: On the Discursive Limits of "Sex."* New York: Routledge, 1993.

———. *Gender Trouble: Feminism and the Subversion of Identity*. New York: Routledge, 1990.

Callinicos, Alex. *Theories and Narratives: Reflections on the Philosophy of History*. Durham, N.C.: Duke University Press, 1995.

Caserio, Robert. "The Antisocial Thesis in Queer Theory." Forum: Conference Debates. "The Antisocial Thesis in Queer Theory." *PMLA* 121.3 (2006): 819–21.

Chisholm, Dianne. "Biophilia, Creative Involution, and the Ecological Future of Queer Desire." *Queer Ecologies: Sex, Nature, Politics, Desire*. Ed. Catriona Mortimer-Sandilands and Bruce Erickson. Bloomington: Indiana University Press, 2010. 359–81.

Chisholm, Hugh. "Irrigation." *Encyclopedia Britannica*. 11th ed. Vol. 14. New York: Encyclopedia Britannica Company, 1910. 841–53.

Chris, Cynthia. *Watching Wildlife*. Minneapolis: Minnesota University Press, 2006.

Christian, Laura. "Of Housewives and Saints: Abjection, Transgression, and Impossible Mourning in *Poison* and *Safe*." *Camera Obscura* 19.3 (2004): 92–123.

Colborn, Theo, Dianne Dumanoski, and John Peter Meyer. *Our Stolen Future: Are We Threatening Our Fertility, Intelligence, and Survival? A Scientific Detective Story*. New York: Plume, 1997.

Clare, Eli. *Exile and Pride: Disability, Queerness, and Liberation*. Cambridge, Mass.: South End Press, 1999.

Clark, David L., and Catherine Myser. "Being Humaned: Medical Documentaries and the Hyperrealization of Conjoined Twins." *Freakery: Cultural Spectacles of the Extraordinary Body*. Ed. Rosemarie Garland Thomson. New York: New York University Press, 1996. 338–55.

———. "'Fixing' Katie and Eilish: Medical Documentaries and the Subjection of Conjoined Twins." *Literature and Medicine* 17.1 (1998): 45–67.

Cliff, Michelle. *No Telephone to Heaven*. New York: Vintage International, 1987.

CNN. "Bush Calls for Ban on Same-Sex Marriages." February 25, 2004. Accessed July 7, 2010, at http://www.cnn.com/2004/ALLPOLITICS/02/24/elec04.prez.bush.marriage/.

Connell, Kathleen. "Green Is Not Just Another Pretty Color in the Rainbow Flag." *San Diego Gay and Lesbian News*. April 21, 2010. Accessed November 27, 2011, at http://sdgln.com/commentary/2010/04/15/green-not-just-another-pretty-color-rainbow-flag.

Corr, John. "Affective Coordination and Avenging Grace: Dionne Brand's *In Another Place, Not Here*." *Canadian Literature* 201 (Summer 2009): 113–29.

Crenshaw, Kimberlé. "Demarginalizing the Intersection of Race and Sex: A Black Feminist Critique of Antidiscrimination Doctrine, Feminist Theory and Antiracist Politics." *The Politics of Law: A Progressive Critique*. Ed. David Kairys. New York: Pantheon, 1990. 195–217.

Cronon, William. "The Trouble with Wilderness; or, Getting Back to the Wrong Nature." *Uncommon Ground: Rethinking the Human Place in Nature*. Ed. William Cronon. New York: Norton, 1996. 69–90.

Curry, Patrick. "Nature Post-Nature." *New Formations* 26 (Spring 2008): 51–64.

Davis, Glyn. "Health and Safety in the Home: Todd Haynes's Clinical White World." *Territories of Desire in Queer Culture: Reconfiguring Contemporary Boundaries*. Ed. David Alderson and Linda Anderson. Manchester, UK: Manchester University Press, 2001.

Dean, Tim. "The Antisocial Homosexual." Forum: Conference Debates. "The Antisocial Thesis in Queer Theory." *PMLA* 121.3 (2006): 827–28.

Deleuze, Gilles, and Félix Guattari. *Anti-Oedipus: Capitalism and Schizophrenia*. Minneapolis: University of Minnesota Press, 1983.

DeLillo, Don. *White Noise*. New York: Penguin, 1986.

DeLoughrey, Elizabeth M., Renée K. Gosson, and George B. Handley, eds. *Caribbean Literature and the Environment: Between Nature and Culture*. Charlottesville: University of Virginia Press, 2005.

D'Emilio, John. "Capitalism and Gay Identity." *Powers of Desire: The Politics of Sexuality*. Ed. Ann Snitow, Christine Stansell, and Sharon Thompson. New York: Monthly Review Press, 1983.

Di Chiro, Giovanna. "Polluted Politics? Confronting Toxic Discourse, Sex Panic, and Eco-Normativity." *Queer Ecologies: Sex, Nature, Politics, Desire*. Ed. Catriona Mortimer-Sandilands and Bruce Erickson. Bloomington: Indiana University Press, 2010.

Doane, Mary Ann. "Pathos and Pathology: The Cinema of Todd Haynes." *Camera Obscura* 19.3 (2004): 1–21.

Dreger, Alice. *One of Us: Conjoined Twins and the Future of Normal*. Cambridge, Mass.: Harvard University Press, 2005.

Duggan, Lisa. *The Twilight of Equality? Neoliberalism, Cultural Politics, and the Attack on Democracy*. Boston: Beacon Press, 2004.

Edelman, Lee. "Antagonism, Negativity, and the Subject of Queer Theory." Forum: Conference Debates. "The Antisocial Thesis in Queer Theory." *PMLA* 121.3 (2006): 821–23.

———. *No Future: Queer Theory and the Death Drive*. Durham, N.C.: Duke University Press, 2004.

Ensslin, Astrid. "Women in Wasteland: Gendered Deserts in T. S. Eliot and Shelley Jackson." *Journal of Gender Studies* 14.3 (2005): 205–16.

Estok, Simon. "Theorizing in a Space of Ambivalent Openness: Ecocriticism and Ecophobia." *ISLE* 16.2 (Spring 2009): 203–25.

Evans, Mei Mei. "'Nature' and Environmental Justice." *The Environmental Justice Reader: Politics, Poetics, and Pedagogy*. Ed. Joni Adamson, Mei Mei Evans, and Rachel Stein. Tucson: University of Arizona Press, 2002. 181–93.

Far from Heaven. Dir. Todd Haynes. Perf. Julianne Moore, Dennis Quaid, Dennis Haysbert, Viola Davis. Universal Studios. 2002. DVD.

Farmer, Paul. *Pathologies of Power: Health, Human Rights, and the New War on the Poor*. Berkeley: University of California Press, 2003.

Feinberg, Leslie. *Stone Butch Blues: A Novel*. Ithaca, N.Y.: Firebrand, 1993.

———. *Transgender Warriors: Making History from Joan of Arc to RuPaul*. Boston: Beacon Press, 1996.

Felman, Shoshana. *Writing and Madness*. Ithaca, N.Y.: Cornell University Press, 1985.

Felski, Rita. "Fin de Siècle, Fin du Sexe: Transsexuality, Postmodernism, and the Death of History." *The Transgender Studies Reader*. Ed. Susan Stryker and Stephen Whittle. New York: Routledge, 2006. 565–73.

Foucault, Michel. *Discipline and Punish: The Birth of the Prison*. New York: Vintage, 1995.

———. *The History of Sexuality vol. 1: An Introduction*. New York: Vintage, 1990.

Fox, Karen M. "Leisure: Celebration and Resistance in the Ecofeminist Quilt." *Ecofeminism: Women, Culture, Nature*. Ed. Karen J. Warren. Bloomington: Indiana University Press, 1997.

Francis, Margot. "The 'Lesbian National Parks and Services': Reading Sex, Race and the Nation in Artistic Performance." *Canadian Woman Studies* 20.2 (2000): 131–36.

Freud, Sigmund. *Three Essays on the Theory of Sexuality*. New York: Basic, 2000.

Gaard, Greta, ed., *Ecofeminism: Women, Animals, Nature*. Philadelphia: Temple University Press, 1993.

———. "Hiking without a Map: Reflections on Teaching Ecofeminist Literary Criticism." *Ecofeminist Literary Criticism: Theory, Interpretation, Pedagogy*. Ed. Greta Gaard and Patrick D. Murphy. Champaign: University of Illinois Press, 1998. 224–45.

———. "Toward a Queer Ecofeminism." *Hypatia* 12.1 (1997): 114–37.

Gaard, Greta, and Patrick D. Murphy, eds. *Ecofeminist Literary Criticism: Theory, Interpretation, Pedagogy*. Champaign: University of Illinois Press, 1998.

Giffney, Noreen, and Myra J. Hird. *Queering the Non/Human*. Hampshire, UK: Ashgate, 2008.

Glotfelty, Cheryll, and Harold Fromm, eds. *The Ecocriticism Reader: Landmarks in Literary Ecology*. Athens: University of Georgia Press, 1996.

Gosine, Andil. "Non-White Reproduction and Same-Sex Eroticism: Queer Acts against Nature." *Queer Ecologies: Sex, Nature, Politics, Desire*. Ed. Catriona Mortimer-Sandilands and Bruce Erickson. Bloomington: Indiana University Press, 2010.

Green, Jamison. *Becoming a Visible Man*. Nashville, Tenn.: Vanderbilt University Press, 2004.

Grosz, Elizabeth. *Volatile Bodies: Toward a Corporeal Feminism*. Bloomington: University of Indiana Press, 1994.

Grover, Jan Zita. *North Enough: AIDS and Other Clearcuts*. Minneapolis: Graywolf, 1997.

Guha, Ramachandra. *Environmentalism: A Global History*. Oxford, UK: Oxford University Press, 2000.

Hagood, Amanda. "The Domestication of U.S. Environmentalism, 1945–1962." Diss. Vanderbilt University, 2010. Print.

Halberstam, Judith. *Female Masculinity*. Durham, N.C.: Duke University Press, 1998.

———. "The Politics of Negativity in Recent Queer Theory." Forum: Conference Debates. "The Antisocial Thesis in Queer Theory." *PMLA* 121.3 (2006): 823–25.

———. *In a Queer Time and Place: Transgender Bodies, Subcultural Lives*. New York: New York University Press, 2005.

———. "Theorizing Queer Temporalities: A Roundtable Discussion." *GLQ: A Journal of Lesbian and Gay Studies* 13.2 (2007): 177–95.

Hallberg, Carl. "Water in Wyoming." Wyoming State Archives, n.d. Accessed No-

vember 12, 2011, at http://wyoarchives.state.wy.us/Research/Topics/SubTopic.asp
?SubID=4&nav=1&homeID=1.

Haraway, Donna. *Simians, Cyborgs, and Women: The Reinvention of Nature*. New York: Routledge, 1991.

Hastie, Amelie, ed. *Todd Haynes: A Magnificent Obsession*. Durham, N.C.: Duke University
Press, 2005.

Hays, Samuel P. *A History of Environmental Politics since 1945*. Pittsburgh: University of
Pittsburgh Press, 2000.

Hennessey, Rosemary. "Queer Visibility and Commodity Culture." *Cultural Critique* 29
(Winter 1994–95): 31–76.

Herring, Scott. *Another Country: Queer Anti-Urbanism*. New York: New York University Press,
2010.

———. "Brokeback Mountain Dossier: Introduction." *GLQ* 13.1 (2007): 93–94.

———. "Out of the Closets, into the Woods: RFD, *Country Women*, and the Post-Stonewall
Emergence of Queer Anti-Urbanism." *American Quarterly* 59.2 (2007): 341–72.

Hoffman, Andrew J. "The Culture and Discourse of Climate Change Skepticism." *Strategic
Organization* 9.1 (2011): 1–8.

Hogan, Katie. "Detecting Toxic Environments: Gay Mystery as Environmental Justice."
New Perspectives on Environmental Justice: Gender, Sexuality, and Activism. Ed. Rachel Stein.
New Brunswick, N.J: Rutgers University Press, 2004. 249–61.

———. "Undoing Nature: Coalition Building as Queer Environmentalism." *Queer Ecologies: Sex, Nature, Politics, Desire*. Ed. Catriona Mortimer-Sandilands and Bruce Erickson.
Bloomington: Indiana University Press, 2010. 231–53.

Hoving, Isabel. "Moving the Caribbean Landscape: *Cereus Blooms at Night* as a Re-imagi-
nation of the Caribbean Environment." *Caribbean Literature and the Environment: Between
Nature and Culture*. Ed. Elizabeth M. DeLoughrey, Renée K. Gosson, and George B.
Handley. Charlottesville: University of Virginia Press, 2005. 154–68.

An Inconvenient Truth. Dir. David Guggenheim. Perf. Al Gore. Paramount Classics. 2006.
Film.

Ingram, Annie Merrill, Ian Marshall, Daniel J. Philippon, and Adam W. Sweeting, eds.
Coming into Contact: Explorations in Ecocritical Theory and Practice. Athens: University of
Georgia Press, 2007.

Ingram, Gordon Brent. "Marginality and the Landscapes of Erotic Alien(n)ations." *Queers
in Space: Communities, Public Places, Sites of Resistance*. Ed. Gordon Brent Ingram, Anne-
Marie Bouthillette, and Yolanda Retter. San Francisco: Bay Press, 1997. 27–54.

———. "'Open' Space as Strategic Queer Sites." *Queers in Space: Communities, Public Places,
Sites of Resistance*. Ed. Gordon Brent Ingram, Anne-Marie Bouthillette, and Yolanda
Retter. San Francisco: Bay Press, 1997. 95–126.

Ingram, Gordon Brent, Anne-Marie Bouthillette, and Yolanda Retter, eds. *Queers in Space:
Communities, Public Places, Sites of Resistance*. San Francisco: Bay Press, 1997.

———. "Strategies for (Re)constructing Queer Communities." *Queers in Space: Communities, Public Places, Sites of Resistance*. Ed. Gordon Brent Ingram, Anne-Marie Bouthillette,
and Yolanda Retter. San Francisco: Bay Press, 1997. 447–58.

———. "Surveying Territories and Landscapes." *Queers in Space: Communities, Public Places,
Sites of Resistance*. Ed. Gordon Brent Ingram, Anne-Marie Bouthillette, and Yolanda
Retter. San Francisco: Bay Press, 1997. 91–94.

Isaac, Steven. Review of *Brokeback Mountain*. Focus on the Family's Plugged-In Online, n.d. Accessed November 11, 2010, at http://www.pluggedin.com/videos/2005/q4/brokebackmountain.aspx.

Jackson, Shelley. *Half Life: A Novel*. New York: Harper Perennial, 2006.

Jagose, Annamarie. *Queer Theory: An Introduction*. New York: New York University Press, 1997.

Jameson, Fredric. *The Political Unconscious: Narrative as a Socially Symbolic Act*. Ithaca, N.Y.: Cornell University Press, 1981.

———. *Postmodernism, or, the Cultural Logic of Late Capitalism*. Durham, N.C.: Duke University Press, 1991.

Jones, Aphrodite. *All She Wanted: "Brandon Teena," the Girl Who Became a Boy but Paid the Ultimate Price*. New York: Pocket, 2002.

Kane, Ariadne. "Cross-Gendered Persons." *The International Encyclopedia of Sexology*, 1997–2001. Vols. 1–4. Accessed March 5, 2009, at http://www2.hu-berlin.de/sexology/IES/xmain.html.

Kerber, Linda. "Separate Spheres, Female Worlds, Woman's Place: The Rhetoric of Women's History." *Journal of American History* 75.1 (1988): 9–39.

Kilgore, Christopher. "We Are 'I': Narrative Paradox and Identity in Shelley Jackson's *Half Life*." International Society for the Study of Narrative. MLA Annual Convention. Philadelphia. December 2009. Address.

Kitses, Jim. "All that Brokeback Allows." *Film Quarterly* 60.3 (Spring 2007): 22–27.

Kolodny, Annette. *The Lay of the Land: Metaphor as Experience and History in American Life and Letters*. Chapel Hill: University of North Carolina Press, 1975.

Kristeva, Julia. *Powers of Horror: An Essay on Abjection*. New York: Columbia University Press, 1982.

Kroeber, Karl. *Ecological Literary Criticism: Romantic Imagining and the Biology of Mind*. New York: Columbia University Press, 1994.

Kutzinski, Vera M. "Improprieties: Feminism, Queerness, and Caribbean Literature." *Macalester International* 10 (2001): 165–206.

LaDuke, Winona. *All Our Relations: Native Struggles for Land and Life*. Cambridge, Mass.: South End Press, 1999.

———. "Foreword." *New Perspectives on Environmental Justice: Gender, Sexuality, and Activism*. Ed. Rachel Stein. New Brunswick, N.J.: Rutgers University Press, 2004. 1–2.

Lease, Gary, and Michael E. Soule, eds. *Reinventing Nature? Responses to Postmodern Deconstruction*. Washington, D.C.: Island Press, 1995.

Lee, Wendy Lynne, and Laura Dow. "Queering Ecological Feminism: Erotophobia, Commodification, Art, and Lesbian Identity." *Ethics & the Environment* 6.2 (2001): 1–21.

Leung, William. "So Queer Yet So Straight: Ang Lee's *The Wedding Banquet* and *Brokeback Mountain*." *Journal of Film and Video* 60.1 (2008): 23–42.

Lynch, Lisa. "The Epidemiology of 'Regrettable Kinship': Gender, Epidemic, and Community in Todd Haynes' [*Safe*] and Richard Powers' *Gain*." *Journal of Medical Humanities* 23.3/4 (Winter 2002): 203–19.

MacGregor, Sherilyn. "From Care to Citizenship: Calling Ecofeminism Back to Politics." *Ethics and the Environment* 9.1 (2004): 56–84.

Machor, George. *Pastoral Cities: Urban Ideals and the Symbolic Landscape of America*. Madison: University of Wisconsin Press, 1987.

Manalansan, Martin F. "Colonizing Time and Space: Race and Romance in *Brokeback Mountain*." *GLQ* 13.1 (2001): 97–100.

Manes, Christopher. [Miss Ann Thropy.] "AIDS and Population." *Earth First!* 7.5 (1987): 32.

Martinez, Roy. *On Race and Racism in America: Confessions in Philosophy*. Philadelphia: Pennsylvania State University Press, 2010.

Mazel, David. *American Literary Environmentalism*. Athens: University of Georgia Press, 2000.

———. "Annie Dillard and the *Book of Job*: Notes toward a Postnatural Ecocriticism." *Coming into Contact: Explorations in Ecocritical Theory and Practice*. Ed. Annie Merrill Ingram, Ian Marshall, Daniel J. Philippon, and Adam W. Sweeting. Athens: University of Georgia Press, 2007. 185–95.

McBride, Dwight A. "Why I Hated that I Loved *Brokeback Mountain*." *GLQ* 13.1 (2001): 95–97.

McKibben, Bill. *The End of Nature*. New York: Random House, 1989.

Metz, Christian. *The Imaginary Signifier: Psychoanalysis and the Cinema*. Bloomington: Indiana University Press, 1982.

Meyer, Stephen M. "The Economic Impact of Environmental Regulation." *Journal of Environmental Law & Practice*, 1995. http://web.mit.edu/polisci/mpepp/Reports/Econ%20Impact%20Enviro%20Reg.pdf.

Miller, D. A. "On the Universality of *Brokeback Mountain*." *Film Quarterly* 60.3 (2007): 50–60.

Miller, Timothy. *The 60s Communes: Hippies and Beyond*. Syracuse, N.Y.: Syracuse University Press, 1999.

Mitchell, David T., and Sharon L. Snyder, eds. *The Body and Physical Difference: Discourses of Disability*. Ann Arbor: University of Michigan Press, 1997.

Moore, Mignon. "Color Us Invisible: In the Shadows of Communities Black and Gay, Black Lesbians Forge Lives, Loves, And Family." *The Huffington Post*, November 4, 2011. Accessed November 24, 2011, at http://www.huffingtonpost.com/mignon-r-moore/black-lesbians_b_1075251.html.

Mootoo, Shani. *Cereus Blooms at Night*. New York: Grove, 1998.

Morris, David B. *The Culture of Pain*. Berkeley: University of California Press, 1997.

Mortimer-Sandilands, Catriona, and Bruce Erickson, eds. *Queer Ecologies: Sex, Nature, Politics, Desire*. Bloomington: Indiana University Press, 2010.

Morton, Timothy. "Queer Ecology." *PMLA* 125.2 (March 2010): 273–82.

Muñoz, José Esteban. *Cruising Utopia: The Then and There of Queer Futurity*. New York: New York University Press, 2009.

———. "Dead White: Notes on the Whiteness of Queer Cinema." *GLQ* 41.1 (1998): 127–38.

———. *Disidentifications: Queers of Color and the Performance of Politics*. Minneapolis: University of Minnesota Press, 1999.

———. "Thinking beyond Antirelationality and Antiutopianism in Queer Critique." Forum: Conference Debates. "The Antisocial Thesis in Queer Theory." *PMLA* 121.3 (2006): 825–26.

Nabokov, Vladimir. *Pale Fire*. New York: Vintage, 1989.

Naess, Arne, and George Sessions. "Eight-Point Deep Ecology Platform." *Clear Cut: The Tragedy of Industrial Forestry*. Ed. Bill Devall. San Francisco: Sierra Club Books, 1993.

Naismith, Gaye. "Tales from the Crypt: Contamination and Quarantine in Todd Haynes's [*Safe*]." *The Visible Woman: Imaging Technologies, Gender, and Science*. Ed. Paula A. Treichler, Lisa Cartwright, and Constance Penley. New York: New York University Press, 1998.

Nash, Roderick. *The Rights of Nature: A History of Environmental Ethics*. Madison: University of Wisconsin Press, 1989.

Orton, David. "Deep Ecology and the Left—Contradictions." *Deep Green Web*, January 2011. Accessed March 30, 2011, at http://deepgreenweb.blogspot.com/2011/01/deep-ecology-and-left-contradictions.html.

Osterweil, Ara. "Ang Lee's Lonesome Cowboys." *Film Quarterly* 60.3 (Spring 2007): 38–42.

Pearl, Monica. "AIDS and New Queer Cinema." *New Queer Cinema: A Critical Reader*. Ed. Michele Aaron. Edinburgh, UK: Edinburg University Press, 2004.

Perez, Hiram. "Gay Cowboys Close to Home: Ennis Del Mar on the Q.T." *Reading Brokeback Mountain: Essays on the Story and the Film*. Ed. Jim Stacy. Jefferson, N.C.: McFarland, 2007.

Phillips, Dana. "Don DeLillo's Postmodern Pastoral." *Reading the Earth: New Directions in the Study of Literature and the Environment*. Ed. Michael P. Branch, Rochelle Johnson, Daniel Patterson, and Scott Slovic. Moscow: University of Idaho Press, 1998. 235–46.

Pingree, Allison. "America's 'United Siamese Brothers': Chang and Eng and Nineteenth-Century Ideologies of Democracy and Domesticity." *Monster Theory: Reading Culture*. Ed. Jeffrey J. Cohen. Minneapolis: Minnesota University Press, 1996. 92–114.

———. "The 'Exceptions that Prove the Rule': Daisy and Violet Hilton, the 'New Woman,' and the Bonds of Marriage." *Freakery: Cultural Spectacles of the Extraordinary Body*. Ed. Rosemarie Garland Thomson. New York: New York University Press, 1996. 173–84.

Pöhlmann, Sascha. "How the Other Half Dies: Narrating Identities in Shelley Jackson's *Half Life*." *COPAS: Current Objectives of Postgraduate American Studies* 9 (2008). http://www-copas.uni-regensburg.de/articles/issue_09/09_01_text_poehlmann.php.

Potter, Susan. "Dangerous Spaces: *Safe*." *Camera Obscura* 57/19.3 (2004): 124–54.

Proctor, J. "The Social Construction of Nature: Relativist Accusations, Pragmatist and Critical Realist Responses." *Annals of the Association of American Geographers* 88.3: 352–76.

Proulx, Annie. "Brokeback Mountain." *Close Range: Wyoming Stories*. New York: Scribner, 1999.

Publishers Weekly. Review of *Half Life*, by Shelley Jackson. *Publishers Weekly*, July 3, 2006. Accessed February 1, 2011, at http://www.publishersweekly.com/978-0-06-088235-8.

Quart, Alissa. "When Girls Will Be Boys." *The New York Times Magazine* (March 16, 2008): 32–37.

Raymond, Janice G. *The Transsexual Empire: The Making of the She-Male*. New York: Teachers College Press, 1994.

Reid, Roddey. "Un*Safe* at Any Distance: Todd Haynes' Visual Culture of Health and Risk." *Film Quarterly* 51.3 (Spring 1998): 32–44.

Rhodes, John David. "Allegory, mise-en-scène, AIDS: Interpreting *Safe*." *The Cinema of Todd Haynes: All that Heaven Allows*. Ed. James Morrison. London: Wallflower Press, 2007. 68–78.

Rich, B. Ruby. "Hello Cowboy." *The Guardian*, September 23, 2005. Accessed November 10, 2010, at http://www.guardian.co.uk/film/2005/sep/23/3.

Richardson, Brian, ed. *Narrative Dynamics: Essays on Plot, Time, Closure, and Frames*. Columbus: Ohio State University Press, 2002.

Robisch, S. K. "The Woodshed: A Response to 'Ecocriticsm and Ecophobia.'" *ISLE* 16.4 (Autumn 2009): 697–708.

Roof, Judith. *Come as You Are: Sexuality and Narrative*. New York: Columbia University Press, 1996.

Roughgarden, Joan. *Evolution's Rainbow: Diversity, Gender, and Sexuality in Nature and People*. Berkeley: University of California Press, 2004.

Safe. Dir. Todd Haynes. Perf. Julianne Moore, Xander Berkeley. 1995. Sony Pictures, 2001. DVD.

Sandilands, Catriona. *The Good-Natured Feminist: Ecofeminism and the Quest for Democracy*. Minneapolis: University of Minnesota Press, 1999.

———. "Sexual Politics and Environmental Justice: Lesbian Separatists in Rural Oregon." *New Perspectives on Environmental Justice: Gender, Sexuality, and Activism*. Ed. Rachel Stein. New Brunswick, N.J.: Rutgers University Press, 2004. 109–26.

———. "Unnatural Passions? Notes toward a Queer Ecology." *Invisible Culture: An Electronic Journal for Visual Culture* 9 (Fall 2005). http://www.rochester.edu/in_visible_culture/Issue_9/sandilands.html.

Savoy, Eric. Review of *Days of Obligation: An Argument with My Mexican Father*, by Richard Rodriguez. *ARIEL: A Review of International English Literature* 24.4 (1993): 130–34.

Sedgwick, Eve K. *Epistemology of the Closet*. Berkeley: University of California Press, 1990.

Selzman, Lisa Jennifer. Review of *North Enough: AIDS and Other Clearcuts*. *New York Times*, April 6, 1997. Accessed December 2, 2010, at http://www.nytimes.com/books/97/04/06/bib/970406.rv094507.html.

Serano, Julia. *Whipping Girl: A Transsexual Woman on Sexism and the Scapegoating of Femininity*. Emeryville, Calif.: Seal Press, 2007.

Shabecoff, Philip. *A Fierce Green Fire: The American Environmental Movement*. Rev. ed. Washington, D.C.: Island Press, 2003.

Shaviro, Steven. "Geek Love Is All You Need." Review of *Half Life*, by Shelley Jackson. *Electronic Book Review*, May 14, 2007. Accessed January 2, 2011, at http://www.electronicbookreview.com/thread/fictionspresent/conjoined.

Siamese Twins. PBS. Dir. Jonathan Palfreman. 1995.

Singer, Linda. *Erotic Welfare: Sexual Theory and Politics in the Age of Epidemic*. New York: Routledge, 1993.

Slicer, Deborah. "Toward an Ecofeminist Standpoint Theory: Bodies as Grounds." *Ecofeminist Literary Criticism: Theory, Interpretation, Pedagogy*. Ed. Greta Gaard and Patrick D. Murphy. Champaign: University of Illinois Press, 1998. 49–73.

Smith, Eric Todd. "Dropping the Subject: Reflections on the Motives for an Ecological Criticism." *Reading the Earth: New Directions in the Study of Literature and the Environment*. Ed. Michael P. Branch, Rochelle Johnson, Daniel Patterson, and Scott Slovic. Moscow: University of Idaho Press, 1998. 29–40.

Smyth, Heather. "Sexual Citizenship and Caribbean-Canadian Fiction: Dionne Brand's

In Another Place, Not Here and Shani Mootoo's *Cereus Blooms at Night*." *ARIEL* 30.2 (1999): 141–60.

Snediker, Michael. *Queer Optimism: Lyric Personhood and Other Felicitous Persuasions*. Minneapolis: University of Minnesota Press, 2009.

Solnit, Rebecca. *Savage Dreams: A Journey into the Landscape Wars of the American West*. New York: Vintage Departures, 1994.

Somerville, Siobhan. *Queering the Color Line: Race and the Invention of Homosexuality in American Culture*. Durham, N.C.: Duke University Press, 1999.

Sontag, Susan. *AIDS and Its Metaphors*. New York: Farrar, Straus, and Giroux, 1989.

———. "Notes on Camp." *Against Interpretation*. New York: Farrar, Straus, and Giroux, 1964.

Spade, Dean. "Fighting to Win." *That's Revolting! Queer Strategies for Resisting Assimilation*. Ed. Matt Bernstein Sycamore. Berkeley, Calif.: Soft Skull Press, 2004.

Stein, Arlene. "Sisters and Queers: The Decentering of Lesbian Feminism." *Socialist Review* 22.1 (January 1992): 33–55.

Stein, Rachel, ed. *New Perspectives on Environmental Justice: Gender, Sexuality, and Activism*. New Brunswick, N.J.: Rutgers University Press, 2004.

———. "'The Place, Promised, That Has Not Yet Been': The Nature of Dislocation and Desire in Adrienne Rich's *Your Native Land/Your Life* and Minnie Bruce Pratt's *Crime against Nature*." *Queer Ecologies: Sex, Nature, Politics, Desire*. Ed. Catriona Mortimer-Sandilands and Bruce Erickson. Bloomington: Indiana University Press, 2010. 285–308.

Stone, Sandy. "The 'Empire' Strikes Back: A Posttranssexual Manifesto," July 2004. Accessed October 14, 2010, at http://www.actlab.utexas.edu/~sandy/empire-strikes-back.

Stryker, Susan. "(De)Subjugated Knowledges: An Introduction to Transgender Studies." *The Transgender Studies Reader*. Ed. Susan Stryker and Stephen Whittle. New York: Routledge, 2006. 1–17.

Stryker, Susan, and Stephen Whittle, eds. *The Transgender Studies Reader*. New York: Routledge, 2006.

Sturgeon, Noël. *Environmentalism in Popular Culture: Gender, Race, Sexuality, and the Politics of the Natural*. Tucson: University of Arizona Press, 2009.

———. "'The Power Is Yours, Planeteers!': Race, Gender, and Sexuality in Children's Environmentalist Popular Culture." *New Perspectives on Environmental Justice: Gender, Sexuality, and Activism*. Ed. Rachel Stein. New Brunswick, N.J.: Rutgers University Press, 2004. 262–76.

Surf Party. Dir. Maury Dexter. Perf. Bobby Vinton, Patricia Morrow. Twentieth Century Fox Film Corporation. 1964. Film.

Szerszynski, Bronislaw. "The Post-Ecologist Condition: Irony as Symptom and Cure." *Environmental Politics* 16.2 (April 2007): 337–55.

Unger, Nancy. "Women, Sexuality, and Environmental Justice in American History." *New Perspectives on Environmental Justice: Gender, Sexuality, and Activism*. Ed. Rachel Stein. New Brunswick, N.J.: Rutgers University Press, 2004. 45–60.

U.S. Bureau of Reclamation. "The Bureau of Reclamation: A Very Brief History." U.S. Department of the Interior, n.d. Accessed November 10, 2010, at http://www.usbr.gov/history/borhist.html.

Valverde, Mariana. "Justice as Irony: A Queer Ethical Experiment." *Law and Literature* 14.1 (2002): 85–102.

———. "A New Entity in the History of Sexuality: The Respectable Same-Sex Couple." *Feminist Studies* 32.1 (2006): 155–62.

Vanderhaeghe, Stéphane. "What's Black and White and Read All Over? Shelley Jackson's *Half Life* (2006), or a Strange Game of I and Seek." *Revue LISA* 12.2 (2009): 158–68.

Vogel, Steven. *Against Nature: The Concept of Nature in Critical Theory.* Albany: State University of New York Press, 1996.

Warner, Michael. *The Trouble with Normal: Sex, Politics, and the Ethics of Queer Life.* New York: The Free Press, 1999.

Warren, Karen J., ed. *Ecofeminism: Women, Culture, Nature.* Bloomington: Indiana University Press, 1997.

Weeks, Jeffrey. *Against Nature: Essays on History, Sexuality, and Identity.* Concord, Mass.: Paul and Co., 1991.

Weston, Kath. "A Political Ecology of 'Unnatural Offences': State Security, Queer Embodiment, and the Environmental Impacts of Prison Migration." *GLQ* 14.2–3 (2008): 217–37.

Whittle, Stephen. "Where Did We Go Wrong? Feminism and Trans Theory—Two Teams on the Same Side?" *The Transgender Studies Reader.* Ed. Susan Stryker and Stephen Whittle. New York: Routledge, 2006. 194–202.

Williams, Linda. *Hard Core: Power, Pleasure, and the "Frenzy of the Visible."* Berkeley: University of California Press, 1999.

Winnett, Susan. "Coming Unstrung: Women, Men, Narrative, and Principles of Pleasure." *PMLA: Publications of the Modern Language Association of America* 105.3 (May 1990): 505–18.

Wu, Cynthia. "The Siamese Twins in Late-Nineteenth-Century Narratives of Conflict and Reconciliation." *American Literature* 80.1 (2008): 29–55.

Young, Al. "Silent Parrot Blues." *The Colors of Nature: Culture, Identity, and the Natural World.* Ed. Alison Hawthorne Deming and Lauret E. Savoy. Minneapolis: Milkweed Editions, 2011.

Zuk, Marlene. *Sexual Selections: What We Can and Can't Learn about Sex from Animals.* Berkeley: University of California Press, 2003.

Index

Abbey, Edward, 6, 188n11
abjection, 28, 100, 107, 112, 129, 140
abuse. See violence
academia, 15, 33, 148, 176
acting. See performance: acting
ACT UP (AIDS Coalition to Unleash Power), 94–95
affect, 33, 77
Against Nature (Weeks), 3–4
Aguirre, the Wrath of God (Herzog), 111
AIDS: allegorization of, 73–74, 76, 80, 83; crisis, 29, 31, 72, 80, 92–95, 164, 187n3, 188n11, 193nn13–15; in deep ecology discourse, 91–92; and film, 79, 103; as "natural," 76, 93; risk groups, 80–83, 94. See also HIV
Alaimo, Stacy, 168, 193n6
alienation: of African-Americans, 54; of labor, 52, 56–57, 68; from nature, 121, 124, 181; in *Safe*, 82, 88; of transgender persons, 37, 44, 48, 53–54, 56, 68
All That Heaven Allows (Sirk), 71
American Literary Environmentalism (Mazel), 14, 24, 139–40, 188n15, 197n12
American West: romanticization of, 31, 166; settling and development of, 32, 108, 116, 127–28, 132, 140. See also desert
Anderson, Jill E., 22, 25
"animalistic" sexuality, 115, 124
anti-capitalism, 39, 56–60
anti-colonialism, 25, 59–60

anti-domesticity, 32, 108–9, 118, 123, 126, 128, 133
anti-essentialism, 3, 25, 98, 173
anti-identitarianism, 14, 28–29, 161, 163, 171, 180, 184. See also non-identitarianism
Anti-Oedipus (Deleuze and Guattari), 61–62
anti-social thesis (queer theory), 5–7
Armbruster, Karla, 53
Atomic Age, 33, 151, 152, 154–55, 196n1
atomic bomb, 29, 33, 152–53, 163, 169, 175. See also Japan, U.S. bombing of; nuclear testing; radiation sickness
Azzarello, Robert, 23, 189n27

Bachelard, Gaston, 100
Bagemihl, Bruce, 21
bars: gay, 20, 36, 44, 48, 105, 114, 133–35; mixed, 134–35
Barthes, Roland, 174
Baudrillard, Jean, 42, 177, 192n19
beach, the, 32, 106, 113–14, 135, 142–43, 145–46
Bell, David, 22, 189n26
Berila, Beth, 94–95
Berlant, Lauren, 9, 188n9, 189n34
Bersani, Leo, 5, 10, 173, 187n3
Bérubé, Allan, 93, 134
bikers, 106, 126, 137–38, 144
biocentricity, 22, 27, 62, 68, 74, 91, 182
Biological Exuberance (Bagemihl), 21
Bookchin, Murray, 17, 91–93, 96

Bouchard, Danielle and Jigna Desai, 192n4, 193n7, 193n15

Bowers v. Hardwicke, 114

Boys Don't Cry (Peirce), 20, 189n21

BP (British Petroleum), 8, 188n7

Brokeback Mountain: as historicist, 32, 116, 128, 132; and neoliberalism (*see also* neoliberalism); as postmodern/self-reflexive, 108–9, 116, 135–38, 141–42, 146; as queer, 5, 25–26, 31–32, 107, 132

"Brokeback Mountain" (Proulx), 111, 123, 125, 132

Brooks, Peter, 79

Bruhm, Steven and Natasha Hurley, 187n1

Buckingham-Hatfield, Susan, 78, 101, 195n31

Buell, Lawrence, 13–14, 57, 74, 188n16, 190n35, 193n11

Bullard, Robert, 26, 74, 88, 164, 194n26

Bureau of Indian Affairs, U.S., 169

Bureau of Reclamation, U.S., 127, 195n3, 195n12

Bush, George H., 8

Bush, George W., 8, 19, 21, 151, 189n20, 189n25

Butler, Judith, 13, 14, 42, 157, 173, 187n3

Byers, Thomas, 121, 132

camp, 150, 163

camping, 115, 121

cancer, 72, 99, 152, 163, 170, 196n6. *See also* radiation sickness

capitalism: accumulation, 8, 28, 58, 118, 122, 125; as anti-ecological, 5, 8, 32, 57, 107–8, 111–13; as anti-futurist, 7–8, 10, 183; and GLBTQI existence, 5, 43, 62–65, 107, 128, 134, 192n16, 195n9; global/late, 29, 42–43, 52, 63, 108–9, 118, 133–34, 183. *See also* alienation: of labor; anti-capitalism; pre-capitalism

"Capitalism and Gay Identity" (D'Emilio), 62–63, 192n16

Carson, Rachel, 189n29

Caserio, Robert L., 5, 187n4

Castro District, 156, 159

Cereus Blooms at Night (Mootoo), 9, 11, 37, 41, 45, 48, 59, 65, 69, 70, 204, 206, 209

chemical sensitivity, 80, 193n5. *See also* environmental illness

Chernobyl, 175

Chisholm, Dianne, 167–68, 187n5

Chris, Cynthia, 22

Christian, Laura, 74, 91, 100, 193n7

Christmas Carol, A (Dickens), 7

cisgender persons, 39, 47, 49, 52, 56, 191n6

Clark, David and Catherine Myser, 157, 159

class consciousness, 122, 125, 139, 193n7

classical narrative cinema, 73, 83, 99, 104. *See also* Hollywood cinema

classical narrative form, 27, 79, 152. *See also* narrative conventions

classism, 74–75, 101–2, 111, 114, 120–22, 181

Cliff, Michelle, 30, 37, 44–46, 50, 52, 55, 60, 62, 66, 90, 191n3

climate change. *See* global warming

coalition building. *See* solidarity, of the oppressed

Cold War, 152, 153, 197n8

Collins, Floyd, 182–83

colonialism, 9, 43, 57, 59–60, 70, 184. *See also* anti-colonialism

commodification: of the body, 36, 44, 56, 61–63; of nature, 59, 107, 122–24, 139–41, 146, 181; of queerness, 125, 140–42, 181, 195n9; of safety, 132

communes, 122, 182

communism, 68, 148, 158–59, 197n8

conjoinment: compared to queerness, 33, 148–49, 156–61, 173; twins, 33, 147–49, 156, 160, 173, 177–78. *See also* medical establishment: treatment of conjoined twins

counterculture, 24, 122, 137, 144–45, 182

cowboys, 105, 113, 122–23, 135, 137–38, 142, 195n10

Crenshaw, Kimberlé, 160

criminalization: of gay men, 9, 114; of minority youth, 80, 95, 100, 134

critical race studies, 2, 16, 160, 180–81

Cronon, William, 138

cross-species identification, 28, 30, 37, 55, 162, 171

cruising, 137, 146

Curry, Patrick, 6, 58

Dean, Tim, 6, 10, 187n4

deep ecology, 31, 74–75, 91, 95–96, 188n17, 190n36

dehumanization, 12, 24, 39, 44, 157, 162

Deleuze and Guattari, 61–62

DeLillo, Don, 163–64, 170, 197n17

D'Emilio, John, 62–64, 192n16

versus transsexuality, 30, 40–43, 56, 70.
   See also "organic transgenderism"
transhistorical GLBTQI identity, 63, 157
transnationalism, 30, 37
Transsexual Empire, The (Raymond), 41
Treichler, Paula, 82

"ugly" landscapes, 51, 161, 163–66, 171, 174
Uncommon Ground (Cronon), 138
unions, 68, 144. *See also* labor: activism
universality. *See* gay universality
unrepresentability: of injustice, 99, 102, 104;
   of labor, 99. *See also* visibility of suffering
urbanity. *See* queer urbanity vs. rurality
utopianism. *See* queer utopianism

Valentine, Gill, 22, 189n26
value: aesthetic, 163; communally-consti-
   tuted, 11, 58; exchange, 56, 113; human
   scale of, 39; intrinsic, 113, 171; revalua-
   tion, 32, 166, 171; sport, 122
Valverde, Mariana, 142, 150, 196n20
Vanderhaeghe, Stéphane, 174, 197n19
veganism/vegetarianism, 182, 197n1
Vietnam War, 68–69
viewer identification, 73, 75–77, 83, 85, 137
violence: homophobic, 12, 52, 108, 114,
   126; misogynist, 63; racist, 44, 67, 96;
   sexual, 44, 48–49, 55, 60; structural, 73,

99; transphobic, 44, 48, 52, 55, 64, 67,
   191n5
visibility, of suffering, 73, 75, 83, 99,
   102–4, 117
visibility, regimes of (Reid), 84–85, 97
visual epistemology, 72–73, 76, 79–80, 85,
   87, 97

Warner, Michael, 5, 128, 142
War on Drugs, 31, 80
wealth gap. *See* income gap
Weeks, Jeffrey, 3–4
West, Cornel, 187n1
West. *See* American West
Weston, Kath, 1, 13, 133
White Noise (DeLillo), 163–64, 170, 197n17
Whittle, Stephen, 40–41
Williams, Linda, 79, 193n12
Winnett, Susan, 79
woman's film, the, 71, 75, 88
workplace un/safety, 52, 78, 91–92, 98–99,
   194n27. *See also* environmental injustice
World Health Organization Europe, 7
Wu, Cynthia, 159

Young, Al, 58–59, 190n33
youth, 80, 106, 113, 134–35, 143

Zuk, Marlene, 161, 191n7, 197n15

Nicole Seymour is an assistant professor of English
at University of Arkansas at Little Rock.

The University of Illinois Press
is a founding member of the
Association of American University Presses.

University of Illinois Press
1325 South Oak Street
Champaign, IL 61820-6903
www.press.uillinois.edu